Margie & Hugh

'Don't laugh at me —
'cos I am a fool!'

With all good wishes

Bill
2003

IN AND OUT OF AFRICA

by

Bill Barton

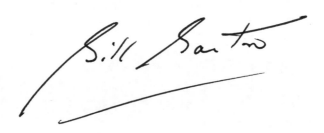

New Edition August 2003

Second edition Paperback published by
Blaisdon Publishing
3 Park Chase, Hornby, Bedale
North Yorkshire DL8 1PR
www.blaisdon.f9.co.uk

First Edition produced in association with
Bound Biographies
Boundary House, 23 Thompson Drive,
Bicester, Oxon OX6 9FA

ISBN 1 90283825 4

Cover: Bruce Webb

Bill

Dedication

This book is dedicated to Libo and the family
without whose coercion it would not have been written.

Contents

Illustrations Index

Introduction

The main purpose of this effort is to satisfy the request of my two children, Lesley and Ian, to relate the 'story' of my early life and leave an anecdotal record for them - a story which they can share later with their own children.

Choosing a title for my autobiography has not been easy; I considered *Excorde Caritas*, the motto of my senior school, George Watson's Boys' College in Edinburgh. The translation of the motto is 'out of the heart comes love'.

A reflection of my life demonstrates that this motto has been proven over and over again, for truly from the heart comes love: the love of parents, the love of family and, in my case particularly, the love of friends.

It was at George Watson's that I found so much which in time proved to be a basis for my future, where I gained so much knowledge and wisdom, where I was taught sport and the true meaning of fair play and, above all, where I learned much about the values of life. It was at George Watson's principally, that I learned the Scottish values of education, of morality, good manners and behaviour, and of religion, all of which provided me with a basic code for living and which were to rest with me and guide me throughout my life.

It was also here that I was introduced to what was then known as The Schoolboys' Club, later to become The Scottish Schoolboys' Club. The aim of the club was 'to help its members understand the full meaning of the Christian faith for themselves and the rest of the world'.

It was through the club, at the age of thirteen years, that I became a firm believer in the power of Christ and, in the words of John, was 'born again'.

It was at George Watson's that I found the basic foundations on which I later tried to develop my character and build my life. So, *Excorde Caritas* seemed an appropriate title for my autobiography. But after reflection I have chosen *In and Out of Africa*, which I hope will become clear as the story unfolds.

My career has had four quite distinct phases, following sequentially and with a pattern. I never had time to become bored, for my career of forty-two years was divided into these four relatively short phases. Eighteen years in the British Colonial Service were followed by eight years in the academic world of post-graduate medicine at the London School of Hygiene and Tropical Medicine (LSH&TM). I then spent nearly eleven years in the World Health Organisation (WHO) in its HQ in Geneva, Switzerland. This phase comprised two years in the Division of Family Health and eight years as Programme Manager of Staff Development and Training. Retiring at the age of 60, I finally worked as Personal Adviser to the Director General of the Department of Health and Medical Services in Dubai.

My Colonial Service experience, with the chance given for post-graduate study in the UK and USA in public health, fitted me to design and teach in a programme of 'Public Health Administration in a Developing Situation' at LSH&TM. During this relatively short academic career, given the opportunity of consultancies, along with operational research offered to me in Afghanistan, Indonesia, Thailand and others and with participation in International Conferences, I became equipped for an appointment in WHO. There, combining the collective experience of the two earlier phases I was qualified for the post of Programme Manager of SDT.

After retirement from my active career service I was able to stand back and, in maturity, provide the advice required by the DG of Dubai for three years.

Four separate but interlinked careers, each building on the earlier phases.

The story is not for general distribution, but specifically for the family and any close friends who may be interested in various phases of my career.

Bill Barton

6th April 2000

Earliest Recollections

Kisumu and Namasagali

In compiling an autobiography I presume a start is made from one's earliest recollections, which are surely always assisted by photographs kept in family albums.

Certainly in my case I can vividly remember early days when I could have been no older than two years of age, in Kisumu, my birth place. I can recall the house in which we lived and its situation with regard to the old *Kisumu Hotel*. Such recollections for me are certainly recalled with the help of the photographs. There I am sitting at my father's feet while he is drinking a pint of beer from a glass tankard.

Years later, in 1946, on returning to Kisumu as a young Medical Officer of the Kenya Government Services, I was able to locate the house where we had lived in Wandsworth Road. Not only that, but with the directions given me by my parents before setting off for Kisumu, I was able to trace the house in which I was actually born. Imagine my surprise to find the name on the gate was 'Barton'! Had I really been so important that they had retained my name for posterity?

No! It turned out that there was a new Marine Officer posted to the Lake, who by chance had the same name - a strange coincidence when one is trying to search for one's roots.

Writing about the early days on the Lake and the ships of the KUR&H it is worth recalling a small piece of history, reflecting on the very rapid

17

development in the Marine Service that occurred at that time. It was only in 1904 that the railway from the Coast to Lake Victoria first reached Kisumu. The history of this great achievement, with its many political, financial and human interactions, is so well recounted in the *Lunatic Express* by Charles Milner. For anyone interested in the early colonial development of this area of Africa it is surely required reading.

With the opening of this single line track through Africa, the development of communications round the Lake became feasible for the first time. Plans were laid for the design and building of appropriate vessels to be constructed in the UK. They were then disassembled and sent out by sea to Mombasa, thence by rail to Kisumu to be reassembled and launched. The first major vessel was launched in 1907, barely three years after the railway first reached Kisumu Port.

Within sixteen years, in 1923, the year of my birth, a fleet of vessels was operating round the Lake, each with one, two or more European Officers manning the bridge and engine-room. By that time also, hospitals, schools for Europeans and major Settler developments had been established and were operating. Fifteen years is a relatively short period of time, especially when one considers the very slow communication sea-link system operating between the UK and Kenya, not to mention the time element in rail travel between the Coast and Kisumu in Kenya itself.

My parents had met in Dunfermline in Fife in 1918. Having a day off from housework and looking after my grandfather, my mother, Vi Godley, had gone there with her friend, Mary Henderson, later Mary Bertram. My father, Billie Barton, was based at Rosyth and, it being his day off from his ship, he had gone to Dunfermline and was standing at the bandstand. It was here that he met my mother; they were married in Swansea in August 1918.

My sister, Margaret, was born in Edinburgh in 1921. At that time Father was in Bombay sailing with the Karimjee Jivanjee fleet of coastal trader ships.

The Clement Hill

The company later had financial difficulties and Father was on his return journey to the UK, when, stopping off at Mombasa he was offered a post with the *Lloyds Surveyors*, later accepting an appointment with KUR&H and being posted to Kisumu.

Another early memory of events in Kisumu was the arrival of the inaugural flight of the *Imperial Airways'* two-winged aeroplane around 1925. I can still see the giants now as they taxied up along the air-strip. Offers were made to the public to make flights and I well recall holding on firmly to my mother's skirt, pleading with her not to go up... she never did!

We went on home leave in 1925 and had a spell in Edinburgh to meet Grandfather Godley and Mum's brothers, John and David. On our return to Kenya Dad was posted to be the Skipper of the stern-wheeler ship *SW Stanley* on Lake Kioga at Namasagali, where my early recollections of life in Africa really begin.

Dad was one of three officers manning the SW steamers, *Grant*, *Stanley* and *Speke*, which operated from Namasagali on Lake Kioga, running up to Masindi Port; Jim Clark was Skipper on the *Grant* and Jim Wood on the *Speke*. Mr Clark was the Senior Officer in the station. He was married to Florence, and their son Roger, being a year younger than myself, was my great chum.

My parents later served at Butiaba on *SS Coryndon* on Lake Albert, before being posted to Packwach, Dad to be Skipper of the *SW Lugard I*. Mum was the first officer's wife to serve at Packwach, and she was allowed to travel on the ship on journeys to Nimule in the Sudan. A feature of the Packwach posting was the tourist trips to the Murchison Falls - many albums of photos record my parents' assignments to Butiaba and Packwach.

I will return to my memories of Namasagali for they are many. Our house was just above the wharf and is seen clearly in a photo of the *Stanley* docked at Namasagali. It was a typical Marine Officer's bungalow - large rooms surrounded by a verandah all the way round the house. Security in those days was of no concern and the only protection from any intrusion was wire mosquito netting on the outside of the verandahs.

Our home had only two bedrooms, one for my parents and the other occupied by Margaret. My bed was on the verandah outside the window of my parents' bedroom and had a cotton mosquito net on a box-style frame. I still remember the terror I suffered in bed when I heard the hippos wandering around the garden, chewing the grass and often rubbing themselves against the exterior walls of the house. I could see their large frames meandering so close by, and on so many nights I would lie awake shivering with fear, knowing I only had mosquito netting to separate me from these brutes, as I considered them. There was no way I could express my fears to Mum and Dad!

The following day we would wander around the garden and 'laugh' at how the hippos must have scratched themselves against the building. Only I knew the terror I used to feel. I did eventually become convinced that I really was in no danger. While crocodiles did not wander up to the garden, they were a constant threat round the shores of Lake Kioga.

Dad's ship was always escorted by three lighters in front of her as she sailed in. It was our usual habit, when home from school, to go down to the wharf to watch for the first sight of the front lighter rounding the corner in the river, behind the papyrus grass.

I still recall, almost like a bad dream, the sight of an African woman washing her clothes at the end of the wharf, which ran down into the lake like the end of a railway platform. I was standing on the wharf waiting to see Dad's ship to greet him when he docked. Suddenly there was a scream and the sight of a struggle as a crocodile had taken the woman by her leg and was dragging her down under the water. Nothing could be done by anyone. It was all over so quickly and the body disappeared in a few seconds.

21

Kisumu - circa 1926 Margaret, Mother and Me

Another time I was similarly waiting on the wharf for the ship. Dad docked and called me up to the bridge, while he finalised the paper work. The crew left to get into their dug-out canoes to cross the river to their homes. While there was always the potential danger of a hippo surfacing and upsetting a canoe, such an accident was very rare. On this occasion an angry hippo attacked a canoe, which was almost unheard of, and all the passengers were thrown into the river. Before anyone could go to their rescue crocodiles appeared from under the surface and picked off each crew member, dragging them down. Those who had been missed started to swim frantically back to the shore, but other crocodiles surfaced and took those still in the water.

I still see the scene as a nightmare; the screaming, the sense of helplessness, and naturally the total horror, confusion and shock to all those witnessing the tragedy unable to do anything to help. It was followed by the terrible wailing of the relatives who had been waiting on the other shore to welcome their loved ones.

Yet another crocodile memory is when we were taken up the river for a swim. We were in a small launch and, as we moved along, our fathers all had their guns at the ready. We passed a sand bank on which lay several crocodiles basking with their jaws open whilst the birds inside their mouths picked at their teeth. Dad and the others all fired at the crocs, shooting a few which remained on the bank, while the others slithered into the water. We turned into a small inlet for the swim. The launch was placed across the mouth of the inlet while our fathers set watch with their rifles ready. All the time we bathed, a lone crocodile lay off at a distance watching us. Nothing happened at the scene, but on the way back we had to pass the bank again and we noticed that the crocodiles which had been shot had been dragged into the water by the others. We then realised they were cannibals.

Another threat living near the Nile was snakes, and on one occasion we had a confrontation with a python. My father had a motor-cycle which was kept in the garage. One day the garden boy came to raise the alarm; a python had wrapped itself round the motor-cycle. It had obviously come from the lake and out of fear it had curled up in the corner and started swinging across the garage. The boys finally beat it to death as it swung backwards and forwards.

Despite these isolated incidents, most of my memories of Namasagali are pleasant ones. Several times a year we had fancy-dress parties for the children in the station. Margaret, my sister, always went as a daffodil and later a gypsy, while I dressed as a little Dutchman with clog shoes, tall peaked hat, and the inevitable pipe! Roger Clark was a Red Indian, but his mother always stole the show. 'Auntie' Florence, Flo for short, would appear as a fairy and hand out the presents. We always had a great tea party, with various games and a tug-of-war, with fathers involved as the climax.

My father would sail up the Lake for eight days and then have six days at home before setting off again, so as a child growing up in Namasagali I only saw my father for six days every fortnight, or twelve days every month. When he was back in the station he was tremendous fun as he loved children and used to enjoy romping around the garden playing all sorts of games with us.

Our dog, Gyp, was a smooth-haired fox-terrier, a true friend and companion whom I remember so well. He was very intelligent and a great watchdog, warning us if there were any snakes or anything else untoward. On one occasion Gyp alerted the family when Margaret and I were being followed by a python. Mum called us back into the house just in time.

I can still picture the last time I saw Gyp. He came down to the wharf from whence the train departed to see us off back to school in Nakuru. We already knew that it would be the last time we were to see him as he was

24

old and had been so ill. We all felt miserable. Suddenly we were aware that Gyp had gone off and we thought that he probably felt as we did. But to our joy, short lived, there he was awaiting us at the next stop down the line, Mbulamuti, standing on the platform, with scarcely the energy to wag his tail. I often wonder if the tombstone bearing Gyp's name still stands in Namasagali. I doubt it.

The post office was in Mbulamuti and our letters were collected by our gardener who carried the mail in the proverbial cleft stick.

We travelled on the train from Namasagali to Mbulamuti where we picked up the main line train to Nakuru to school or en route to the Coast. The drivers were all European in those days and we were always spoilt by being allowed to climb into the driving cab before the train moved off.

More exciting still, we were often allowed to sit on the seat placed in front of the engine for part of the trip down to Mbulamuti. This was rather like a large garden bench, and as the train only travelled slowly, it was pleasantly cool to sit there. However, we were only allowed this privilege if there was an adult with us to hold us in. It was a thrill that I will always cherish, but it certainly dates me as far as East African railway travel is concerned.

Our journey to Nakuru took two full days, with one night spent sleeping on the train, again a thrill for children going to school. Many photos exist of our departure from Namasagali and the train journeys, all dressed in our school uniforms; an interesting feature of which is the shape of our double terrai hats, all stiff-brimmed for the first term... thereafter all limp, soft and certainly unshapely! You could always tell who was going off to school for the first term, by the condition of their hat! Yes, they were double terrai or cork pith helmets that we had to wear. The red felt-like material we wore as spine pads was discarded when we went to school.

Attitudes on the effects of the sun changed in the following decades but there has now been a reversal to the old respect we used to have for it.

The Family in Kisumu

Travelling to School

*Swimming with
Crocodiles!*

26

Kenya School Days

In 1928 the family returned again to the UK for Dad's home leave. We often travelled on German passenger ships, which were comfortable and cared particularly well for children. There were many fancy-dress parties and I again wore my Dutch costume. A happy memory I have of such a trip is of sneaking downstairs and sitting on the staircase when the adults were at dinner. On spotting Margaret and me, the steward would bring us ice-cream.

We stayed in Edinburgh on our home leave and my sister and I were entered for a term at the Parsons Green School, which was in the Royal Park at the end of Royal Park Terrace. I recall little of the school, but I do remember my first cold winter!

During this time we also visited Western Avenue in Cardiff, the home of Grannie Barton and our cousin Kenneth. Ken was the son of Dad's sister Maimie, but was brought up by Granny Barton and thus took the family name. I learned that Grandad Barton had gained his Master's Certificate and skippered four-masted sailing ships. These ships were based in Cardiff and, I understand, belonged to Granny's family. It was also rumoured that the family had owned the *Cardiff Arms Hotel*... before it became bankrupt!

I started at the Government School Nakuru in 1929. It was the first school I attended in Kenya... the school 'on the hill' overlooking the Lake, with playing fields at the foot of the hill along with 'our' little gardens to be cultivated and cherished by the children. The Headmaster, Mr Pratt, later became Col. Pratt and was in charge of the East African Military Labour

27

Service (EAMLS). My father served under him during the Second World War in the East African Campaign in Somaliland and Abyssinia.

Mr White was the Sports Master and how well I can remember him. On one occasion, several of us were summoned to the Headmaster's room, having been caught in a dormitory rumpus. We saw the Head's arm was in a sling and so the powerfully-built Mr White was called in to inflict the cane... with full vigour!

We were taught ballroom dancing at Nakuru School, for which I will always be grateful, for having learned to dance at the age of six and seven I never suffered from the shyness of having to learn later in my schooldays in Edinburgh. At our dancing lessons we mastered not only the quickstep, fox trot and waltz, but also the charleston, on its first time round in the late twenties, and the sailor's hornpipe. I recall the time when Margaret and I gave an exhibition of the hornpipe and the charleston, at the local *Stag's Head Hotel* in Nakuru, as well as ballroom dancing.

Fifteen years after leaving Nakuru School and completing my school and university education in Edinburgh, I returned as a young Medical Officer in the Kenya Medical Service. I was driving from Nairobi with my newly engaged houseboy, Manjari, to my first posting in Kisii. After Lake Elemteita I turned to Manjari and said, "If I am not mistaken we shall soon round a bend in the road and there on the right, high up on the hillside, we should see Nakuru Government School where I started my education." Sure enough there it was. An impulsive reaction took me off the main road and I found myself driving straight up to the front door of the school. Parking the car I entered the building, turned right along the corridor, stopped at the first door on the right and knocked! I waited feeling rather stupid. The door opened and a lady teacher enquired "Yes! Can I help you?"

I gulped out, "This will sound rather stupid, but fifteen years ago I used to sit in this classroom and was taught by a Miss Goodwin."
"I am Miss Goodwin. And what is your name?"

"Barton, Miss!"

"Oh yes! I remember you well, Bill; you had a sister Margaret and you both came from Namasagali."

The proverbial feather did not strike; I merely gulped in amazement and relief!

My three years at Nakuru came to an end with our home leave back to the UK in 1931. Father's tours were three years, so after his post as Skipper of the *Stanley* in Namasagali we set off for 'home'. What I had not realised was that after this leave I would not be returning with my parents to Kenya but was to be left in the UK for schooling. But where?

Our leave was spent mainly in Withernsea on the east coast of Yorkshire, where Margaret and I were enrolled at the local school. While at Withernsea, one day Dad turned up with a secondhand *Fiat* car, an open tourer, which meant we could travel with the roof folded back. It was the first car I ever remember us possessing. It allowed us to travel to Cardiff to visit Granny Barton and my cousin Ken. Ken was a keen motor-cyclist but also had a 'Baby *Austin*' car. As he was about 6'4" tall, he looked quite incongruous getting into the car. Ken worked in Philog Garage with Dai Morgan, who was Dad's close friend.

We stayed with the Morgans while visiting Gran and together we spent a short holiday at Lavernock near Barry. I shall always remember the Equinox autumn high tide at Lavernock, which required everyone with a beach hut or temporary café building to remove same for two days before and after the highest tide. The combination of the Bristol Channel full tide and the Equinox created this annual phenomenon.

It was on this trip to Cardiff that I had my first meeting with my two younger cousins Dick (Dickson) and Annie Williams, children of Auntie Maimie. It was to be years before we met up again, for my schooling was to take me to Edinburgh, and after Gran died we had no real reason to revisit Cardiff.

With Granny Barton at Withernsea

An incident occurred while we were in Cardiff staying with the Morgans which was to affect my thinking for many years ahead. One night I was in bed upstairs and was awakened by adult voices which, while not raised, were certainly engaged in intense discussion. I crept out of bed and sat on the top step upstairs and listened in. Evidently the discussion had been about Dad's imminent return to Kenya and the decision that had been taken for Mum to join him after a short while and for my sister and myself to be left behind in the UK. "How can you possibly leave your children for three years?" was the question put to my mother.

Her reply was clear: "I married Billie and we have been blessed with our two lovely children; but I repeat I married Billie. He is my husband, the one I married with a solemn vow, and he must come first in my life."

Little did I realise the significance of what this was to mean to my sister and myself, but when the time came for Mum to leave us to rejoin Dad in Kenya, I was able to accept it.

My favourite picture of my parents - the one I carried for years in my wallet

131 WPR

The family moved north to Edinburgh in time for Margaret and me to start the new term in January 1932 at the George Watson's Colleges for Boys and for Girls. The Girls' School was always known by its location as 'George Square', later to become part of the University of Edinburgh.

It must be recorded that my father chose Watson's for myself and my sister because when he was in Uganda between 1923 and 1929 he came across the Watsonian Club and thought that any school that had a club and an association of former pupils overseas must have some tremendous feature and character about it. So we went to Watson's, otherwise I might well have been entered for Daniel Stewart's or Heriot's.

Our first stopping place in Edinburgh was in Wellington Street, Portobello, opposite the indoor swimming pool and but a few yards from the promenade and beach. This is all recorded by the pictures taken of my sister and me outside No.13 Wellington Street, as we set off on our first day at our new schools. The occasion was later recorded by a snap taken at *Jeromes the Photographer*!

Margaret and I travelled to school by tram car, with changes to get us up to the Meadows; I to the old school, which was then in Lauriston Place facing the Meadows and Margaret to George Square. While in the early days we were escorted to school by a parent, after a few trips we travelled alone - the safety of children going to school by themselves was never doubted. Those tram rides I remember so clearly, sometimes sitting out in the open upstairs, either at the front or back. The trams were not turned round at the terminus; the pole connected to the overhead power cables was merely swung round to the new rear of the tram, thus allowing it to travel in the opposite direction!

Margaret and me in uniform
and with Mum

It soon became important for our parents to find alternative accommodation for us to be nearer the schools, and certainly before Dad had to return to Kenya at the end of his leave.

It so happened that a Miss Whyte, who was a spinster and who had sacrificed her own happiness to care for her father, especially in his later retirement period, lived in a flat at 131 Warrender Park Road. After her father's death, her doctor, Dr Carmichael, told her that she should have people to share her home to provide her with company and prevent loneliness. She originally had had a final year medical student, Peggy Paxton, the daughter of a headmistress in a small village near Hawick, who left on qualifying. Dr Carmichael insisted that Miss Whyte re-advertise for new tenants and that is where we came in.

My parents had seen Miss Whyte's advertisement offering accommodation and visited the flat. It was agreed that it was very adequate for our immediate needs and in due course my sister and I were informed that we would be picked up from school and taken round to meet Miss Whyte. Margaret had been taken round first and Miss Whyte was delighted with her, remarking what a sweet child she was and how nice it would be to have her in the house. My father apparently remarked, "Ah, but wait till you see the wee laddie." This story about my entry to 131 Warrender Park Road (WPR) was repeated by Miss Whyte many times in the years ahead, and I can still hear her remarking, "and I remember very well Mr Barton saying, 'Ah, but wait till you see the wee laddie,' and when the laddie finally appeared he was such a tiny wee boy, who just came up to the level of the door handle."

In due course, and before Dad returned to Kenya late in January 1932, we all moved to '131 WPR' where my parents had rented two large bedrooms and what had been the dinning-room, sharing the kitchen and bathroom. Our rooms were part of a large flat comprising three bedrooms, a large drawing room with characteristic bow windows and an attached box room,

34

a dining room, kitchen, bathroom and what was obviously a maid's room off the kitchen. The flat overlooked Bruntsfield House, at that time owned by Lord Bruntsfield, but later purchased by the City Council and converted into James Gillespie School.

The flat was in a typical up-standard Edinburgh tenement block, with a common entry without a lift. The 'stair' comprised three storeys, two flats on each floor, totalling six flats, and a rear entrance to a common 'back garden'. Ours was the first flat on the first floor.

The rooms had been rented as they were convenient for both schools, thus allowing Margaret and me to go down the Bruntsfield Walk, alongside Warrender Park Terrace, through the Whale Jaw Bone, thence across the Meadows to our respective schools.

Our Edinburgh Home - 131 WPR

Although I did not know it at the time, this was to be my home for the next eight wonderful years as I went through school, and then, in 1940, for a further six happy years as I studied at university. I remained with Auntie Whyte until I set off for Kenya in the Colonial Medical Service in 1946.

I returned later to 131 WPR for a further period of post-graduate study, taking my Diploma in Tropical Medicine and Hygiene in 1949 and 1950, and yet again between 1953-54 for my studies for the Diploma of Public Health. By 1953 I was already married and our first child Lesley was born from the house, at The Simpson Memorial Wing of the Royal Infirmary.

After my father's return to Kenya, he was posted to the Kigera River to build up the port there, so Mum could not join him immediately. The plan was for Mum to look for someone prepared to act as guardian for Margaret and me. My parents could not afford to enrol either of us into one of the school boarding houses (for boys, Crowden's, Allan's, Penman's and possibly others) which would provide care for us over the holiday periods. It must be remembered that there were no aeroplanes to carry us out for holidays, while ships took four weeks to reach Mombasa from Tilbury.

Mother's family was in Edinburgh; Grandad Godley being looked after by Uncle Dave and a housekeeper, Mrs Davidson. Uncle Dave himself was an invalid as a result of the 1914-18 war; he had a crippled leg, was deaf and had very reduced sight. He worked for his brother John, in his gents' tailoring shop in Abbeyhill. Uncle John was married to Auntie Jean (née Scougall) but they had no family and lived in a one-bedroomed flat in Wellington Street, near Easter Road in Abbeyhill. Certainly there was no possibility of us children being cared for by Mum's relations.

As we were settled in at 131 WPR before my father left to return to Kenya, at least he had the comfort of knowing we were housed. It has to be remembered that when one said goodbye to one's parents in that situation, one was saying goodbye for a minimum period of three years, because tours in the East African Colonies were at least of that duration. Added to

36

that there was the month on the ship travelling either way. I still well remember saying goodbye to my father in January 1932, realising with deep anguish that I would not see him again until 1935 at the very least.

I feel I should expand on this aspect of my separation from my parents. It was customary for Mum to go out to Kenya three months after Dad had arrived there, and to come back 'home' three months ahead of him at the end of their tour. This allowed us to see Dad for six months every three years and Mum for a twelve months period. Accordingly, Dad came back in 1935 for six months, then disappeared again for another three years. As a result I only saw my father in 1935 and again in 1938.

Dad was expecting to retire in 1940 and had planned to return to the UK to be with us while we were going through our university education, but the war intervened and I did not see him again till November 1945 when I was already 22½ years old and a qualified doctor. All this meant that between the age of nearly nine years till I was 22½, those very vital fourteen years of the growing up period of my life, I actually was in my father's presence for a total of only twelve months. I did not see very much more of my mother either, only a total of approximately twenty-six months during those fourteen formative years.

My experience was not much different from that of other children left at 'home' for education by parents serving in the British Crown Colonies. I myself am quite convinced that separation from my parents without any close ties with grandparents, meant that friends played such an important role in providing happiness, and contributed so much to my development and wellbeing. I certainly learned at an early stage in my life that I would feel more strongly, and experience more emotion towards my friends than they would ever feel towards me. I realised that they did not need my love and attachment as I needed theirs, for they had the natural give and take of emotion and affection that exists between parent and child, which I was

37

denied. This reality prevented me from being hurt by friends and helped me to accept and understand my emotional development.

Miss Whyte, our landlady, was in her early sixties and, being a spinster, my parents did not consider that she would be either prepared or suitable to take on the responsibility of looking after two children aged, at the time, 10 and 8. So Mum continued to look for an alternative suitable solution. One day Miss Whyte asked Mum why she kept on looking for a guardian - could she not take us on? It seemed that Miss Whyte had become very attached to the 'wee ones', especially 'the laddie'. So it was agreed that, after our first summer holidays spent at Lower Largo in Fife, Mum would leave us with 'Auntie Lizzie', and she set off in early autumn to rejoin Dad. By this time I had turned 9 and Margaret 11 years.

Miss Whyte or 'Auntie' as she had become known, was to be our guardian for many years. For my sister this was to be for the nine years to 1941 when she returned to Kenya, while I stayed for a further five years until I set off for the next stage of my career in Kenya in the summer of 1946.

As I have mentioned, Auntie never married, her mother having died when she was still a young woman. Auntie's elder sister, Jessie, had died shortly after her mother and so Auntie decided to sacrifice her own personal life in caring for her father. Her eldest brother, Willie, had already left for Australia where he later died. She had two other brothers, David and James, both living in Edinburgh and both married. James, the youngest brother, and his wife Chrissie had no family, but David and his wife Annie had a son and three daughters: David, Annie, Eliza and Jessie, of whom all but Jessie married. I got to know David and Annie and their children very well. Eliza married Bill Williamson and they had two children, Dorothy and Gordon. Whilst these children were much younger than Margaret and myself, we saw quite a lot of them in the early years.

How lucky we were to be left with 'Auntie', who was the most loving and adorable person. She certainly adored me, a feeling I can genuinely say I

38

reciprocated. She did not spoil me but gave me every comfort that a child could ever have looked for. She never tried to usurp or replace my parents' affection or love for me, but would always question me with, "What would your parents think?", "Would they be proud of you if you did that?", "Would you think they would be ashamed?", or, "Would you like your parents to know about that?"

Auntie constantly talked about my parents and kept them as the model for me to follow as the precious beings in my life. They were always to be considered, always to be remembered and thought about, never to be taken for granted, but rather always to be loved and cherished.

Auntie Whyte

At the same time, it was impossible for me not to love Auntie very deeply. She taught me so much about life and about the true values. Discipline was strict in those days and life and pleasures were very simple. We did not have a wireless or radio, as we know them now. However, we did have a crystal set, which we tuned by delicately adjusting the 'cat's whisker'. We used headphones and had reasonable reception; we could even attach two headphone sets and still get a clear sound. However, with three sets, which we often tried if there was a good programme, the reception tended to be very faint. Of course, there was not a great selection of stations, but music and the news were always favourites.

When I was about 9 or 10 I was very keen on rugby and I enthusiastically 'tackled' Auntie in the hall. With my arms round her legs, she crashed to the floor. Thankfully, she was unhurt, and she took it all in good part... although the procedure was never repeated.

Seven years after moving into 131 WPR, Auntie replaced the gas lighting with electricity and bought a wireless set, a *Cossar* I think. The sets were still called wirelesses and not radios. With such simple pleasures, music played a major part in our spare time activity.

Auntie had persuaded my parents to allow Margaret and me to have piano lessons. We were enrolled as students with Miss Janet Collins, a small and rather petite, quaint woman - a leftover from the Victorian era, certainly as regards her dress sense. She was a true artist, in both music and painting. She and her sister, both spinsters, lived in Blantyre Terrace, if I recall correctly. Margaret and I would walk over the Bruntsfield Links to their house, otherwise Miss Collins would come to us at 131 WPR. My sister always preferred to have the first lesson of half an hour, which meant that when I arrived she would get away with just thirty minutes, whereas I had much longer as Miss Collins would never finish on time; it was often three quarters of an hour, or even an hour before I was released. I was obviously her favourite, and as a result benefitted greatly from the extra hours of instruction. I certainly enjoyed the instrument.

After several years of piano lessons, time for practice had to compete with my new interests of rugby and cricket! In due course, my parents decided that they could not afford such lessons when I was practising so little and so not making the progress I had shown earlier. Miss Collins was a great teacher and as a youngster, with modesty, I think I can claim that I played the piano well. I always had a good ear, and after practising with the music I was soon able to play by 'ear'.

Margaret was a better reader of music and we had a lot of fun playing duets, a joy often shared with our teacher - *Marche Militaire* was our favourite piece. After Margaret left for Kenya in 1941, Auntie and I would frequently play the duets, or I would accompany her as she played the violin. She persevered too in teaching me how to play the violin, but the piano was always my favourite instrument.

Many hours of music were enjoyed, especially on Sundays, playing hymns, Gilbert and Sullivan or songs from the *Student Song Book*. Auntie would often go through the book on the piano while I tried my hand with the violin, but always singing with great gusto! In later years this enjoyable habit was carried on with Gus McKnight, who was three years my senior at school and at university. Gus qualified in Medicine in 1942 and served in the Scots Guards with many later well known public figures; including Lord MacLean, Chief Scout and Lord Chamberlain, the Very Reverend Lord Runcie, Archbishop of Canterbury, and Lord Whitelaw.

Gus was an excellent pianist and during his medical studies would often visit 131 WPR and join Auntie and myself in a musical evening, often singing and playing G & S.

I was taught the value of music when I was young and Auntie insisted on me having a musical education. She took me to many of the weekly Saturday afternoon concerts where famous pianists played with orchestras of equally high repute. The resident and university orchestra was The Reid Orchestra, developed and led by Professor John Reid. The Orchestra usually performed every Friday night and provided a wide range of music. I was privileged to watch and hear Moiseovitch, Myra Hess, Solomon,

41

Rubenstein, Rachmaninov, Padrewsky, Moira Lympany and others - memories I will never lose.

Other concerts we attended at the Usher Hall were to hear famous singers of that time. I particularly remember Isobel Bailey singing *The Messiah* on New Year's Day; Richard Tauber and Joan Hammond were two others I well recall.

I was also introduced to opera: *Rigoletto, Madame Butterfly, La Bohème, Carmen* and *The Barber of Seville* to name just a few. In addition there was the full range of the D'Oyly Carte operas, which were performed at the King's Theatre. I was allowed to queue up for seats in the 'gods' at very cheap rates for young students. I reckon, on looking back, that I saw them all! This wonderful exposure to a classical music education was always with the encouragement of Auntie.

I had a very early introduction to the famous Scottish comics of the theatre, whose style of entertainment I later often followed in my various amateur stage performances. On many occasions I saw appearances by Sir Harry Lauder in his kilt. Included in his repertoire were such famous titles as *Keep Right on to the End of the Road, Roamin' in the Glomin', I Love a Lassie, Just a Wee Doch and Doris* and others. Then there was Will Fyffe as the ship's stoker, with his famous *I Belong to Glasgow* and *Sailing Down the Clyde*, and Dave Willis with his collection of *The Smartest Looking Warden in the ARP, I'm Don Jaun, Dressed in Indian Feathers* and countless others. Tommy Lorne and Jimmy Logan were the great Panto Dames of the earlier period. The *King's Theatre* was the home for such artists, while the *Empire Theatre* was the home of variety and vaudeville. Later artists included Stanley Baxter and Jimmy Stewart.

As far as my literary education is concerned, I was not read to as a child, except on Sunday afternoons when Auntie would read *Pilgrim's Progress* and 'John Halifax Gentlemen'. Of course there were also the Dickens novels!

42

Religion was very important in our lives. I was taken to Church most Sundays with Auntie to the Robertson Memorial Parish Church in Kilgraston Road at the Grange. Dr Rev Dunnett was the first Minister I recall and he was succeeded by the Rev Stevenson. Naturally I attended Sunday School there for several years.

Every Sunday afternoon Margaret and I set off on the number 15 tram, later a 15 bus, to visit Grandpa Godley and Uncle Dave, at 29 Royal Park Terrace, overlooking the Royal Park with Arthur's Seat nearby. In the summer we often walked through the Royal Park to '29 RPT' where Mrs 'Sandy' Davidson, who always had the day off on Sundays, would have left a cold meal for us. Grandpa would be sitting there, in his black velvet smoking cap with its tassel, smoking his pipe and always reading his book. He was an avid reader and often also sat quietly writing poetry. After our greetings, Uncle Dave would give us 4d (there were 12d to a shilling and 20 shillings to £1 and so in today's value it would be worth just over 1p) to go down to the local sweetie shop to buy our week's 3lb ration for consumption that afternoon! Grandpa was the first to be offered a sweet.

During the summer we would go along to visit 'Auntie' Bessie McCulloch and her niece Elizabeth Dougary, who lived in No.25 in the Terrace, or to No.31 to visit 'Granny' Mills. All these people had been close friends of Mum and had helped her when she was young. She had lost her mother when she was 12 years old and had taken on responsibility for running Grandpa's home while still trying to continue at school.

This could be a good place to identify some of Mother's family more fully. She had an older sister, Agnes, and three brothers, Willie, John and Dave, all of whom initially worked with Grandpa in his tailoring business in Hanover Street. Uncle Willie was the 'black sheep' of the family and was instrumental in ruining Grandpa's business. I never met him, and only one of his family was at Grandpa's funeral in 1937. We have completely lost contact with that side of the family.

43

Uncle John was been injured in the Great War, having suffered from shell-shock in the Dardenelles. After the war he went out to Ceylon (Sri Lanka) but returned home to Edinburgh to open his own business. Uncle John married Jean Scougall who was a trained seamstress and so helped in the shop with minor alterations to suits.

Uncle John and Auntie Jean had no family and were very kind to Margaret and myself during our stay with Auntie Whyte, visiting us frequently and taking us out to the circus and, in due course, to a cinema show. Uncle John died quite young, leaving Jean a widow for many years; she finally died in her eighties.

Uncle Dave's greatly reduced eye-sight meant that he had to use a magnifying glass, his poor hearing necessitated a hearing-aid and his deformed left ankle gave him a severe limp - he had to use a stick as a support if walking any distance. However, despite all this I never once heard him complain, although I know he suffered severe pain. Uncle Dave always had a smile and a joke and was certainly our favourite uncle. Having worked initially for Uncle John, he later set up his own outfitters shop in Gorgie Road, where during my last year at school and in my student days throughout the war I would often serve on Saturday evenings. I became quite skilled at selling caps, hats, ties and shirts.

Mother's sister, Agnes, was much older, and shortly after Granny's death she left home and married Ralph Calder, settling in the Manchester area. They had five sons and one daughter: Ralph, a Congregational Minister, Stanley, Lester, Douglas, Graham and Irene. Years passed before I had the chance to meet Aunt Irene, her husband and, in time my cousins. I cannot in fact remember ever meeting cousin Lester.

Vina and Annie Godley, two of Mum's cousins, lived in Dumfries and we visited them occasionally. They remained spinsters, spending their lives caring for other members of their family, their mother, uncle and, finally, Uncle Dave, for it was with them that he lived his last days. It was always

44

said that Vina was in love with him and wanted to marry him before the First World War, but upon his return he decided that with all his injuries he was too much of a burden for any marriage, so they both went through life unmarried. It was poignant that Vina was given the privilege of caring for him in his last illness.

After Uncle Dave's death, Vina and Annie had a sad life, for they were mugged and seriously injured by a burglar. They were naturally terrified and quickly moved into a church home, but died shortly after, both in their eighties.

Margaret and I lived with Auntie Whyte from 1932 till late 1941 when Margaret went to join our parents in Kenya. She returned towards the end of 1944 to marry Eric Baxter, her fiancé for several years; Eric had been seriously injured in the Burma campaign.

George Watson's College For Boys

It is very unlikely that anyone born after 1927 can claim to have attended George Watson's College when it was still in the Meadows, off Lauriston Place, down Archibald Place. The last session of the school there was 1931-32.

We had arrived in the UK from Uganda in July 1931 for my father's spell of six months' home leave, and spent the summer in England where I was entered in the village primary school in Withernsea, Yorkshire, for the autumn term.

I started at George Watson's in January 1932 in the spring term. I was eight years of age and was placed in Class F, the lowest class grade of the top three classes of the preparatory school.

'Grannie' Louise Milne, as she was affectionately known, was my teacher. She was the sister of Dr Milne, the Headmaster of Daniel Stewart's Boys' College, our brother school in the four Merchant Company schools of the city; the other two were girls' schools - George Watson's Ladies' College (George Square) and Queen Street School, later known as The Mary Erskine School for Girls.

Grannie was quite definitely the last of the line of what I suppose was the 'Victorian Era'. Her black dresses and frills were certainly of that period and obviously she had been born and grew up under the influence of Queen Victoria's great reign. Grannie was unashamedly a lady with strong Christian ethics and beliefs.

We started each school day with a prayer and a reading of one verse from the Bible, repeated daily for a week. All boys were expected to memorise one verse, so Grannie started at the head of the class and, working down from the top, each boy in turn was called upon to quote his verse.

Back row: Far right Alec Drysdale
3rd row: Haig, xxx, xxx, Bill Barton, xxx, Norman Smart, xxx,
Gibson
2nd row: xxx, xxx, xxx, Willie Swanson, Miss Milne, xxx, xxx, xxx,
Watson
Front row: xxx, xxx, Hislop, xxx, xxx

When a boy was reached who did not have a verse, he was expected to learn the verse of the week. Every day all verses were repeated and by the end of the session one was familiar with about 30 verses from the Bible, having heard them quoted daily. As I joined the class in the second term, naturally I was soon expected to pick up the verse of the week. The verse was underlined in my Bible by Grannie so that I would not forget it. Mine was John Ch.1 V.4., remembered to this day. "In Him was life and the life was the light of men; and the light shineth in darkness and the darkness comprehended it not."

Grannie made a lasting influence on me, not only through the verses I learned, but also by her fine example.

Following the Bible verse reading, the class went through the exercise of mental arithmetic - the tables! We were not only expected to know the tables from 2 to 12, but 2 through to 20. Again, by the end of the session we all knew the tables... forwards and backwards. First we would recite the odds forwards and backwards, and then the same for the evens. We learned by the daily repetition of tables from beginning to end, adding a new number once the earlier ones had been mastered. How grateful I have always been for that learning process, and to this day I can always work out the costing of a shop bill by mental arithmetic and beat the assistant using the adding machine. I once made the mistake of calling out the total before the assistant had finished and received the reprimand, "Do be quiet, you are putting me off and I haven't finished." Surprise, surprise when he finally agreed that we had the same answer!

I still recall the battles that raged during the class breaks, when our separate gangs struggled for possession of the big field guns that stood in the gravel forecourt in front of the school. Again, I suppose because I was a new boy and seemed taller than some, I became the leader of one gang, with my chief rival being a ginger-headed lad, Jim Watson.

At the end of the session the Watsonian Dinner was held in the school. It was the last function to be held in the building before Watson's moved to Colinton Road. The old boys saw this as an excuse to run berserk, and in their drunken stupor they rampaged round the classrooms tearing up books, jotters and causing havoc. When we turned up the following school day poor Grannie was in tears, for among the items they had torn up were several of our personal Bibles. All those who lost a Bible had them replaced, I think by Grannie, each with their verse underlined. I have mine to this day.

Maybe it was because of the educational grounding I received in Nakuru School, that after only two terms I was placed top of the class and took 1st prize for the session.

My prize was a book, *EDINBURGH - Mine Own Romantic Town*, written and illustrated by Gordon Home, 1927. I have always treasured it and it still has its place on my bookshelves. It is a beautiful book with an excellent text from the town's earliest history and there are 24 full-page reproductions from pencil drawings by the author. It carries the label shown on the next page.

22nd September 1932 saw me standing in the front row, in front of the school as His Royal Highness Prince George, youngest son of King George V, turned the key in the front door and formally opened the new school in Colinton Road.

Having taken 1st prize in Class F, I was placed in the top class in the first year of the Junior School, entering 3LJ (Lower Junior) with Miss Lamont as teacher. My two further years in Junior School were in 6MJ (Middle Junior) with Mr Budge and finally 9HJ (Higher Junior) under 'Pa' Lennie, Headmaster of the Junior School. What a large, formidable but loveable man he was, always wearing his gown and mortar board. In fact, all teachers wore gowns in class, but only Pa Lennie wore his mortar board, seldom removing it.

Vol. I

THE EDINBURGH MERCHANT COMPANY · A.D. 1681 ·

Edinburgh
Merchant Company Schools.

GEORGE WATSON'S COLLEGE
✢ FOR BOYS. ✢

SESSION 1931-1932.

1ˢᵗ PRIZE *(Aggregate)*

AWARDED TO

William C. Barton

FOR

General Excellence.

Class F.   *Louisa F. M⸍ᵉ⸍...*

GEORGE ROBERTSON, M.A., Headmaster.

George Watson's College, Edinburgh

The Junior School saw us introduced to rugby, and how deeply we threw ourselves into the game. Mr J C Rattray, teacher in 7HJ, was himself a player and was the chief coach for rugby in the Junior School. I was playing regularly in the top team of the juniors. As we were nearing the end of the season and about to have the team photo taken, disaster struck. In a practice game I was feeling very unwell, but nothing would make me ask to be excused and so I played. At the end of the game Mr Rattray came to me and remarked, "I see your knees are still clean. You can't have tackled anyone, so you're not good enough for our team." I was dropped and never got into the team photo. At that early age it was a great tragedy.

At the end of the Junior School we had to face the Promotion Grading Exam to Senior School. I made it to the university class level for Senior School - two years at the U level in 1U and 2U with Paddy McLean as form master.

In the Junior School the form teacher taught all subjects, but once into the Senior School we were introduced to the system of having different teachers for each subject and so one faced many new teachers. Mr 'Teddy' Albert and Mr Findlay taught English. Here I must break off as I recall two true stories regarding my time with John Henry Findlay. I was reading from Shakespeare and pronounced the word 'whore' as 'huer'! Mr Findlay gasped and exclaimed, "The word is whore, boy... whoo-wore, boy!"

On another occasion I had obviously replied to a question from Mr Findlay with the words, "I don't know, Sir!"

"Well you should know boy. You are here to learn; your parents have paid good money for you to learn; it is my job to help you learn and so surely you will learn!"

Another English teacher was Jim Collie. Maths was taken with Messrs F J H Williams, A W Edmunds and W S Catto, and French with Messrs

R T Currall, Charlie Dawson, J S C Brown and Paddie McLean. History was taught by Mr W R Cooper, who took over Pa Crowden's boarding house. Interestingly, Graham Crowden, the senior male lead in the on-going TV show *Waiting for God*, is the son of our old teacher Pa Crowden. Graham and I were in 3MJ with Miss Lamont, before he moved on to Edinburgh Academy.

I learned my Latin with Mr A Mackenzie (renowned as one of *The Scotsman's* crossword puzzle writers), Mr Penman or Mr 'Pip' Paulin; Chemistry was with Mr W C 'Titch' Forsyth and Mr Bill Dickson, the latter also being Captain in charge of the Officer Training Corps (OTC). Other teachers who come to mind are Messrs A S Jamieson and D Jeffrey both of whom taught Physics.

One could go on about all the other subjects and the teachers, but I cannot close without remembering Mr F B Holmes, who taught me to sing, and Freddie Lemmon who taught me to swim. Art and Woodwork were taken by Messrs Hay, Parnell and Dunbar, not forgetting Gymnastics by firstly Miss Esme Park and, latterly, P E C 'Percy' Honeyman.

Throughout all my years at Watson's our Headmaster was Mr George Robertson, a learned, scholarly, quiet, humble 'gentleman' who was respected by pupils and staff alike. Six years after I left school, in my application to the Colonial Service I was required to have a character reference from my school. While not a prefect, nor holding 1st XV or XI colours, I still felt that my former Headmaster was the one to ask. I felt very humbled by what he wrote, and I treasure his reference to this day.

Like so many young children, my first recollection of walking the boards was in *King Arthur and the Burnt Cakes*, but my first real stage performance was in a Warrender Park Church (Edinburgh) production of *Princess Chrysanthemum* in 1932/33. This was a Chinese musical show in which I remember all male characters wore pig-tails, which was considered the traditional dress of Chinese males at that time.

However, it was at George Watson's that my real passion for the stage was kindled when I became involved with the Dramatic Society under the direction of J 'Scott' Allen. The school had a recognised tradition of drama and in 1937 I was cast in my first production with the Society, J M Barrie's play, *Dear Brutus*. My character was Joanna Trout - having no girls in the school at that time, boys had to play the female parts! Could I ever forget my entry, for not only was it my first major stage appearance, but I had the opening line of the play, as part of the following dialogue,

Me: "Go on Coady, lead the way."
Other: "I don't see why I should go first."
Me: "The nicest always goes first."
Other: "It's a strange house if I am the nicest."
Me: "It is a strange house."

Years later I saw a professional performance of the play and was amazed at how many of the lines I had remembered.

The Admirable Chrichten and *You Never Can Tell* followed. My last appearance at school was in *The Merchant of Venice* playing Jessica, Portia's close friend.

Too much involvement with dramatics, singing, Scouts, rugby and camping etc affected my studies and I dropped out of the U class in the third year to 3A with Mr Naismith as form master.

After the Promotion Examination at the end of the third year, it meant that there were just two more years of Senior School. I went into 4C and 5C with Mr Jim Collie as form master for those years - what a delightful man and an encouraging form master and English teacher.

The new school in Colinton Road opened up new sports opportunities. We had always had rugby and cricket, but now swimming, gymnastics, squash and tennis were added, to name a few.

We also had Scouts, OTC and many extra-mural activities, including the literary club, photographic club, choir and orchestra. Nearly all these sporting and club activities were led by members of the staff, giving their own time after school to provide us with these wonderful opportunities.

Most of my school colleagues were undergoing adolescent changes, growing into maturity with muscular development. Many of them went forward to play rugby for the 1st or 2nd teams... I made the 3rd XV.

Sandy Montgomery, form master of 4M was coach for the school 1st and 2nd cricket teams. He taught me how to keep wicket, and finally I obtained my 2nds Colours. It was a hard apprenticeship for I had to 'keep wicket' at practices inside the nets behind the stumps.

I left school with few honours - although I did achieve my 'Highers' which gave me entrance to Medical School. I was not a prefect, only a Lance Corporal in the Corps and a Patrol Leader in the Scouts.

The school's Scout troop was the 9th Morningside. Our Troop Master was the unforgettable Sandy Sommerville, more of whom later. The troop was divided into four Sections; I was in C Section, with Graham Burge as my Patrol Leader and John Gauldie as our Section leader. I joined in 1936, and in 1937 was lucky to be among the very last chosen for the troop's contingent to attend the World Scout Jamboree held at Vogelenzang, Holland. This was the last great world-wide Jamboree, with scouts from Poland, Czechoslovakia, Romania and many other countries from which scouting was outlawed after 1945. Our founder, Lord Baden-Powell, was there and we in the Scots contingent, wearing our kilts, danced our 32, 16 and 8-some reels and 'dashing-white sergeants', before Holland's Queen Wilhemina.

C Section won the Morningside District Shield with a seven scout patrol. They were to represent the District in the County Flag Competition, but needed another scout, a tenderfoot. At a troop meeting, Sandy

Sommerville congratulated the Section on their success and then called me up. He shook my hand, turned me round to face the troop and said, "This is the tenderfoot who is going to help the patrol bring back the Community Flag"... and we did!

Apart from Section camps, the troop held its annual camp at Gullane, and each Easter had a five-day trek through the Borders pulling trek-carts and sleeping in farm barns on palliasses filled with straw. The trek generally followed the Scottish Schoolboys' Club (SSC) Easter Camp. My first Gullane camp, and SSC camp and trek were in 1937. The SSC camp was held at Naemoor, where we also returned for the next two years. With the outbreak of the war all such activities had to be modified and took place in a different form.

We were entering our final year at school in 1939, so our last year was somewhat restricted, with black-outs, travelling restrictions and, of course, rationing. We had to work harder to ensure success in our studies and we trained harder in the OTC in preparation for any future service in the Forces.

Because I had been late in developing and so was small in stature while in the 5th Form, several efforts were made by friends to persuade me to return to the 6th Form. I was told I would become a prefect and would most likely make the 1st XV etc. This would provide me with more confidence and maturity for university life! However, I was so keen to enter Medical School that I could not be persuaded to carry on to Form 6. The present day practice is to have a year off before starting on one's career studies; the tradition for us was to get on with it and complete one's studies. I have never regretted leaving school at the end of Form 5.

Before moving on to the years of my medical studies let me just reflect that my nine years at Watson's were full of happiness, joy and, I suppose, success, not in the normal schoolboy criteria of being a prefect, playing for the 1st XV or XI etc, but in terms of a good education, healthy sportsmanship, introduction to Christian values and life lasting friendships.

I was blessed with having a happy home provided by my beloved guardian Auntie Whyte, in the absence of my parents. Without her loving care and the support of many friends, those vital character-forming years and education for life could have been a miserable failure.

I must record that throughout my schooldays we received corporal punishment; in Kenya with the cane, while at Watson's it was with leather straps to the palm - two, three or more strips comprising the 'taws'. It did not take any time to learn the required discipline demanded by each teacher!

The argument goes on today, but I think one is entitled to have a personal opinion formed on the basis of experience. For myself, I am convinced that such punishment helped me, along with other influences, for example, the SSC, the Scouts and Sunday School impressions, not forgetting the standards set by those whom I greatly admired, Auntie, Abe Wallace, Sandy Sommerville and so many dear friends, to set my own standards and especially not to fail myself, my parents, guardian and friends.

The Scottish Schoolboys' Club

As I have previously explained, I came to realise very early in life that I had to depend on the love of friends and I was certainly very lucky to have so many wonderful people around me all my early life. Several were older than myself, acting in the role of 'foster fathers' or as 'big brothers'.

I cannot write of friends without mentioning the Scottish Schoolboys' Club (SSC), which has had such an impact on my life. Originally called The Schoolboys' Missionary Camp, it was the vision of Stanley Nairne, who with a few close friends took boys camping in 1912; its success ensured an annual series of Scottish Schoolboys' Camps. In 1919, at a post war conference, it was acknowledged that the movement had become a club.

The aim of the Club is "To help its members discover the true meaning of the Christian faith for themselves and the rest of the world." A full history of the Club has been written and reference should be made to that. Its motto is Teneo et Teneor - I hold and am held.

Stanley Nairne was one of those people whom one is occasionally privileged to meet in life. He was quite brilliant intellectually and could have followed a professional career, but he dedicated his life to the cause of youth, helping them to develop deep convictions so that they could face life with strength, courage and faith and identify themselves as Christians.

Stanley was ably helped by so many others worthy of mention here: Sandy Sommerville, Jack Tait, Neil Campbell, Alistair Wallace, Gibby Galloway, Alec Weston, Hugh Beatty, David Williamson, Joe Ewart (who during the war was Field Marshal Montgomery's personal ADC), and so many more.

For me, probably the most memorable was Sandy Sommerville. He had been severely injured in the First World War and the story goes that he had even been laid out for burial. His batman came to pay his last respects and saw Sandy move. His life was saved but he suffered poor sight and so could not follow his career in the Ministry. Instead, like Stanley, he dedicated his life to the cause of youth, serving the young and future generations. He was truly a devout and practising Christian, pure in heart and spirit and totally unselfish, giving to others always of his best. Sandy survived with little in the way of luxuries; he did not seem to need them as the rest of us do. Sandy, Stanley and so many others had the strength of God and the Spirit of Christ in their souls.

While Sandy may have been the most memorable, Alistair, or A B Wallace, had possibly the greatest influence through my formative years. I met 'Abe' as he became known to me, in 1937 at my first Scottish Schoolboys' Club Camp at Naemoor when he was the Marquee Officer. Abe was a renowned plastic surgeon and general paediatric surgeon.

The SSC camps were held at Easter, involving boys from various Edinburgh Schools - Watson's, Heriot's, Stewart's, The Royal High School and Melville College. The camps used to attract between 180-200 boys from the age of 13 years through to school leaving age. There would often be frost on the ground in the mornings... and we were expected to wash in the freezing water of the nearby River Devon.

After breakfast, the older boys would retire to discussion groups to consider topics of relevance to our lives, while the younger boys would collect in 'Thinking Sessions', led by one of the camp leaders. The rest of the day was spent in camp games: volleyball, tenniquoit, touch rugby - all the games which were not played at school. Walking or climbing expeditions were popular, as, believe it or not, was bathing in the cold rivers!

Sandy Somerville

It is hard to believe that in those days we all wore shorts and thin shirts, no long trousers, jeans, tracksuits or anoraks.

The evenings came to an end with a sing-song, a range of camp songs with words written to well-known tunes of the day, e.g. *Hometown* and songs from *White Horse Inn* etc. There were 'turns' by officers and boys, who could become 'famous' overnight by the success of their turn! Donald McEwan, a classmate of mine at Watson's, and I were look-alikes, often called the 'heavenly twins'... or more usually the 'abominable pair'. We were involved in the old music hall skits like blowing out the candle. Gus McKnight and I were partners in *The Wee Cock Sparra* and Arthur Askey's *Busy Busy Bee*, which we were called upon to repeat in many further camp sing-songs.

After the singing every night the day closed with one of the leaders reading from the Bible and leading us in prayers. There was also a short talk on a personal Christian experience which might help us school boys to better understand the true meaning of the Christian faith.

On the last night we all collected around a huge campfire of friendship. Each camper collected a twig and as the fire blazed Stanley or Sandy would call forward the different groups of boys; those on their first, second, third, fourth or even their fifth camp. We would throw our twig onto the fire, link hands and experience the spirit of friendship which encircled the whole campfire.

I will never forget that experience at my first camp in 1937 at Naemoor standing at the fire for the first time, in front of Abe, his arm placed round my shoulder. As my group was called out he gripped my shoulder and gave me that wonderful feeling of friendship. It was a deep emotion for a young lad who had not seen his parents for three years. The experience made me realise I was not alone, but surrounded by a wealth of friends and a spirit of Christian fellowship. It was at these Scottish School Boys' camps that I was able to find the true meaning of the Christian faith for myself, and how I could be involved with that throughout the world for the rest of my life.

A feature of the camps was that, because it was always so cold at Easter, we used to sleep in bell tents which were pitched inside marquees. Robin Winchester was our Tent Officer while Abe was the i/c or Marquee Officer.

Abe realised that with my father overseas I probably had no male guardian relationship and so took it upon himself, as the good Christian he was, to watch over me and to support Auntie on behalf of my parents. On his rounds, moving to and from the Sick Children's Hospital at the end of Warrender Park Road, he would on occasions stop, come upstairs, just for a few minutes, and chat to Auntie as to how I was getting on, to encourage me, help me, guide me and always support me. Before he married, Abe lived with his parents in Argyle Place, further down Warrender Park Road, and I was always welcome there if I had any problems.

Abe married dear Marney, a Canadian, in 1937. When they returned from their honeymoon to live in Comely Bank, she too accepted me as a kid brother. I suppose I had been anxious about losing my 'best friend'. Far from that, I gained a big sister. It was wonderful for me to have Abe and Marney always there to turn to, to love and to be loved. As in time they had their family, Christine, Alison and twins Alistair and Mary, so I gained further little sisters and a brother, who have always remained part of my life.

At my first SSC camp in 1937 I also met Norman Horn, who had been School Captain at Watson's, later studying Medicine and becoming a Consultant in Chest Diseases and Tuberculosis and settling in Edinburgh. He made a great impression on me, for he was always ready to give his time just to encourage this little schoolboy who was lost and wandering around, needing affection, guidance and God, and the understanding of what life was really all about. He was marvellous.

62

Abe

Our paths parted when I left for Kenya and I doubt if Norman even remembers me. He might even be embarrassed if he was told of the impact that he had on the young Barton at that time, and of the gratitude that I have always held for all he did to help me in those early formative years of my life.

* * * * *

Craigmillar Boys' Club

The Craigmillar Club was supported by funding from George Watson's Boys' College, to provide a boys' club facility for the families moved from the slums of the Cannongate in the High Street to the new housing estate at Craigmillar. Sandy Sommerville was the driving force behind the project and was the Club Leader for many years.

Sandy was also the Scoutmaster of our Watson's troop, the 9th Morningside Scout Troop, which I joined in 1937. Instead of having a Rovers Troop, those who had been Scouts of the 9th Troop followed on to the Craigmillar Boys' Club, which was a member of the Edinburgh Association of Boys' Clubs (EABC) and naturally the Scottish Association of Boys' Clubs (SABC). Those among the leaders whom I recall, and who were all great friends, included Gus McKnight, Ado Scott, Stuart Aikman, Walter Jamieson, Donald McEwan, David Young, Bobby Calder, the Wishart twins, George Goodall, Norman Smart, Rae Lyon, Kenny Lyon and others.

Some of the club lads were quite tough and one always had to be on one's guard. Sandy was quite incredible in the way he was able to handle the boys and every delicate situation.

Two stories of personal amusing incidents must be recorded:

I went along to the Club every Friday night, generally with Gus McKnight and Walter Jamieson. That was the night-out when my student friends went for a few beers. I could not afford to join them and so went straight to the Club from home. On one occasion I was prevailed upon to join the crowd at the pub, to have a half pint to celebrate a birthday. After my quick drink, I slipped away and when I walked into the Club I passed Sandy who turned round and with a smile remarked, "The first pint always smells the worst!" Never again did I dare have even a half pint before going on to the Club on a Friday!

To raise funds for the Club we decided to have our first Club Dance. What a risk! I asked Helen Crowden to come as my partner; she was the daughter of one of our school teachers, Harry Crowden, and went to a posh Edinburgh school. I had warned her of the possible behaviour of some of the lads.

It was well into the evening and I was sitting quietly with Helen when young Tommy Taylor came up and asked me, "Can I ask yer dame fur a dance?"
"Of course," I replied, "Just ask her."
"Whit's her name?"
"Helen."
"Oh Nellie!" And, turning to Helen he said, "Here Nellie. See's a len of your chassis for the next wiggle."
"Pardon?" was Helen's reply.
"Come and rub bellies and swap breath with me," was Tommy's response.
I turned again to Helen and with a smile remarked, "Tommy is asking you to dance with him."
'You could have fooled me,' was obviously in her mind!

The following week Helen was walking along the Bridges, north of the Waverley Station, when suddenly a wild finger-whistle rang out, followed by a scream. "Hi! Nellie, how yer doin'!" Helen's friend looked on with disbelief!

Helen became a great supporter of the Club, helping with future musical productions organised and run by Gus McKnight and Kenny Lyon.

SSC ~ camp advance parties

I could not close this chapter without at least listing those whose friendships I cherished then and so well remember now, even though many have since died. I have mentioned Gus McKnight who was older by three years but who taught me so much about music. I shared a common bond with Ian MacLean in that his parents lived in India and so he was left alone for schooling as I was. He was one of my own idols throughout school. He achieved so much of which any schoolboy would wish: School Captain, Captain of Rugby 1st XV while also CSM of the OTC, yet he never boasted and was at all times humble in his success. Then there was Walter Jamieson who was School Captain in my last year of school. We went through medical studies together and helped at the Craigmillar Boys' Club and as officers in the SSC. Then there was Kenny Lyon, I think the youngest in our year, who was a skilled pianist playing by ear. His parents lived in South Gilsland Road adjacent to the school and were a great support to me, as were the parents of another dear friend, Ivan Scott. So many others died in the war: Ian Laidlaw, JB Smith, Jimmy Hunter, Ken Park, Jim Brotherston and David Calder to name only a few.

The Outbreak of War

Those born before 1930 must surely remember just what they doing, where they were and what happened on 3rd September 1939, the first day of the 2nd World War, immediately following Prime Minister Neville Chamberlain's announcement to the nation that "A state of war exists between ourselves and Germany."

We can all recall the famous lines of the comedian Rob Wilton which started every war-time broadcast of his: "The day war broke out!"

We, that is sister Margaret, Auntie Whyte and myself were in Lower Largo, Fifeshire, throughout August for our annual summer holiday, where we had been going every August since 1932. We returned by train to Edinburgh on 30th August, having been closely in touch with the depressing news and feeling we should get home before any hostilities broke out, hence our return to Edinburgh a day early.

Awaiting our return was a notice to me from our Scout Leader, Sandy Sommerville, informing me that I had been placed for duty as a Boy Scout Messenger to the Air Raid Precaution (ARP) Centre, at 6 South Oswald Road, in the event of war being declared or being advised beforehand. I was to wear Scout uniform and preferably take my bicycle.

In the event, on 2nd September I received a message telling me to report the following morning, Sunday, to the Centre at 6.00 am. Fortunately, it was daylight at 5.45 am when I set off on 3rd September ready to do my bit. My first instruction was to fill the baths in the three bathrooms in the large house, in preparation for the fires expected following the first bombing raids.

Everyone in the UK on that day remembers the events that followed. At 11.00 am Mr Neville Chamberlain the PM spoke to the nation and within a few minutes of the end of his speech, before we had time to take stock of what it all might mean, the first genuine Air Raid Warning was sounded.

The start of the autumn term at school had been postponed to allow for the digging of the necessary air raid shelters, so I continued to report daily to the Centre to act as messenger boy, carrying messages round the various other centres and HQ. In due course school opened and my duties at the Centre were limited to Sundays.

The OTC parades were intensified, with regular rifle practise in the school range. In the Scouts we were expected to engage in fire-watching duties, which involved us standing on the roof tops whenever the alarms sounded at night, ready to push any fire bombs off the roofs, or if not that, then in stretcher-bearing work in the hospitals. We still continued to hold our regular Scout meetings but they had to be held in private homes. I was by this time a Patrol Leader and so Auntie agreed that my Patrol should meet weekly at our home, 131 WPR.

Looking back I wonder how and when we had time for studying for our Highers due at the end of the session. It all seemed so exciting and rather fun, though when the bombs did finally drop it was no longer funny. We were lucky in Edinburgh for we had few direct raids and it was not until after Dunkirk in 1940 that the Germans turned on the pressure and made regular raids on Glasgow and the Clyde shipping.

It was during one of those raids that I had a frightening experience. I was on air raid duty at the Medical School during my first year at 'varsity. We used to report to the ARP duty room where we were expected to stay all night. Naturally we were allowed to study, if not called upon to go on to the roof in the event of an air raid. This particular night, the first of three nights of raids on the Clyde, I was on duty. When the raid started I put on my steel helmet, grabbed my incendiary bomb shovel (long pole with a

69

scoop on the end), and a sand-bag and rushed up onto the roof of the Medical School. There I stood with my helmet on, my pole at the ready, with the sand-bag in the other hand, knees shaking and feeling very lonely. The bombers were passing overhead and our flack was going up and of course coming down! I prayed that the Jerries would not drop any incendiary bombs, and if they did that they would not land on the Medical School.

I could not help smiling though when I suddenly thought, 'the whole future of the Medical School depends on me, Mrs Barton's little boy!' It really did seem quite a music hall comedy sketch! On reflection now, I was like a character from *Dad's Army*, though it was long before that television programme came onto the screen... indeed, it was a long time before television!

Having dropped all their bombs, the Jerries returned on their way home. Again the flack went up and came down and landed around me, but fortunately with no incendiary danger. The following night I was on duty back at 131 WPR, again up on the roof. On reflection, as I say, it was all rather comical but at the time I was terrified.

On the outbreak of war my parents started sending urgent telegrams instructing my sister and me to get passages to Kenya as quickly as possible. They wanted their children to be safely in Kenya with them, which was quite understandable, especially as my father was not due to retire until 1940. I pleaded with my parents to allow me to remain in Scotland to complete my schooling and hopefully obtain my Higher School Leaving Certificates. It was finally agreed that my sister would go out and that I should remain with Auntie.

Margaret departed for Kenya, sailing from Liverpool in March 1941. Naturally it was a very anxious time for the family for we could receive no word regarding her safety until she eventually reached Mombasa, many weeks later.

I had always wanted to be a doctor, having been deeply affected by the caring Dr Carmichael, Auntie Whyte's doctor, and during my final year at George Watson's I applied for and was provisionally accepted for entrance to Medical School at the university. I wired my parents advising them of this and expressing my desire to become a doctor. The reply I received was, "Can't afford to put you through Medicine why not try banking or accountancy with your success in arithmetic at school!"

I replied, "If I can't enter Medicine I will go onto the stage and in time save enough money to finally train in Medicine!"

I really was serious about wanting to be a doctor. Everyone thought the war would only last a couple more years and I did not want to go out to Kenya. Father's reply to my 'ultimatum' was the most unselfish of any parent. "Have decided to commute my pension, so am sending you £1,085 which is all we have. This must take you through your studies."

It has to be realised that there were no available funds for me to go through Medical School, for Social Services and educational allowances for students were not in existence in 1940.

Auntie received a cheque from my father for £1,085, which was to last me, and did last me, through the five years of Medical School. I do remember that the university fees for the five years of medical training were £285! Admittedly the fees were increased a little during the five years, but only very minimally.

Naturally, because of the war, there were no holidays on the continent, no cars and few luxuries on which one could spend excessively. So I can proudly claim that I went through Medical School, all fees, books, food and lodging with Auntie, and of course pocket money, within the total my father had provided.

My father's decision about my future meant that my alternative choice of a career on the stage was put aside. Fortunately, however, I was able to continue my great interest in the theatre in the amateur environment.

My attraction to the theatre had been influenced by the fact that I had been lucky to have had an introduction to the Wilson Barrett Repertory Company. They played their seasons at the *Lyceum Theatre* in Edinburgh, and through this I got to know Wilson Barrett and Richard Mathews.

I cannot recall the names of the other players, but I do remember that Richard Mathews was a diabetic, and I always respected his great courage in playing so many major parts while taking his insulin injections during intervals.

With the demise of many repertory companies, few now realise that those in such a company, while performing every evening and even playing matinees, were rehearsing the following week's play in the mornings.

I finished my days at Watson's successful in my 'School-leavers', with three Highers and three Lowers. These grades exempted me from taking the qualifying exams for entry to Medical School.

My last year at Watson's was a happy one, interrupted occasionally by sad news of the death of one of the older boys whom we had idolised at school. In some cases they had been playing for Watsonians or even the School XV only two years before. The frequency of such news accelerated in the years following my own leaving, ie from 1940-45.

Like everyone who left school in 1940 after the first year of the war, one recalls the long list of those who shared that year together and who sacrificed their lives for the rest of us. For me the names of Jimmy Hunter, JB Smith, Ian Laidlaw, David Calder, Tom Park, Graham Burge and Bobby Budgett are but a few of the many which rush to mind.

Several of our teachers were also called up, but there was not too much disturbance to our studies in the first year of war. All that changed when our expeditionary forces withdrew from Dunkirk and Mr Winston Churchill took over from Neville Chamberlain as Prime Minister. I remember that I was in the chemistry laboratory when the news came through. Will we ever forget that first speech 'Winnie' made on taking over? "I offer you blood, toil, tears and sweat," later followed by another speech, "We will fight them on the beaches, in the streets... we will never surrender!"

As a young schoolboy just turned 17, I felt proud to be British and have so ever since. I always remember that it was the only time in my life when I felt real hatred in my heart - a deep hatred for the Germans. How dare they think they could invade us, far less defeat us! Just let them come!

Edinburgh University Medical School

In my first year at Medical School we studied chemistry, physics, botany and zoology. The final exams for the first two were at the end of the second term, and the other two at the end of the summer term. Along with these subjects we had anatomy lectures and dissections along with lectures in physiology, the exams for which were to be at the end of the second year.

We received notices instructing us to register for the chemistry and physics exams with the necessary qualifying certificates, at 10.00 am on a specific day; we were told the dates of the exams to be held, starting at 9.00 am, on successive days at the end of the spring term. I duly registered and felt confident about the exams. For some unknown reason I had it fixed in my mind that the start of the chemistry exam was 10.00 am and not 9.00 am, as I discovered when I turned up, as I thought, twenty minutes early. There were only about ten other students waiting outside the hall, which I thought was a little strange. By 9.50 we panicked and one of us looked into the hall to find the others sitting there. The shock was immense! The exam supervisor at first refused to allow us to enter, but after hearing our pleadings, gave in and so we started the impossible task of trying to complete the four questions in one hour, instead of the two hours allocated for the exam.

Will I ever forget going in for my oral exam? Professor Marrion started it by saying, "Barton you have made a great effort but have not obtained the 50% required on the paper. If you obtain 100% marking in your oral we may take that into consideration, but otherwise it will have to be a resit." All ten of us who had made the same mistake on timing had to resit in

September. It was a hard lesson which I never forgot throughout my working life - viz always double check on important timings!

So many stories come to mind when I reflect on my first year at Medical School. First there was the Anatomy Department, with dear old Dr E B Jamieson, affectionately known as 'Jimmy', who was in charge of the dissecting room. He always wore a white coat, a velvet skull cap, and smoked a pipe with the stem and mouthpiece joined by a length of bunsen burner rubber. He was greatly respected by all students. The story is told that, on entering the dissecting room, the student pushed the swing doors a split second after Jimmy had already pushed from his side. The student jarred backwards exclaiming, "Jesus Christ!" As Jimmy walked through, passing the student he remarked, "Ah yes! but strictly incognito."

Another tale tells of Jimmy taking the final exam for a student at the end of the dissection of the upper limb. Jimmy picked up the humerus bone and asked the student "What is this?"
"A bone Sir."
"Good! Which bone?"
"The upper limb, Sir."
"Which bone boy?"
"Please Sir, I am not going for honours, just a pass."

The student was faced with a resit!

Then of course there was Jimmy's famous men-only lecture or talk on 'sex'. The women students, who numbered about 50 in a year of 200, were furious, but in those days sexual discrimination did operate, and anyway you could not expect to have talks or discussions on sex in a mixed audience. Certainly Jimmy would never have agreed to giving such a talk to women. His talk was more as guidance on the temptations and problems of sex facing young males. It was given at the end of the anatomy course just weeks before the final exam in anatomy and physiology, which had to be passed together and for which only one resit was allowed - they therefore had to be taken very seriously. Jimmy's last sentence as he closed the talk and started to move to the door was, "Gentlemen, my advice to you is you must now screw your scrotums to the chair and get down to serious study! Good luck!"

What an experience it was to be suddenly thrown into the academic world where no one set you 'homework' or bullied you into study. You were the master of your own fate.

Success in the second year in anatomy and physiology provided immediate security for me to continue my studies into the real world of Medicine.

The names of Professor Brash in anatomy, Professor Gaddam in physiology, Sir 'Willie' Wright-Smith in botany, along with, of course, 'Jimmy' in dissection, have remained with me over these last 60 years.

The third year covered bacteriology with Professor Mackie, pathology with Professor Drennan, materia medica with Professor Derek Dunlop, later Sir Derek, and, in time, clinical medicine and clinical surgery. I found the opportunity to junior in the wards was a real introduction to true medical practice.

Our clinical studies took us into the Royal Infirmary of Edinburgh (RIE). I was lucky to be accepted to junior in surgical wards 7-8 under Sir John Fraser, Regius Professor of Clinical Surgery, with Sister Sutton in charge of the wards, Sister Bertram in charge of the theatre and Dr John Gillies as his anaesthetist. At that time Sir John's number two was 'Wattie' Mercer, later Sir Walter, Professor of Orthopaedics.

Other Consultant Surgeons were Mr Graham (5-6), Mr Jardine (15-16), Mr Patterson-Brown (13-14), Mr Dott (20), Mr Quarry-Wood (9-10) and Sir James Learmonth (11-12). The Clinical Medical Chiefs were Professor Murray-Lyon, Dr A Rae Gilchrist, Professor Derek Dunlop, Dr Todd and Dr Fergus Hewitt.

The following years introduced us to forensic medicine with Sir Sydney Smith, the Dean of the Medical School, obstetrics and gynaecology with Professor J W Johnstone, ENT with Mr Simpson, venereal diseases with Dr Batchelor, psychiatry with Professor Henderson, ophthalmology, dermatology and other subjects.

Every student remembers the anecdotal stories which they shared in their clinical studies. I relate three:

The advice given by Sir James Learmonth to us just before we went into our finals: "In your orals, if asked 'What is the bird sitting on the telephone wire?' do not give the reply, 'a canary'! Start with the sparrows and only if they don't satisfy your examiner then start thinking of the canaries."

Professor Derek Dunlop's legend provides many stories: Sitting beside the patient in a clinical in the ward, he asked Euan Douglas, our 6'4" rugger star, "How do you test for ascites?" Douglas paused, looked at the patient, looked at Derek, paused again and stammered out "Shoogle her and see if she splashes!" Derek sank to his knees, buried his head in his hands, and cried out, "Shoogle her and see if she splashes! My God! My God! Shoogle her and see if she splashes!" Poor Euan wished he could have disappeared... the rest of us were anxious, waiting for the explosion! Derek finally looked up, smiled, turned round and said, "Tell him someone!" None of us there would ever forget how to test for ascites!

On another occasion, again sitting beside a patient, Derek Dunlop, enquiring about her symptoms asked, "Do you feel scunnered?" All the Scots knew exactly what he meant, only the English students looked lost!

Derek was always ready to give guidance to final year students to help them function in their chosen profession. The following story demonstrates this well:

77

Professor Dunlop always dressed immaculately with matching tie and top pocket handkerchief. His advice to us was, "Don't worry too much about the suit you are wearing. What's important in facing a patient is that you have polished shoes, clean collar and clean cuffs. When the patient enters the consulting room, get up, go to meet them and ask them to take a seat, sitting in front of them. Their eyes will drop - they will not look you straight in the eye. They will see your shoes, and from the state of them may form a first impression of your clinical standard. As you continue the consultation they will raise their eyes, but still not straight eye-to-eye. Rather, they will look at your neck and see your collar - clean? Finally, when they are lying on the couch waiting for your examination, as soon as you place your hand on their chest or abdomen, their eyes will drop to watch your hand. What will they see? Your cuff. Those three - always remember: clean shoes, clean collar, clean cuffs!"

Few opportunities existed during the war years at university in Edinburgh to participate in any student drama presentations, but almost yearly there was a major production at the Usher Hall, to raise funds for the Services - either buying a *Spitfire*, a destroyer, tank or other wartime armament need.

The productions were staged by professionals, with amateur actors or singers being used as the supporting cast. I was lucky to be chosen to appear in two such productions, as a Battle of Britain pilot in one, and a naval officer in another.

Holidays were out during those years. It was either felling trees in lumber camp, bringing in the harvest, Home Guard duties, or helping in ambulance services or in special hospitals, e.g. mental asylums, as they were called then. I used to go every holiday during my last two years as a student resident at the Fife District Asylum in Springfield, Cupar. The Medical Superintendent was Dr W Boyd with Dr Mitchell as his Assistant. Dr Boyd and his wife played the role of parents to me during those happy days. Their son was like a kid brother and he became a Psychiatrist, Dr Bill Boyd.

I always remember entering our fourth year final professional exam. It was the time of 'D' Day and was difficult to concentrate on something like exams when the whole future of our country was at stake. We all listened to the wireless whenever we could for news of the landings and, in time, of the advance. It was a long year.

Then the finals were looming. It was clear by this time that victory was ours, i.e. the Allies. The black-out had been slackened and people were beginning to await the final news of surrender. I had been invited to Frances Campbell's 21st Birthday Party, to be held in *Gibsons* in Prince's Street on 8th May 1945. She was to be 21 at the bewitching hour of midnight. The surrender had been declared and so everyone was on the streets and particularly Prince's Street. At midnight we all went onto the balcony at *Gibsons* and waved to the crowds below as if we were Royalty. Those of us who were about to sit our finals had to return to reality very quickly for time was running out and there was still so much to learn!

Finals consisted of six written papers: systematic and clinical papers on medicine, surgery and obstetrics/gynaecology.

These papers were then followed by six clinical case studies (three short and three long) and finally three orals. In all there were fifteen examinations over a period of three weeks. As my name started with 'B' I was at the top of the lists for the clinical case studies and orals. I therefore finished my exams after fifteen days. Rather than sit around for the results to be posted, as I was a leader I decided to go to the annual Edinburgh Union of Boys' Clubs camp, down in the Borders, with the lads from the Craigmillar Boys' Club.

Will I ever forget seeing Sandy Montgomery (the same Sports Master of my school days) drive up in his little 'Baby *Austin*', with Katharine Barratt, who had been my loving companion for my last year at university. They stepped out of the car, approached Walter Jamieson and myself and quietly said, "Dr Barton and Dr Jamieson I presume." That wonderful, wonderful moment of joy and relief was one never to be forgotten.

Four memories of the most wonderful moments of my life are: being addressed as Dr Barton for the first time; taking my marriage vows; being told I had a daughter; being told I had a son.

To conclude this chapter there is one point which requires clarification... my name.

Few people can have experienced the embarrassment I did through the early years of my life. Most children when asked their name proudly repeat it with clarity and without interruption.

I was always know as Bill. When I set off for my first school in Nakuru I had a photo taken of me standing there wearing my new double terrai hat and holding my little attache case in front of me. The case measured about eighteen inches long, ten inches wide and six inches deep. It had the letters W.C.B. on it in white paint. That was 1929.

Next came my entry into George Watson's Boys' College in Edinburgh in January 1932. I was entered as William Barton with no mention of my middle initial 'C'.

Thereafter, Father came back on his home leave in 1935 and on reading my school report he questioned me about my middle name.
"What middle name Dad?"
"Your middle name, Cochran."
Mother retorted, "You know quite well that he was never given Cochran as a middle name'. He is just plain William."
"Nonsense," responded Dad, "go back to school and get them to insert your middle name."

So after being four years at Watson's I went up to my teacher in 9HJ 'Pa' Lennie, who was also Headmaster of the Junior School, to explain,

"Please Sir, my father tells me that my name was wrongly recorded and I should have 'Cochran' inserted as my middle name."

So, duly my middle name was reinserted. Unfortunately Dad had not told me that the name 'Cochran' did not have an 'E' at the end. So I was registered as William Cochrane Barton.

For the next five years I suffered the embarrassment of having to reply to the question in every new class: "What is your name?"
"Barton Sir."
"Your initials?"
"WC Sir."

This was met with sniggers all round the class and I was open to many nick-names, e.g. piss-pot Bill! I learned to live with my embarrassing initials WC!

I went through the next five years of senior school at Watson's and entered and achieved my Scottish Higher School leaving certificate, with entry to university, as William Cochrane Barton.

As I was about to start my studies at the University I had a letter from my mother to tell me that Cochrane was not my middle name and I should register as plain William! Back again I went to the Registrar to request him to remove my middle name! I was relieved to think that I could go through my student years as plain William. I was told by the Registrar that I would have to bring in my birth certificate before I qualified and was formally registered with the General Medical Council.

Another five years went past, but still no birth certificate had come through from my parents. In due course it did arrive, just before my final exams. Enclosed with it was a note from my mother which simply stated, "You'll be surprised to see that you have a middle name which is not Cochran but is Leftwich! I am sorry you haven't heard of it before but please don't bring the subject up with your father and never ask any questions about it... Please! You will now have to register your official name with the University."

Again I had the embarrassment of going back to the Registrar explaining that now, at 22 years old, I discover I have a middle name which I had never heard of before... and it is Leftwich!

When Sandy Montgomery drove up to the camp to tell me I had passed, in conversation he told me that he had registered my name for the graduation ceremony and for the preparation of my certificate. He had never seen me write my new name and so registered me as William 'Leftwitch' Barton.

So it is that I have a school leaving certificate with William Cochrane Barton and a graduation certificate with William Leftwich Barton! I have gone through life as William C.; William; William Cochrane, again plain William, and finally William Leftwich... yet all the time my name has been William Leftwich Barton.

The family sometimes call me Lefty and I will never know why or from where I got my middle name, but we will just leave it at that!

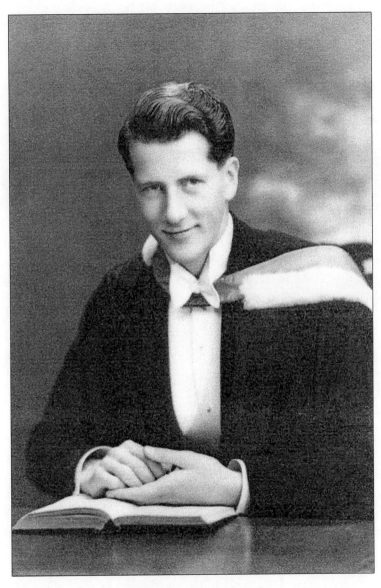

Dr Barton I presume?

Starting Off as a Doctor

In my last year at university Professor Sir John Fraser, Regius Professor of Clinical Surgery, was appointed as Vice-Principal of the University of Edinburgh and so gave up his Chair and being Chief of Wards 7-8 in the Edinburgh Royal Infirmary (RIE). This was a great honour for him, but a great disappointment for myself for he had earlier suggested that he would seriously consider me as his house surgeon after I qualified, starting in August 1945. As Professor of Clinical Surgery, he was also Chief of the Surgical Out-patients Department (SOPD), now generally known as 'Accident and Emergency'. After giving up his wards, Sir John recommended me to the Chief of SOPD for selection as one of the three housemen there. This duly happened and I took up 'residence' in the Infirmary Mess in August 1945 along with Dr Hamish Watson and Dr John Littlejohn. Mr Curr was Chief of SOPD and the Sister in charge was Sister Maggie Dewar.

I hold wonderful memories of my six months in SOPD for several reasons. Firstly, it proved to be the ideal training for my future service, that of working in a 'native hospital' in a district in Kenya. Attending to emergencies which turned up in SOPD truly gave me the confidence to tell the difference between a medical and surgical emergency and to handle all types of accidents, particularly fractures of the wrists and arms, as well as operating on the flow of septic hands that one saw as part of the daily routine.

In those days, we had no penicillin at our disposal for treating such bad infections. Penicillin was a new drug which was only being issued for trial purposes to special units, of which we were fortunate to be one. Daily, we received horrific septic infections of the hands, generally following a cut or even a nick which had become infected. It was quite usual for the whole hand, including the fingers and palm, to become painfully swollen and fill with pus, necessitating an incision to allow the pus to escape. Small rubber drains were inserted across the three phalanges in each finger and then further incisions were made into each web between the fingers. Drains were inserted deep into the palm, again to allow the pus to drain out. Before the common use of penicillin, it was then up to nature to heal the hand after the pus had fully drained out. Supplemented with the new drug, the healing process was hastened. In time, penicillin given by intra-muscular injection prevented the spread of the infection and soon the crippling problem of septic palm was seldom seen. Naturally, when I first arrived in Kenya, such infections still existed and so my experience in SOPD stood me in good stead.

The significance of a functioning thumb was brought seriously to my attention in one case. I was called to see a miner whose thumb had been caught in a machine at the coal face. He was still covered in coal dust and the distal phalanx of his thumb was being held only by a narrow strip of skin. With a local injection I tried to clean up the area which was embedded with coal dust. I decided that the only solution was to cut off the distal phalanx and try to build up an adequate cover for the stump. I told the miner of my decision. There was a long pause before he looked me straight in the eye and said, "You realise, Doctor, that if you remove my thumb I will become unemployable. I must be able to grip a tool in my right hand to carry out my job." In the days before National Social Security benefits, unemployment benefits and accident compensations that we know today, he and his family would be seriously affected by my planned action.

I thought again and decided that it was up to me to save the situation for him and his family. So, with painstaking patience, determination and perseverance, I found all the nerve endings, muscle tendons and sheaths and cleaned up all the tissues before rebuilding the thumb. Finally, after many hours of labour and sweat, I enclosed his arm, hand and thumb in plaster-of-paris and he left with a thumb in place again. Whether it would be an adequately functioning thumb, time alone would tell. It transpired that he was left with a fixed terminal joint to his thumb, but returned to work and continued his lifestyle. It was a lesson I never forgot during the rest of my medical career: never take a short cut to save yourself time or inconvenience.

I have a notion that the residency for housemen no longer exists, having been replaced by night rooms for doctors on duty. The traditions of the residency must not be allowed to be forgotten. Each resident had his own bedroom. In charge of the residency was the house-steward, who served as a butler at our meals. Breakfast and lunch were flexible meals in time because of the demands of work, but one was expected to attend dinner every night, unless yours was the 'waiting ward' or you were involved with an emergency.

The eldest resident or 'Father' sat at the head of the table with the rest of us occupying our allotted places. When we first entered the residency we were individually asked whether we could play a musical instrument, sing or tell a story. If deemed by 'Father' to have committed a misdemeanour, he would call upon you to perform as indicated, play, sing or speak! Swearing was deemed a misdemeanour and so until we all settled down and controlled our language, punishment was frequently handed out to the amusement of the rest! Another misdemeanour was a fart. If you were guilty you were expected to confess it by raising you right index finger. It was left to the discretion of Father whether or not you would be punished. If you did not own up and someone challenged you over the event, you were honour bound to confess, when you certainly would be ordered a punishment.

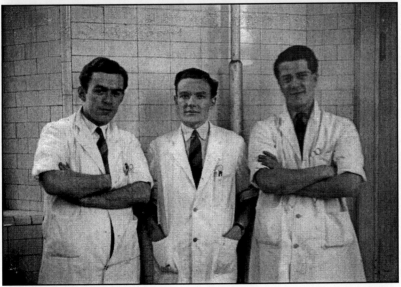

Dr Hamish Watson, Dr John Littlejohn and Dr Bill Barton!

87

The large, wooden residency dining table was scrubbed clean daily. It was engraved with the signatures of all the residents over the many years. Naturally there were several tables filled up with such signatures. One signed the table then chiselled out the signature, leaving the engraving for all time.

The three of us in SOPD also had a photo for our six month residency period and similarly engraved our own wooden table which we left hanging on the wall along with those of the famous earlier residents. Each group was expected to have its own topical theme of the period of their residency. Ours was a picture of the three of us each with our index finger raised and each wearing a small school cap, for we had gained a reputation of always farting in the residency and being sent to stand in the corner like naughty little boys! When I revisited the residency in 1995 (fifty years after qualifying) I looked for, and found, my signature on a table now hanging on a wall. Similarly, I found the table in SOPD with my signature. How proud I felt.

At Christmas, one or two residents traditionally dressed up as Santa and went round all the wards delivering stockings to all the children in the side wards. I went round with Dr Watty Gillies, another resident, and we arranged how to split up the wards.

Something went wrong! I was in a side ward having wakened up one of the kids to give him his stocking of presents. As I announced myself as Father Christmas, suddenly Watty entered with his bag of stocking presents. Oh dear! The little boy looked at him and then at me. "You said you were Father Christmas?"
"Yes, that's right."
"Then who's this yun?"
"Him? Oh, he's Santa Claus!"
Watty quickly disappeared and the little fellow snuggled down satisfied!
Wow! A near thing!

Residency parties to celebrate special occasions were the norm. We had a real feast on Christmas Eve, as Christmas Day was to be an off-day for the residency staff. At the end of the dinner we decided that we should give the Medical Superintendent of RIE a Christmas present. He was an ex-Indian Army officer, Colonel Stewart, not at all popular with the residency. His house was right opposite and so it was easy to watch the lights of his house being extinguished. We crept out and, with plaster-of-paris, decorated his wall with 'Happy Christmas Stewpot'. We then decorated the tree in his garden with toilet paper rolls, a bed-pan, urine bottle, and such similar medical or surgical equipment we could lay our hands on. Our boldest effort, however, was to go along to the maternity ward and remove a recently delivered placenta to hang from the tree top. Rather unsavoury and disgusting, but at the time we thought it amusing!

The next morning we received a message from the Colonel that we were all to appear in the residency at lunch time to be faced by the Board of Governors who had been summoned to meet us and, we were told, they were likely to sack us. It appears that the Governors were not amused by the Colonel calling them out on Christmas Day for what they reckoned was an amusing joke. In the event only three turned up and it all became an embarrassment for the Colonel and no more was heard of the incident. In fact he had no real proof that we were involved, for none of the RIE staff saw anything!

It is probably true to say that every group of residents were threatened with dismissal during their six months. The problem for the Superintendent was that there was no possibility of finding any replacements, so we were really pretty secure. This was all the more so because salary payments for residents were a paltry £6 per month. What's more, we were the first group to receive any payment at all, for it had always been considered an honour to be selected and so previous residents had received no remuneration!

89

During the time of my residency, my parents arrived back in the UK after eight years. My father had been discharged from the army and granted LILOP (leave in lieu of pension) as he had not been able to take his terminal home leave upon retiring from KUR&H in 1940. I had not seen my parents during those years and both sides were apprehensive of the reunion.

I was given 'off duty' to allow me to meet my parents at Waverley Station in Edinburgh, and for my parents to settle in with Auntie Whyte at 131 WPR. On our first evening, Dad, while opening a bottle of beer, asked me if I drank. I replied in the affirmative, to which he responded, "This will be an expensive home leave."

After the 9.00 o'clock news Dad got up stating, "Well, time for bed." "Yes," I replied, "I'll have to get back to the RIE - I'm on duty at SOPD as from midnight." Dad's response was, "Now, young man, you must learn; you cannot burn the candle at both ends. You need adequate kip to perform effectively." He found it difficult to accept that I was 22 years of age and a doctor. To him, I was still the 14 year old schoolboy he had left behind in early 1938.

Mother had accompanied Dad on leave. Dad returned on a troop ship after six weeks, but there was not room for Mother so she had to wait for another passage back to Kenya.

Coming to the end of my residency in SOPD at the end of January 1946, I became aware that, unlike my colleagues, I had received no communication concerning my military call-up. While the war was over, with both VE and VJ Days behind us, call-up of medics was being continued to allow those in service to be speedily released. Accordingly, I contacted our local War Medical Council Office in Edinburgh to enquire why I had not heard anything.

I was soon advised that I was not going to be called up. It was explained that as I had been born in Kenya and was financially supported by my parents presently resident there, I came under the Kenya call-up regulations. Kenya had cancelled her call-up programme, the war in East Africa having long since ended. It was then that I decided I should do my 'service' in the Colony of my birth and accordingly applied to join the Colonial Medical Service, intending to complete but one tour, which in those days was 3-3½ years, thus fulfilling, as I thought, my obligation of service.

I decided to apply to the Colonial Office for service in East Africa. In due course, in April 1946 I was called for a selection interview in London. This, to my conscious memory, was my first visit to London.

At the interview, after being asked to sit down, I was offered a cigarette, obviously to put me at my ease! I accepted, lit up, took my first puff and inhaled. Obviously nervous, I spluttered, coughed and could hardly speak!

The interview continued, each member of the committee being invited to question me. Finally the Chairman, Dr Jewell, looked at me and enquired, "How is your mother? Do give her my regards. Though we have never met before, I have known of you for many years." I was totally confused, but all was revealed later, when I told my mother of the question and Dr Jewell's remarks. She smiled and told me that Dr Jewell had been in charge of her ante-natal during her pregnancy with me. He should in fact have delivered me, but Father was transferred from Mombasa to Kisumu where I was eventually delivered!

At my interview an attempt was made to encourage me to go to Uganda. I made my ultimatum, Kenya or nothing!

I was selected and offered an appointment as a Medical Officer in Kenya and in due course received my travel directions. I was to sail on the *RMS Alcantara* from Southampton in August, four months hence.

While I had been waiting for my application for the Colonial Medical Service to be processed, I was lucky to be offered a post as resident junior assistant in the practice of Dr Lowell Lamont with his wife Janet, in Bruntsfield Terrace, as from early February 1946.

A severe 'flu epidemic was raging that winter which made an already busy practice pretty hectic, but I learned a great deal of life. Remembering the fact that penicillin was not available for general use, only *M&B 693* and *760*, one had to visit 'flu cases every day, and in severe cases sometimes twice.

I was generally released from being present at the evening surgery to allow me to work through the long list of calls for the day. I well remember climbing three flights of tenement stairs, ringing the bell and, after waiting a short while, hearing a voice behind the door asking "Who's it?"
"It's the doctor."
"The doctor! At this time of night? We're a' in bed."
"I'm visiting in response to your call; so sorry I'm so late but how's the patient?"
"She's asleep, could ye' call the morn'?"
"Fine."

I looked at my watch to see it was 10.30 pm. No wonder they were in bed!

When I qualified at the age of 22 I looked like a lad of 17, so I always wore a hat. Not only was it the fashion, but was the required dress for the profession. Dr Lamont always wore his 'Anthony Eden'; for me it was a 'pork-pie' trilby style. I always kept my hat on till they answered the door and I was across the threshold, for in the early days when the door opened they would gape and ask, "Yes?"
"I'm the doctor."
"The doctor? Yer too young to be a doctor. I was expecting Dr Lamont!"... and the door would shut. Once I was inside the house and had taken off my hat they found it impolite to throw me out.

On the morning of a Murrayfield rugger international, I appeared at breakfast dressed in a pair of R W Forsyth's blue and white pin-stripe flannel trousers, a Harris tweed jacket, quiet sports shirt and woollen tie. "And where do you think you are going dressed like that?" was Mrs Lamont's comment. I explained that, after completing my list, I was joining a few colleagues for a snack lunch before going on to the match. "Not until you have been home to change back into these clothes!" And that's how it was! To be properly dressed was an essential value operating in the practice!

I studied medicine when students wore grey flannels, tweed jackets and ties, or suits. This was the era when if you saw a male walking along the corridor of the hospital in a white coat, you knew that he was a medical student or doctor if he was wearing a tie, while without one he was probably a painter going out for a leak! Back then, the white coat was the mantle of dignity and not the garb of decadence, which it seems to be considered these days!

I experienced further episodes while in the practice that have lasted in my memory. At breakfast one morning, while reviewing the list of visits, Dr Lamont asked me to make my first call at the *Pooles Cinema*, behind the Usher Hall. He had received a phone message to say that the daughter of the house had been haemorrhaging... they concluded from 'piles'. I duly called at the cinema and met 'father', who told me, "The wife is waiting for you upstairs." So up I climbed to the top and was met by 'mother' who seemed distressed. "Oh doctor! It's terrible! Jeannie will tell you about it." When I entered the room I realised immediately that there had been a childbirth. Enquiring what had happened, Jeannie explained that in the middle of the night she had had a severe stomach ache and a bearing down pain. She thought she must have haemorrhoids. Feeling faint and needing air, she went to open the window. "I got up, and when I was crossing the room to open the window it just popped out!"

93

"Just popped out! So where's the baby now?"

"In a paper bag on the top shelf in the cupboard!"

Sure enough there it was! She was still retaining the placenta with the umbilical cord, which she had tied with string to cut herself free. I later questioned Jeannie and her mother about missing the pregnancy. Mother replied, "Well, I thought Jeannie was getting a wee bit fatter, but she has always been a big girl!" In reply to my question, "But surely you had noticed that you were not having your periods?" Jeannie commented, "Aye, but I thought it was very convenient!"

Realising the concealment of pregnancy to be a crime in Scotland, I contacted Dr Lamont who turned up without delay! The phone call before the delivery was the saving grace.

In another case, I was surprised by an interview I had with a young couple consulting about sterility. He was an airman in the RAF. I saw the wife first, and from the discussion I could see no reason why she should be sterile. My interview with the husband made me realise that their knowledge of the sexual act was certainly lacking. It was obvious from his description that they had never consummated their marriage. On examination of the wife this suspicion was confirmed for she was certainly still a virgin.

Another episode was one which many young recently qualified doctors may have had to face. In the evening surgery I called out Miss L from the waiting room. After taking the history, I told her to retire behind the screen, lie on the couch and loosen her clothing so that I could palpate her abdomen. When told she was ready, I went round the curtain to find her lying on the couch, totally naked and without the sheet covering her. I quickly covered her up, and making the excuse that I had forgotten to warm my hands, withdrew from the scene. I slipped out and called Mrs Lamont who was in surgery with me. I explained my dilemma. "Not her again! She does this to all our young assistants. I'll pop in and help you out." All went well and Miss L didn't have the time to scream - a terrifying experience for one newly qualified. A near thing?

I finished my six months in practice with the Lamonts, and in August 1946 set sail from Southampton, headed for Mombasa, to take up my first appointment in the Colonial Medical Service.

The Colonial Service

Kenya 1946 - 1956

Arriving in Kenya - 1946

The *Alcantara* had been a passenger liner on the South American route but was commandeered as a troop transport ship to repatriate UK servicemen after their service in East Africa and who were now entitled to LILOP. The ship also transported recruits for the Colonial Service and new Settlers for the three East African Territories, Kenya, Uganda and Tanganyika. As the *Alcantara* was a troop transport ship the sexes were segregated and we were bunked with between four and six in a cabin.

The *Alcantara* was the first passage to Kenya my mother had been able to secure since my father's return six months earlier. This was doubly fortunate for me as, apart from her company on the four week voyage, when we arrived in Mombasa I had no cash and had to borrow £5 from her to enable me to get off the ship and start my Colonial Service.

However, travelling with Mum also had its embarrassing moments, for example, it was thought that I was returning with her after a holiday in the UK. I was asked by one passenger how long I still had to go at the Prince of Wales School, the main secondary school for Europeans in Kenya! I was sailing out to my first assignment as an MO and they thought I was still at school - I looked that young!

The *Alcantara* was a 'dry ship', but one of the privileges I enjoyed, having been acknowledged by the ship's surgeon as a colleague, was being invited to his cabin for the occasional drink!

Many of my fellow travellers on the *Alcantara* remained friends for the rest of my life. They included Desmond Hone who, after his war service was joining the dental firm of Jack Melhuish and Jimmy Guest, and Pat Lidell who was joining the staff at Limuru Girls' School as their Gym

99

teacher. In 1949 Desmond and Pat married. I also met Anne Carrick on the *Alcantara*. She was on her first appointment in the Colonial Service as a Nursing Sister with the Kenya Medical Service. In 1950 she married Bobby Winser, a DO with whom I served in Kisii. Another lifelong friend met on the voyage was Meg Le Blanc-Smith, returning to her Kenya family. She later married Peter Derrick who was DC at Wajir when I first arrived there in 1947.

Desmond Hone did me a great service in introducing me to Jack Melhuish and Joan Waddington, with whom he stayed when he first arrived in Nairobi to work in Jack's practice. They lived in Woodlands Road, not far from what was then Government House. Their house was large and rambling, built of wood and with a large verandah along the front entrance which housed several cages for parrots and a hyrax, while two loveable dogs, an Alsatian and a golden setter, were also always present. Other space on the verandah was taken up with various tropical plants and shrubs. They were close friends of Colonel and Mrs Belcher, who were later to become my 'in-laws'.

Whenever I visited Nairobi during my first tour in Kenya I was always invited to stay with Jack and Joan. Their home was ever full of interesting people and one always felt one belonged to an extended family. It was so comforting to have such a family. At their house I met some very important Kenya Settlers and Officials as well. So many names come to mind: Archie Ritchie, the Game Warden of Kenya, and his wife Queenie; Cliff and Mollie Baimbridge, the Senior Surgeon of the Medical Department; the Nightingales from the Kinancop, and Alan and Joan Davies from Nyeri, who had a holiday home in Kilifi.

Other houseguests included present and future Governors such as Sir Percy Wyn Harris of Gambia, Sir Henry Guerney from Malaysia, Sir Walter Coutts and his wife 'Bones' from Uganda, Sir Fredrick and Lady Crawford of Uganda, and Sir John Waddington from Nyasaland.

100

R.M.S. "ALCANTARA" (22,209 tons)

Two other passengers sailing out with me on the *Alcantara* were later to become well-known figures in East Africa.

Jomo Kenyatta was returning from his self-imposed exile from Kenya. After his role in the Mau Mau he became the First President of Kenya at the time of its Independence on 12th December 1963. Jomo Kenyatta proved to be a somewhat troublesome passenger, constantly complaining about conditions. It was reported that the ship's Captain faced Jomo and informed him that he was travelling on a troop transport ship and so military discipline prevailed; he would either have to comply with the conditions or, if he preferred, the Captain would slow down the ship to allow Jomo to disembark!

The other noteworthy passenger was Juma Aley, who was returning from studies in the UK to join the Education Department in Zanzibar. He later became a Minister of the Government at the time of Independence for Zanzibar on 10th December 1963.

My mother and I were met at the port by the MOH Mombasa, Dr Bill Davies, who later became DMS Uganda. I was very impressed for he was immaculately dressed in white socks, white shorts and white short-sleeved shirt. He took us to his home to meet his wife, Joan. After lunch, Bill went to rest, only having to return to the office at 2.00 pm. He re-appeared after a cold shower with a complete change of his whites.

I was posted to the Native Civil Hospital in Mombasa for about a week before setting off 'up country' for a posting at Kiambu. During my brief stay in Mombasa I had met Dr Bunny Haynes who was then MO i/c but later became the TB Specialist for Kenya based at Port Reitz in Mombasa. Bunny asked me if I would give an anaesthetic to a private case he had in for a haemorrhoid operation that afternoon. I agreed and asked, "Will it be an open or closed circuit anaesthetic?" I was met with a blank stare and a pause before Bunny replied "Oh!... Open."

When I turned up in the theatre, I looked around and, failing to see the machine, I enquired where it was. "There," replied Bunny pointing to a table upon which was laid a face mask with a muslin cover, and a bottle standing beside it. I freely admit that I gasped, for it was a bottle of ether. "I said it was to be an open anaesthetic," was Bunny's comment!

I had never given such an 'open' anaesthetic and was certainly lacking in confidence when Bunny asked, "Shall I begin?" How would I know! Fortunately the operation was a success in that the patient lived!

In due course I was met at Nairobi railway station by Dr Kenneth Martin the DDMS Kenya, who took me to his home and next day took me to Medical HQ in Anderson Road, to meet the DMS, Dr Maclennan, and ADMSs, Dr Alan Howell, who later became DMS Tanganyika and Dr Teddy Trim, later to become DMS Uganda.

Dr Howell told me I would be relieving Dr Edward Rigby at Kiambu for four weeks as MO i/c of the Native Civil Hospital and he wished me the same luck in service as he had enjoyed. As he said, "It was twelve years before I was posted to HQ" - in my case it was ten years.

It may be appropriate here to explain the relationship which existed between 'Officials' and 'Settlers'.

While Europeans from both the UK and South Africa had begun to move into the territories of East Africa at the turn of the 20th century, with some of them being recruited to serve with the then existing Administration, the official turning point in the acceptance of Settlers and their development of the area was The Crown Land Ordinance of 1902. This Ordinance allowed for 99 year leases for the development of land, and therefore gave the go-ahead for large-scale European settlement in Kenya. By 1903 Lord Delamere had been granted a lease of 100,000 acres of sheep country. Would-be settlers rushed in from South Africa as well as from Europe.

While there was considerable opposition by early Governors of Kenya to such settlements, the 1902 Ordinance prevailed.

Many of the early Settlers were from the upper social classes of the UK; many recruited for service in the Administration were not from such backgrounds of education. The Settlers soon made it obvious that they did not readily tolerate nor respect the authority of the officials in the Administration.

It was not till 1910 that selection for the Administration was tightened up and recruitment by the Selection Boards in the UK was to be made from candidates with an educational background from public schools, universities, or regular army commissions. Very shortly after, Settlers were officially recognised, the first East African Agricultural and Horticultural Show was held, while cricket matches and race courses were established.

A healthy and, in time, friendly rivalry between 'Officials' and 'Settlers' continued till the time of Independence, which was fought out not only in the political arena, but more especially on the cricket and rugger fields, the golf course, squash courts, polo field and other areas where sport encouraged such rivalry.

The District Commissioner's authority in a district prevailed, but with resentment from many Settlers from time to time. Officials were essentially in service to maintain law and order, as well as to ensure peace between sometimes warring tribal forces. This naturally involved the establishment of police forces and prison and detention services. Their main purpose however was to provide for an improved quality of life for the Africans by ensuring the basic infra-structure of the district. This encompassed housing, roads and communications, water supplies, power and electricity, as well as the land, health and educational development of the district.

Settlers often operated in remote areas and so they were truly jacks-of-all-trades and provided facilities for their labour in terms of housing, schools and medical care. Naturally they all had to labour for profit, often hampered by changeable weather conditions. Drought was often followed by flood, leading to failure of crops, or disease striking their stock. Many of the early Settlers failed to establish any equilibrium and so became bankrupt. Many others, often supported by remittance funding from the UK in their early years, became very wealthy, but then only after years of hard endurance and personal sacrifice. While the Settler had some respect for the authority of the Officials, at the same time Officials had similar respect and admiration for the efforts of the Settlers. But through it all, the healthy sporting rivalry between the two groups prevailed.

As an Official, one was confronted by a Settler with the question, "Just what do you hope to achieve with Colonialism?" I personally have been guided by the words of Sir Philip Mitchell, Governor of Kenya 1944-52, in his autobiography *African After Thoughts*. He wrote about the challenge facing the Administration (which included all the supportive departments of medicine, education, agriculture, etc) after the last war when so many Africans of East Africa travelled throughout the world in the services.

"What we have had to do is to help the African to believe in that world, feel at home in it and to look with hope and happiness to their future in it."

He continued, "That, at least, is my conception of 'Colonialism' and explains what I have been trying to do throughout my forty years of service."

Shortly after arriving in Kiambu I came face to face with the problems of dealing with members of the Legislative Council as well as with Settlers. One morning I received a call from HQ telling me that Mrs Olga Watkins had phoned to say that she was infested with rats and would I take steps to eradicate them. Just arrived from the UK, I responded by questioning was not this the responsibility of the householder? Maybe, I was told, but she was a member of the Legislative Council and I should therefore visit the

105

farm. I contacted the Health Inspector in Kiambu, one Leslie Lewis, and told him the story. He said that I was quite right, but volunteered to visit the farm himself. His report was that he found one dead mouse in a barn, which had obviously been attacked and half eaten by an owl. I received no reprimand, but certainly learned at an early stage the meaning of Legislative Council.

My other experience was one where I learned a good lesson which I remembered for the rest of my service in East Africa. I was called out to visit a European who was running a temperature and could not be brought into the boma. They lived close to the boma and so I went out to call. They were an elderly couple and the lady was running a high temperature with symptoms resembling 'flu. I prescribed symptomatic therapy and said I would call the next morning. How glad I was I had said so. I met my Nursing Sister at the club that evening and told her of my call out. "Did you take a blood slide?" was her first question. Heavens! She was the one who gave me the lesson on just how easily one can be fooled into thinking that someone with a temperature but no specific symptoms was suffering from 'flu and how malaria must always be excluded first. While there was no malaria in Nairobi at that time, there was at the Coast and the question must always be asked about possible exposure. Furthermore, there was always the possibility of a relapse if the malaria was a vivax parasite infection. I never forgot the lesson, especially as the next morning the blood slide proved positive to vivax. Thankfully, I was able to prescribe treatment in time.

* * * * *

Kiambu District

In Kiambu I found I was on my own with Dr Samuel Mwathi as my assistant. A week after taking over I was called to the maternity ward one night around 1.00 am, to see an obstructed labour; I realised I had a Caesarean operation facing me. As I had never performed such an operation I decided to call the Nursing Sister, Helen Sheppard, from her bungalow. She appeared and I asked where I should send the case. She looked me straight in the eye and replied, "You can't send it anywhere. You will just have to do it! Go and read your books. I will get the theatre ready and will help you through it."

With my tail between my legs, I returned to my bungalow, sought out Dr Rigby's gynaecology book and read and studied the chapter on the Caesarean operation. After a quick prayer, I went to the theatre. There I was, with an open anaesthetic and an open paraffin pressure-lamp above the table. When would the explosion occur?

Skin, superficial fascia, deep fascia, muscles separated and there was the uterus facing me. With a deep breath I took up my scalpel and opened the uterus with a deliberate incision. I had never seen such bleeding! "Hot towels, cautery, forceps, anything!" Sister lent across the table and quietly whispered, "Finish your incision, the uterus will retract and you will find the bleeding stops." I did and it did!

I delivered the baby and was able to complete the operation in a time of 45 minutes. I was thrilled - both mother and baby did well and in due course were discharged.

In the month I was at Kiambu I performed six Caesarean operations and reduced my time for the operation to 24 minutes. It was a great encouragement that all six mothers and babies were discharged in good health.

It should be realised that in 1946 there was no penicillin on the shelves of any Native Civil Hospital (as the district hospitals were then known). While penicillin was being used in the UK, it was still in the experimental stage and not available for general worldwide distribution. We did have the sulphonamides (*M&B 693* and *760*) which were the only drugs available for the prevention of transmission of infection, in the theatre especially. I thought later that I had a truly excellent success rate for my Caesarean and other operations I performed in those early weeks in Kiambu.

No penicillin was on hand to treat gonorrhoea, syphilis, or yaws etc. We treated gonorrhoea with the sulphonamides and mist. potassium citrate per urethra for bladder washouts. Syphilis was treated by intravenous injections of neo-arsphenamine (an arsenical compound). If I recall correctly, the course was twelve weekly injections. Yaws was treated by five intra-muscular weekly injections of bismuth nitrate.

Those four weeks at Kiambu proved to be an exciting experience and a wonderful introduction to what lay ahead. I had never seen such traumatic injuries as a result of fights after bouts of heavy drinking, some of which resulted in death, for which I had to appear in court to provide post-mortem reports. It was one such court appearance to which I was recalled after I left Kiambu, which provided me the opportunity to meet my future wife, Elizabeth (Libo) Belcher.

Kisii District

My next station was Kisii, in the District of South Kavirondo, about 75 miles south-west from Kisumu. On my way from Kiambu to Kisii I passed through Nakuru - my visit to my old school there is recorded in an earlier chapter.

En route to the District I had to call on and be briefed by the Provincial Medical Officer in Kisumu and I was invited to a dinner party at his home on my first night. To say I was nervous was an understatement, for I was unfamiliar with the formality of such an occasion with servants and wine. After the first round of serving the wine, our host lent forward and remarked, "I hope you will excuse me if I speak to my servant, but I feel I cannot let the occasion pass without a slight reprimand." The servant was duly called into the dining room and the following dialogue took place, naturally all in Swahili. "Kimani! How many years have you worked as our houseboy?"

"Over ten Bwana!"

"And how many times have you served wine at dinner?"

"Always with guests Bwana!"

"Precisely! And what is the rule about using a napkin when serving the wine?"

Pause...

"To wrap a napkin round the bottle before bringing it to the table Bwana!"

"So why tonight was there no napkin round the bottle?"

Pause...

"There was no need for the napkin, Bwana; the label had come off the bottle!"

A true example of the well-known management saying, 'The greatest cause of misunderstanding in communication is the assumption of understanding'.

In Kisii I was introduced to witchcraft, the medicine man and the effects of curses. Cranial trephining for the relief of cranial pressure, undertaken by medicine men with crude chisels and other tools, was a feature of 'medical care' among the Kisii.

Having been thrown in at the deep end with Caesarean operations at Kiambu I grew in confidence and tackled all manner of surgical, obstetrical and gynaecological operations, while also handling a wide

109

variety of medical emergencies. I was beginning to love the challenge and the opportunities for exciting medical practice.

When I arrived in the boma of Kisii I booked in at the hotel and then set off through the township to look for the hospital and Dr W G Kerr who was the MO in charge. Dr Kerr was in fact a fully qualified surgeon and was being transferred to the Provincial Hospital Kisumu as the Provincial Surgeon. I found Dr Kerr had returned home, and as I was driving up through the boma I overtook Pat Low who was then the Senior DO under Eric Davis, the DC, whose wife was the delightful Lisette, a popular DC's wife to all.

I asked Pat where I could find the MO's house. He stared at me and asked, "Are you the new MO?" I could see his worry. Was I to be the MO responsible for the health and care of his family - after all I was still only 23 years old?

I first stayed in the home of the MO i/c, the large wooden house next to the DC's overlooking the golf course, but after a short spell Dr Waterston was posted to be MO i/c and so I moved into the house next door. This was a modern Public Works Department house which became the pattern of Government Officers' houses in many other stations.

Just as there was no penicillin nor antibiotics in our hospitals, so in the Districts where we were posted, our bungalows had no electricity and we depended on paraffin lamps. Nor did we have indoor water-borne sanitation. The hot water system for the house was a 44 gallon drum set into a raised brick foundation outside the bathroom, with the heat provided from an open wood fire burning under the drum. The hot water was piped into the bath or kitchen sink!

Our loo was a bucket latrine housed in a corrugated 'specialist shelter' about twenty yards from the back of the bungalow. The sweepers came round nightly, with the rattle of the ox-drawn container often waking us up. The bucket was removed from a flap-trap at the rear of the fixed seating. We got used to the inconvenience of night calls, but a tummy upset could be a real drag.

The story is told of the Official's wife caught short in the middle of the night who had retired to the loo and was performing when there was the sound of the sweeper approaching the rear to remove the bucket. To her horror, the flap was raised and the bucket was about to be withdrawn for the clean one to be placed in position. She called out, "Ngoja kidogo," which, translated, means "Just a minute." The prompt reply was "Haiseru Memsahib"' ("OK Madam") and the old bucket was replaced just in time!

Dr Waterston was doubly qualified in medicine and dentistry and my first experience at tooth extraction was on him. He gave clear instructions on the process before succumbing to the local anaesthetic. Again it provided me with the confidence to perform further extractions in the years ahead.

My mother and sister arrived to stay with me to set up my house, with curtains, carpets and bits of furniture which were passed on to me from my parents' home. They were with me when Dr PCC Garnham, the Senior MO in charge of the Unit for Parasitic Diseases arrived. He had been a young MO when my parents were in Kisumu at the start of his career in Kenya. He was accompanied by Mr McMahon, the Provincial Entomologist. Dr Garnham was searching for the missing link in the life history of the black fly, *Simulium damnosum*, which was incriminated in the transmission of onchocerciasis, well-known as African Blindness, a scourge throughout the east and west of Africa. He had searched all the rivers believing that the fly was laying its eggs on the weeds and grasses growing in the rivers. He arranged to set off early one morning for one of the rivers with Jim McMahon, and requested that I should turn up with a picnic lunch, advising his driver where to bring me. In time we arrived and I called out his name. He replied from down the hill at the river. He had a very high-pitched voice and suddenly I heard him call out, "I've

111

found it! I've found it! Come quickly." I slipped down the hill at speed and there he was holding a fresh-water crab upside down in his fingers. "There look!" I looked but saw nothing strange. "There!" he repeated, pointing to the hind legs of the crab. Still there was nothing for me to see. "Where?" I questioned hesitatingly. He then pointed to several little black dots on the hind legs of the crab. "There they are. The eggs of the fly which I have searched for many months." It was proof to me of the difference between a true scientist and the likes of myself. They look, observe and perceive, while I look and sometimes don't even see!

Dr Garnham's discovery opened up the possibility of eradicating the dreaded disease. We had the insecticide DDT and the technique adopted for the eradication was to treat the sources of the affected rivers. The insecticide would dissolve in the river and kill the eggs on the fresh water crabs, and so interrupt the life-cycle of the fly and the transmission of the disease. Ten years later when I was PMO in Nyanza, Jim McMahon was still personally monitoring the treatment of the rivers in the North Nyanza District with DDT. He did this every day of the year whether Christmas day or any other. His reward was to realise that he had saved millions of Africans being blinded by the disease, but it was encouraging that his efforts were recognised and he was honoured by the Queen with an OBE.

Dr Garnham's brilliance as a scientist led in time to him being associated with the discovery of the exo-erythrocytic cycle in the liver, this being the missing link in the transmission of vivax malaria.

I have always considered it a highlight in my personal professional career in the Colonial Service that I was present when the missing link in the transmission of onchocerciasis was discovered by Dr Garnham in Kisii.

Another episode that occurred while I was in Kisii was the journey I made with Bobby Winser, the DO, through the night searching for Dr Waterston and his family. Dr Waterston had set off with his wife and son to inspect dispensaries west of Kisii. As they had not returned by 8.00 pm I became very anxious and called on Bobby. We decided that we should set off and look for them, lest their car had broken down. We prepared well with food, ropes, chains and other items we considered necessary for such an outing and travelled through the night, calling on several Missions and dispensaries. We followed on through the forest in the Mara, coming out early morning at Sotik. By this time we were very weary, after a long night of worry and imagined hidden terror with elephants and rhinos grazing in the bush alongside the road. Every shadow held potential dangers and even the occasional glimpse of bits of paper brought forth thoughts of a scrawled message for help. We decided to return back to the boma at Kisii. On arrival we found that Waterstons had got back about ten minutes after we had set off to look for them!

Our nursing sister was Margaret Marshall, and Naftali was the theatre assistant who helped me so much. He gave me great confidence in my learning process in operating in Africa under strange circumstances! Our senior clerk was also a keen footballer and with him we set up the Medical Department team, eventually winning the Clarence Buxton Cup... both Bill Waterston and myself playing for the team!

While at Kisii I was posted to relieve Dr Bartlett at Kericho while he went on leave for three weeks. Kericho was the centre of the African Highlands' and *Brooke Bond*'s tea-growing industry in Kenya.

I had a short but exciting ten months in Kisii before I was posted to the Northern Frontier District as MO in charge to be stationed at Wajir for a wonderful two years of medical practice and excitement.

The Northern Frontier District (NFD)

1947 - 1949

Sir Vincent Glenday, with his wife and son, were fellow passengers travelling with me on the *RMS Alcantara* in 1946. Sir Vincent was travelling to take up his appointment as HE The British Resident to HH The Sultan of Zanzibar, Sir Seyyid Khalifa bin Harub bin Thweni. Little did I realise at that time that I would follow Sir Vincent's tracks by serving in the Northern Frontier of Kenya and then later on a posting to Zanzibar.

Vincent Glenday, in January 1914, at the age of 23 years, took up his first appointment in the Colonial Administrative Service as an Assistant District Commissioner in Kenya, posted to Moyale in the Northern Frontier District, as it was then known. He was later to become the most renowned and the longest serving officer ever to work in the Northern Frontier's Administration. In fact he served there a total of 25 years without interruption, only leaving in 1939, later to become Governor of British Somaliland.

Two other well respected names serving in the Northern Frontier during that period after 1913, were 'Long' John Llywelyn Llewellin, who was posted there in May 1914, only five months after Glenday, and Major Eric Dutton, who recorded much about the life and work of Glenday and others in those early years.

The history of the development of the Northern Frontier District (later Province) is well documented by Monty Brown in his excellent book *Where Giants Trod.* Here I quote from his book when he wrote: "Dutton,

114

in recalling the concluding words of an appraisal by Glenday of the vast savage district he had ruled for so many years, succeeded in putting the final and appropriate touch to the matter. 'Yet the fact remains that the only people who know the Northern Frontier are those who have lived in the days gone by... To the newcomers... the real, essential North is a closed book. A firmly closed book.'"

With total humility I ask whether those of us who served in The Northern Frontier during the 1940s, when it was still 'The District', can stake a claim to having lived in the days gone by?

I feel that before memories totally fade, I owe it to those who have gone before to record some of my lasting impressions of those days, and of those with whom I served during the period 1947-49 in the Northern Frontier District.

When I was posted to the NFD I found myself but one Medical Officer in a cluster of Administrative Officers, Policemen, Game, Veterinary and Livestock Officers, with many other categories besides, all serving together, under the paternalistic guidance of 'Uncle' Gerald Reece, and later Dick Turnbull, who were the two Officers-in-Charge (later to be called Provincial Commissioners - PC) during those impressionable years in my life.

The Medical Service, as it was when I arrived in Wajir in August 1947, was truly the creation of Dr Ronnie Heisch who had served in the NFD 1944-45. Dr Heisch served under the DC Wajir, 'Daddy' Cornel, and together they were responsible for building the Wajir Hospital and creating its infra-structure.

After leaving the NFD, Ronnie Heisch became a renowned Parasitologist and succeeded the even more renowned Dr PCC Garnham as the Chief of Parasitology and Entomology in the Kenya Medical Department. Drs Garnham, Heisch and myself met up together later in 1964, in the

London School of Hygiene and Tropical Medicine (LSH&TM), with our respective academic titles - Professor Garnham of Parasitology; myself as a Reader in the Department of Tropical Hygiene and Deputy Director of the Ross Institute, and Ronnie Heisch a Senior Lecturer in the Department of Parasitology. Ronnie died in the 1960s while Professor Garnham died on Christmas Day 1994 aged 92.

I did not directly succeed Dr Heisch in Wajir. He was succeeded by Dr Adams who later handed over to Dr Singleton, who only served there for eleven months.

I set off from Kisii in my truck for the unknown, with Manjari my Kikuyu cook and David, my Kisii houseboy. I had bought my first vehicle when still in Kiambu; it was a : ton *Ford* LDV truck, the back being built up with a frame of expanded metal, with side canvas screens.

When I arrived in Isiolo in August 1947 I was surprised to find Dr Singleton there; his handing-over to me took place the next morning, before he set off for Nairobi. I well remember asking him, "But how do I get to Wajir; where exactly is it?" His advice was of such value that he could well have been quoting from the *Wizard of Oz* with the song *Follow the Yellow Brick Road*. He replied, "In your *Ford* LDV just follow your Medical Department lorry across the desert for the next 250 miles!"

I drove almost non-stop, passing Garbatula, Muddo Gashi and Habaswein, before finally arriving in Wajir. We reached our destination without incident, but not without certain anxiety as we travelled north into the 'unknown'. I grew to love Wajir, my home for the next two years.

Wajir was the replica of any Frontier fort associated with one's idea of the French Foreign Legion. It was the 'Beau Geste' of the famous film; indeed it was the film set of *The Huggetts Go Abroad* which was shot by Shepherds Bush Film Studios in 1948.

116

There were four fort-like houses for the senior officers of the boma or station, namely the DC, DO, Police Officer and Medical Officer. My house was the one nearest to the township and to the swimming pool, but, as it happened, furthest from the hospital.

Each mini-fort was quite different in style but each had a flat roof on which we sat at sunset to imbibe our beer, and where we slept during the long dry season. The rest of the boma was made up of the Dubas lines, Police lines, the hospital and staff lines, swimming pool, squash-court, and a small house which normally housed the Development Officer.

The duka area (shops) was separate but very close to the Government boma. Ali Aden of Haji Ali Sigara's Store and Lalji Mangalji were the two main traders, while Haji Abdulla Farrah, reputedly the illegitimate son of a Baronet, ran the main transport business. Sherrif Kulatein was the popular school Headmaster.

The three main tribes in the District were the Mohamed Zubeir with their Chief Abdi Ogli, the Degodia with Chief Mohamed Onsur and the Ajuran, whose Chief I no longer recall.

My arrival in Wajir had coincided with the handover by Peter Derrick as DC to Anthony (Tony) Galton-Fenzie, who later married and brought his wife, Daphne, to live with him in the boma. Shortly after, Gordon Hector arrived as DO, joined later by the eye-patched ex-Battle of Britain pilot, Don Stones, and then South African Desmond Craib. Tony in due course handed over to 'Wee' Gordon Hector. The Police Officers were Donald Whitehead, Stuart Aikman and later 'Paddy' Lynch, while the Development Officer was Hector Douglas.

Our team over the years in Wajir was a happy and healthy group. We spent many hours playing squash in the open-air court into which we had to climb by way of a wooden ladder.

117

Travelling to Wajir in my first car

Wajir Fort

The occasional camel ride into the bush was another activity, as was shooting dik-dik, gazelle and oryx for the pot; grouse and guinea fowl shooting was a further favourite.

The Swahili word 'boma' originally meant a circular hedge of cut thorn branches to keep livestock in and predators out. By association it came to mean the offices, houses and stores within such a ring fence; and eventually, any government station, with or without a fence.

* * * * *

Medical Services

The NFD comprised six administrative centres at Isiolo, Moyale Marsabit, Mandera, Garissa and Wajir. Each centre had a DC i/c while the Officer i/c NFD and his HQ was stationed at Isiolo. In addition to the hospital at

Moyale, with an SAS i/c, further small hospitals under the control of Hospital Assistants and assisted by dressers, were at Marsabit, Mandera, Garissa and Isiolo. During my stay in the Frontier the new hospital at Mandera was built and opened in 1948, while that at Garissa was expanded. All of these hospitals were supported with wards, but without operating theatre facilities.

The medical service in the Frontier could not have succeeded without the wonderful work of the Hospital Assistants, who for the most part were Kikuyus, but not exclusively so. They were dedicated and hard working as well as being loyal to myself. Amos Gatwach in Wajir, Frederick in Marsabit and Hillary Mitchell, were three whose names come immediately to mind. I have always felt privileged to have worked with them. They were truly wonderful staff with whom to try to do one's best, as well as to train the local Somali staff who had never had the opportunity of being able to attend the Medical Training Centre in Nairobi to train as Hospital Assistants.

The MO i/c NFD had responsibility for the medical services in all the stations. These medical units were respectively Moyale, 180 miles from Wajir, Isiolo 225 miles away, Marsabit 400 miles, Mandera 225 miles and Garissa 250 miles. I had the responsibility of paying frequent visits to all these medical centres in the Frontier and was also asked to supervise the Turkana District Hospitals at Lodwar and Lokitong.

* * * * *

Wajir District Hospital

In 1947 the hospital consisted of two major wards, one male and one female, with a long central administrative block, comprising an out-patient department, a pharmacy/dispensary and a laboratory, with offices for the MO i/c and the Sub-Assistant Surgeon (SAS). In the centre of the hospital compound was the operating theatre unit, while staff quarters, kitchen and stores completed the buildings. During my tenure we were able to

120

construct a badly needed laundry unit. The hospital provided all the services of other 'Native Civil Hospitals' down country, including full medical, surgical and obstetrical care.

Among the medical cases which attracted attention at Wajir were various eye conditions, for example, cataracts, trachoma with complicating corneal ulcers, ectropions and entropions, yaws, venereal diseases (complicated in women by infertility due to obstructed fallopian tubes), obstructed labour resulting from female circumcision, osteomyelitis prior to the advent of penicillin, obstructed inguinal hernias and hydroceles, and all manner of other cold surgical and gynaecological conditions. I faced up to the need to tackle all the problems which presented themselves and during my stay I carried out a thyroidectomy, end-to-end colon anastomoses, obstructed hernias, repairs of vagino-vesicular fistulas as well as many cataracts and other eye operations.

I shall never forget my first cataract operation. We were returning from Isiolo, in our two-ton *Ford* Medical Department lorry, when I saw a woman sitting at the side of the road under a tree. I called on my driver to stop, inquiring why she was sitting there. "Oh! She is holding up the caravan because she is blind and has to be led by hand. They are worried about reaching Wajir in time for the camels to be watered before they are too exhausted. They have left her with a bowl of camel milk and will pick her up on their way back, if she hasn't already been taken by hyenas or a lion." My response was, "Put her in the back of the lorry and we'll take her to the hospital in Wajir." Having got her there, word quickly got around and her family turned up at the hospital, questioning just what I planned.

There was nothing for it but to operate and hopefully give her a degree of sight. I promised that we would keep her with us till they next visited Wajir for watering, by which time I hoped that I would have helped. I had to read up how to do the operation, search out the necessary instruments and study how to give a local anaesthetic for an eye operation!

Boma and Township [hospital in foreground]

122

The time came and with a quiet prayer I entered the theatre, prepared the area, covered the patient with the necessary green operation towels, leaving only the eye exposed. After anaesthetising the eye I picked up the knife and started. Without any problem the lens popped out and there it was, lying in the lens spoon. I felt wonderful and elated but had not noticed that the green towel was being lifted up. Suddenly her hand moved out from under the towel and she grabbed mine, calling out in Somali, "Glory be to Allah! I can see!" I have to confess I burst into tears with emotion and relief. It remains the most moving moment of my total medical career. To give sight to someone and so allow her to continue to live a 'normal' life again, was surely the most rewarding experience for any young field officer just 24 years old.

There were, however, also many distressing experiences, one of which related to my personal houseboy, Abdi. He dislocated his knee when playing football - a rare accident. As I had not treated such a case I studied my text books, especially those on orthopaedics by Watson-Jones, which advised that, after reduction, a skin-tight plaster-of-paris should be applied. This advice I followed but it unfortunately resulted in gangrene of his left leg, the end result of which meant that I had to amputate his leg above the knee. It was a great personal shock and I determined to ensure that Abdi be fitted with an artificial limb. In time this was done at the orthopaedic centre in Nairobi and I shall never forget Abdi's return to Wajir. The whole boma was waiting as he stepped off the lorry and walked to greet me on his artificial leg.

A special medical phenomenon experienced at Wajir was that of the hypnotic condition which often followed prolonged participation in 'ngomas'. This was especially common among the Dubas, the DC's tribal police and grazing guards, who after long periods of dancing would pass into a semi-coma fit, often frothing at the mouth and occasionally inflicting burns on their bodies from hot embers. The strange feature was that the next day there were no signs of such self-inflicted injuries.

It was as this point that penicillin appeared in our hospital pharmacopoeia which revolutionised the treatment of gonorrhoea, syphilis and yaws, with single intra-muscular injections of procaine penicillin being all that was necessary. The dose was 1cc for gonorrhoea and 4cc for syphilis and yaws. With the advent of penicillin, in time we saw the disappearance of osteomyelitis and the need to perform sequestrectomies, to remove the sequestra which had formed, particularly in long bones, from infection of bone marrow. Sequestrectomies were common on every operational list in most hospitals, and their gradual disappearance was wonderful to note.

Albucid eye drops and ointment with later, aureomycin, teramycin and tetracycline eye ointments, were the wonder drugs which allowed for the treatment of trachoma and the consequent development of entropion and ectropion eye conditions, so prevalent in the NFD.

Sterility was another problem with which we were faced. The females had become infected by gonorrhoea and in time, through chronic infection, their fallopian tubes became blocked, thus preventing the ovaries from travelling to the uterus, hopefully to be fertilised by semen after intercourse. The only solution seemed to be to attempt to open the fallopian tubes by inflating them with air. Again, another Heath Robinson apparatus was developed, which allowed air to be pumped along the blocked tubes. I had quite a success rate, which was determined by the number of women who became pregnant after such treatment! The success story reached the PC, Dick Turnbull's, ears. When in due course the Governor, Sir Philip Mitchell, visited Wajir for the celebration of Id-ul-Fitr, I was introduced by Dick Turnbull to Sir Philip in the following manner: "This is Dr Barton who has great success in making many Somali women pregnant!"

Sir Philip Mitchell during the Id-ul-Fitr celebrations
Flanked by Dick Turnbull and Gordon Hector
I'm in the back row

I had the privilege of training my SAS and the various Hospital Assistants posted to Wajir during my stay, in the giving of spinal anaesthetics, and performing hernias and hydrocele operations.

Royal Wajir Yacht Club

One assumes that the club was started by the Kenya African Regiment (KAR) posted to the Frontier in earlier times. Certainly by the time I arrived in Wajir it was almost completely inactive with little pomp or circumstance. It rested with Gordon Hector to revive the spirit and re-establish formality and procedures! The DC was the Honorary Commodore of the club, inheriting the epaulettes, sword and the formal cocked hat.

125

My father had been in the Marine Service of the KUR&H, and on his retirement in 1940 had retained all his old uniforms, caps, three stripe epaulettes of a Commander, buttons and other accessories. On one of my leaves he agreed to bequest all this to the RWYC. This meant that whenever the Commodore called a meeting we were able to distribute the necessary regalia to the various 'officers' of the club. Over time various functions were held, but the most auspicious certainly was the Id-ul-Fitr Dinner held on 7th August 1948 when a menu was prepared and songs, which had become a feature of the club, were printed for the occasion to be left for posterity. The famous log book of the club was brought up-to-date and the activities of the newly revived club were duly entered. A selection of these songs can be found at the end of this chapter.

* * * * *

Travelling Arrangements

I travelled in the Government Medical Department two-ton *Ford* truck to Garissa, Mandera, Moyale, Marsabit and Isiolo, but flew, generally with the PC, to Turkana District. We always carried a 44 gallon drum of fresh drinking water in the truck, as well as my tent and enough food to be able to survive for a week en route, in case of a mechanical breakdown on the road or being held up by swollen luggas (dry river beds).

On occasions I did fly round the various centres, initially in a *De Havilland* piloted by David Whitehead, and later by Jerry Morris. I will never forget my first experience flying with Jerry. How could I? I had travelled by road down to Isiolo to join a team, which Uncle Reece had planned, to visit the various stations in the Frontier. It was the monsoon season and taking off at Isiolo I felt maybe we were overloaded. We tore along the runway and I noticed that we had passed the two lines indicating the end of it. What now? Jerry bounced the plane and somehow we bounced into the air and just cleared the trees at the end of the Isiolo strip! We landed safely at Marsabit.

126

Next morning Jerry looked at the map and made a finger measurement of the distance to Lodwar. He remarked, "It will only take one-and-a-half hours. I don't want to take on any more petrol, due to our weight. We have enough petrol for two hours." We were flying over Lake Turkana when I noticed we had been in the air for over one-and-a-half hours and I reckoned we still had another half hour to go! Approaching Lodwar we did not circle but went straight in, dodging through the hills. We landed and Jerry came back to open up the doors remarking, "That was close. I think we have two minutes of petrol in the tank!" We disembarked shaking but relieved!

Those going on to Moyale boarded the next morning and took off flying east. En route we ran into heavy rain and Jerry could not see the terrain. "I'll fly below the clouds, a bit south of Moyale to avoid the hills. When we hit a road we will fly north to look for Moyale." In due course we saw a road, one of us recognised where we were and finally we found Moyale and landed... only to get stuck in the mud on the strip as it was so wet! I had often pushed our truck out of mud on the road, but now we had to push our plane out of mud!

My experiences flying round the Frontier were building up, as were my anxieties! There was no incident flying to Mandera, but next morning after two abortive attempts to take off I offered to disembark with my luggage to lighten the plane! Jerry accepted my offer and I stood on the runway, watching with relief as the plane again bounced off the ground. It took me another twelve hours to drive back to Wajir via El-Wak, but I got back home relaxed and glad to be still alive!

My next flight was to Nairobi in an RAF *DC3* which had flown up to Wajir with supplies for the RAF squad carrying out an air survey of the Frontier between Kenya and Abyssinia. I had set off in my own *Ford* $^3/_4$-ton LDV, going on local leave to Mombasa, but only reached Habbaswein when the heavens opened; I spent the night on a raised part of the road

127

with lions drinking from the water all around. I was able to return to Wajir next morning and was lucky to pick up the RAF plane. We flew onto Lodwar before moving down to Nairobi, where I had to catch the train to Mombasa.

Jerry Morris later flew a *Proctor Percival* on his trips to the Frontier. Don Stones DFC was our DO; he was a former Battle of Britain pilot and later a test pilot, and Jerry allowed him to fly the 'kite'. Don would take off and beat up the boma, and occasionally would take one of us with him as he did so - an exciting experience.

I flew with Jerry several times and gradually he taught me how to handle the controls and just what to do on take-off. I did indeed take the controls for one flight out of Wajir, but with Jerry always in full command in case of any flap! It was a great experience and stimulated me to learn to fly, but regrettably I never had the opportunity.

Peter Nelson-Gracie was our next pilot in the Frontier. Maybe because he was a married man, he was a much more professional pilot, never taking risks. So flights with him were never quite such fun... although considerably safer.

* * * * *

The Administration

The officer in charge of the NFD 1947/48 was the lovable, endearing, if sometimes awesome 'Uncle' Gerald Reece. Who could ever forget his twitching nose and the clearing of the throat before uttering a word or sentence? So many of us picked up the habit without realising it, only to be told by others, "For Pete's sake, stop impersonating 'Uncle'." Impersonating Uncle! Who me? Never!

I was always proud to have been able to say I served under Uncle and Alys, his lovely wife, for he was nearing the end of his long Frontier service and in 1948 became Governor of British Somaliland.

So many stories can be told of Uncle but, for me, the most significant was his own story of having to walk from Mandera, where he was serving, to Wajir to be invigilated for his standard Swahili examination! He told me, "I had to walk nearly 250 miles there, and then another 250 back again... and I failed it!" I myself was invigilated for my first attempt at the examination in Wajir by John Gardner from Garissa... and I failed it! I always felt that I had been in good company.

Another great story was at the time of Uncle's efforts to control the smuggling of miraa. All DCs were instructed, with the Police Force, to search out and punish those involved with the movement of this drug. We in Wajir could never understand how, even with the greatest of vigilance, the drug still seemed to find access to the boma. We only later discovered that Uncle's driver of his *Chevrolet* used to pack bags of the drug under the back seat of the car, where Uncle was sitting comfortably in state. The bags were later unloaded after Uncle settled for the night in the DC's house!

Gerald 'Uncle' Reece, later Sir Gerald, was succeeded by Richard (Dick) Turnbull, equally at home in the Frontier, having served in many stations for long periods. Sir Richard, who lived to be over 90, endeared himself to those who served under him. He went on to serve as Chief Secretary Kenya, before becoming Governor of Tanganyika, taking it through to Independence and then later serving as Governor in Aden.

In 1949 Dick had arranged for the Governor of Kenya HE Sir Philip Mitchell to visit Wajir for the Id-ul-Fitr celebration at the end of the fast of Ramadan in August. In due course the army arrived for the parade, and Sir Philip arrived by air with his entourage. A crisis had arisen before the evening function, for as the sun set no new moon had been seen and so officially no celebration could take place. Dick Turnbull took the Sergeant of the Dubas up onto the ramparts of the Wajir Fort searching the horizon. Suddenly he pointed, calling out, "There it is, look Sergeant. There it is.

Look there!" The Sergeant seemed convinced and nodded. Whether or not the moon was seen we will never know, but Dick Turnbull persuaded everyone that the moon had been sighted and so the celebrations began.

Uncle Reece

I had completed 25 months duty in the NFD and in fact had postponed my departure on home leave to be able to attend the Id-ul-Fitr celebrations. Sir Philip had very kindly invited me to travel to Nairobi in his aircraft. So I departed in style after a very happy two years of service. I felt very low at the thought of leaving Wajir and asked Dick Turnbull whether he thought I should apply to be re-posted to the Frontier. He told me, "Never go back, hoping you will rediscover the fulfilment of the past." I have never been able to return to Wajir since leaving in August 1949.

Several excitements occurred during my two years stay in Wajir. There was the political pressure of the SYL (Somali Youth League), giving rise to the occasional raid on manyattas, to seek out suspect members of the proscribed organisation.

A great event for us was the arrival of a British film unit from Shepherds Bush, with stars, to take location shots for the film, *The Huggets Go Abroad*. The story was of the Hugget family crossing the Sahara, encountering the French Foreign Legion. Wajir Fort was therefore the central focus for the filming; it was an exciting few days with lovely girls and several camera and other technical staff, not forgetting the director, make-up, wardrobe and continuity personnel.

Another group posted to Wajir towards the end of 1947 was a detachment of the RAF based in Wajir, responsible for surveying the re-alignment of the Frontier between Kenya and Abyssinia. While the team was based near the Wajir airport, their company was an added bonus to us posted permanently, joining in as they did with our various sports activities. I formed a lifelong friendship with Kenneth Butterfield, one of the detachment, and became Godfather to his son. Sadly, I gave the eulogy at Ken's funeral in 1998.

* * * * *

Isiolo District

The District Commissioner of Isiolo was John Pinney, who was considered to be the Senior Commissioner of the Province, acting as the Officer i/c Frontier in Uncle's absence.

In Wajir, early 1948, we had been cut off by heavy rain for six weeks, during which time I had decided that I would try to grow a moustache and so did not shave. At the end of the period I was to visit Marsabit so travelled to Isiolo to stay with John Pinney en route. Uncle and Alys Reece had invited me to dinner that night, without John. I got ready and came through to John's sitting-room before going off to Uncle's house. John looked at me and asked, "Aren't you going to shave for dinner?" I had been so proud of my six week growth but John thought that I just hadn't shaved that day! I crept back to the guest wing and with four brave strokes of my razor removed my six weeks' growth. I have never again attempted to grow a moustache!

John had a stable of two horses which he exercised daily, always expecting any visiting guest to join him on a canter out of the boma after tea. I had never ridden a horse in my life, but that did not deter John who told me I could ride his mount, the quiet horse, and he would lead us to control the speed of the trip out of the boma! Everything was fine until we turned for home when 'my' horse, which John normally rode, decided that was the end of the quiet exercise and it was his prerogative to be first home. As he took off and we flashed past, John called out, "Just let him go, hang on, he's safe and won't slip!"

With both arms round his neck, I kept my head alongside the horse's head to avoid it being stripped off by low branches. In absolute fear we arrived back to the boma, and the safety of John's garden, still intact and well ahead of John on his charger! I enjoyed several further rides with John on other visits to Isiolo, and although I never became a competent horseman, I did lose my fear and so settled well into the camel saddles in Wajir!

The Provincial Team based in Isiolo included George Low, the Veterinary Officer, and George Adamson, the Game Warden, with his renowned artist wife Joy Adamson of *Elsa* and *Born Free* fame.

There were of course various Police Officers who included Freddie 'Brookie' Brooks, the Superintendent i/c, and 'Bulls-eye' Brown the ASP.

* * * * *

Mandera District

Mandera lies 250 miles north of Wajir in the north-east corner of Kenya, sharing boundaries with former Italian Somaliland and Abyssinia. Halfway between the two is El-Wak, an old police outpost, which became famous thanks to the devotion and hard endeavours of Grant McIntosh (Mac), in designing and building the new fort. Mac had been a Police Officer in pre-war days when Uncle and Dick Turnbull had been District Officers.

After retirement from service with the Police, Mac became a Development Officer attached to the Police Force responsible for the El-Wak Fort project. After completing that, he moved to the Coast and became Development Officer based at Gedi. He lived in the DC's guesthouse at the Blue Lagoon, Watamu, from where we had several goggling trips while I was MO i/c at Kilifi. Indeed, for our early efforts, the goggles were old gas masks with tubes, and we had home-made guns to spear our prey.

Mac had suffered from periods of depression and, tragically, during one such spell he took his own life - a sad loss to many friends throughout Kenya.

There were three District Commissioners posted at Mandera during my service at Wajir; Terry Gavaghan, Arthur Loggin and Alan Burkett. The Medical Department Dispensary at Mandera was upgraded to a small hospital, on which project both Terry and Arthur were actively involved and which I finally opened in late 1948 with great celebration.

133

An interesting story can be told of the loss of my sunglasses on a safari to Mandera. They were the latest *Poloroid* shield-type of sunglasses, so quite distinctive and the only pair in the Frontier!

When we were about 60 miles from Wajir, I asked my team to stop and make tea. I obviously dropped my glasses as I returned to the lorry and we drove off heading for Mandera; the sun having faded, I had no need for my glasses. I only realised I had lost them the following day and so had to continue without them for the next few days until I returned to Wajir. To my surprise, when I entered my house, there they were... my glasses were on the table. All was later revealed! Two days after my departure, a Somali with his caravan of camels came to the watering wells at Wajir. He was wearing my glasses and they were recognised by a Dubas who confiscated them, returning them to my house in time for my return. What a surprise!

* * * * *

Garissa District

Three different District Commissioners were posted to Garissa during my stay in the Frontier. John Webster was the Commissioner with John Gardner as his District Officer, relieved later by Arthur Small and later still by Peter Walters.

The interest of Garissa was the mixture of the Pokomo Tana River tribe, with their agricultural traditions, alongside the nomadic Somali tribes and their camels.

My outstanding memory of Garissa was of a drive back to Wajir after a visit, during which I had selected several patients requiring cold surgery to be taken back to Wajir for operation - hernias, cataracts and other eye conditions. As was my custom, we set off from Garissa boma around 4.00 pm with the intention of driving for several hours in the cool of the late afternoon and early evening before setting camp for the night. This

134

meant we could travel almost half the distance of 220 miles in the cool evening, leaving the second half of the journey to be tackled early the following morning, reaching Wajir before the heat of midday.

At around 8.00 pm I instructed my team to stop and prepare supper before we travelled further. My cook, Manjari, said that he thought it might be better to keep going, for there were obvious signs of a storm looming and maybe we could get ahead of it before the luggas filled with water which would restrict our progress.

In my opinion the threatened storm was so far away that it could not possibly interfere with our progress, so my meal was cooked and served. As we were packing my chair, table and kitchen equipment back onto the lorry before finally setting off, the skies darkened and the heavens opened. We were able to keep moving, until we met the next lugga which was now a deep flowing torrent, obviously filled by the rains which had fallen further up-country and which had been augmented by rain falling locally over the last few hours. We thought maybe we could return to Garissa, but the lugga we had already crossed before was now a torrent. So we were between the two luggas and there we stayed for five days, till they reduced to a trickle allowing us to cross.

I was not too worried for, as was my usual practice, I had my tent, enough food for a week, a 44 gallon drum of drinking water, petrol and general supplies. But we did have the extra five passengers whom I had picked up at Garissa, returning them to Wajir for cold surgery!

My tent was pitched and everyone settled down for a long wait. Morning and evening I went down to the lugga to wash in the flowing waters, while toilet needs were met in the bush. After four days my driver came to tell me that our water was running out. How could that be for we had enough water for drinking purposes for days. "Ah yes! but we have had the extra passengers and they had to wash as well!" While I was using a few pints of drinking water daily and washing in the lugga, I discovered the others

135

had been washing in fresh water from the 44 gallon drum! I filled both of my two-gallon containers with fresh water and left the others to work out their solution. I reckoned I had enough drinking water to last me several further days.

Fortunately the lugga dropped and we were able to reach Wajir before a major crisis arose for the others. The 'code of practice' for future safaris was laid down to ensure there was no repeat of the casual attitude to fresh water supplies!

Garissa had a specific interest in that it was a favourite area for game-hunters, mainly Americans. They were always accompanied by one or other of the famous Kenya White Hunters.

* * * * *

Marsabit District

The DC was Honorable HAC (Henry) Howard (of the famous Howard family whose chief is the Duke of Norfolk); his wife and lovely hostess in Marsabit was Barbara ('Baa').

We gathered that Uncle Reece's first posting within the NFD was as DC Marsabit, and it had always been his plan to transfer the PC's office there from Isiolo. So, during his period as Officer i/c NFD, Uncle planned for and saw the building of his new house in Marsabit. He was promoted and transferred to British Somaliland before his hoped-for transfer could occur and before he and Alys and their family could live in the new house.

Because of the distance from Wajir, having to travel via Isiolo, my visits to Marsabit were infrequent but always pleasant and memorable.

* * * * *

Moyale District

Colin Campbell, the DC, handed over to David Christie-Millar in 1946. David, with his famous aviator wife 'Silver Jane', ruled in Moyale during the period of the realignment of the Frontier between Kenya and Abyssinia, with many meetings taking place between the Governor of Boran in Abyssinia and his entourage, and the PC and his senior staff from Isiolo.

Two stories warrant telling! On one such meeting I was included in the PC's entourage and so had travelled from Wajir with Uncle Reece in his black *Chevrolet* saloon car. After meetings during the day, we retired to the DC's house for social drinks. The Governor of Boran, learning that I was the MO, requested that I sit with him while he quizzed me about his wife's health problems! All the discussion was through an interpreter and so was somewhat protracted. All the time, we were drinking neat, or nearly neat, Abyssinian brandy. The time came for me to relieve my bladder. I requested the interpreter to explain to the Governor that I needed to move outside for some fresh air! The reply came, "The Governor would be happy to join you." My next request was to be allowed to move down the garden. "The Governor would be happy to join you." As we descended the steps from the verandah, the Governor took my right hand and we moved down into the garden! "Please explain to the Governor that I need to relieve myself!" "The Governor has no objection." So we walked to the edge of the garden and, with the Governor still holding my right hand, I struggled with my free left hand to unfasten trousers, search, withdraw, then hold on while I uncomfortably tried to relieve myself. The task of replacing everything and buttoning up with only my left hand free, before we had to reappear indoors, was even more taxing! Fortunately the interpreter remained with the Governor and myself throughout so there was no suspicion of anything untoward!

Another memorable evening at the DC's house was when Bulls-Eye Brown suddenly demonstrated with his revolver how a former DC, one Hugh Grant, had spent his evenings sitting in his chair shooting ghekos in the corner of the wall and roof of the living room.

I walked out into the garden! In due course David Christie-Millar came out and asked why I was outside. I told him I would not return until all guns were put on the verandah table and the shooting stopped. "But why?" asked David. "Well, I am your MO ready to help in the event of an accident, and I don't want to have to explain at any inquest who it was who fired what shot and explain what happened." Three guns were produced and put on the verandah table, at which point I returned inside.

Shortly thereafter David himself walked into the room with a 12 bore shotgun and fired it up to the roof. Out I went again! David brought out the gun, so again I returned, but this time Silver Jane appeared. No one realised that she was carrying a small pistol in her hand, which she then fired into the corner! My retiral again was followed by Silver Jane's pistol! The rest of the evening was spent in relaxed drinking!

Stories of Moyale during David and Jane's stay would not be complete without a passing reference to the two occasions when Jane lost her way in her small plane while flying up from Nairobi. She always flew over Isiolo but, instead of following the road via Wajir thence to Moyale, she invariably tried the direct route and finished up following the wrong road twice and having to make emergency landings due to fuel shortage! The crisis caused by her wanderings nearly drove the PC crazy!

In due course David Christie-Millar handed over to Charles Chenevix Trench.

There is so much more that could be related and added to the anecdotal tales of life and service in Wajir in the Frontier, including:

-    Tales of sitting on the flat roofs of our 'Beau Geste' style houses, drinking *Tusker* beer after sweaty games of squash.

-    Camel rides out to the airport, purporting to be Royal Wajir Yacht Club desert races.

-    During the non-stop heavy rains of 1948, watching the desert sprouting spinach, almost in front of one's eyes, transforming the brown sands to green pastures.

-    After those rains watching anxiously for signs of the first lorry to get through to Wajir with vital food and drink provisions... we had had no delivery for over six weeks and had already run out of essential alcohol supplies! Having heard that the new District Officer, Des Craib, had set off from Isiolo with relief supplies, several of us went down the road to Habbeswein and waited for the lorry to appear over the horizon. When it finally arrived, a party started there and then and continued into the boma with *Tusker* beer flowing freely!

-    Numerous Wajir Yacht Club parties on the roof of Gordon Hector, the Commodore's, house and having to dissuade several of the members from jumping off after splitting the yard arm!

-    The visit of American author Negley-Farsen (*Behind God's Back*) in 1947;

-    The handover from 'Uncle' Gerald Reece to Dick Turnbull as Officer i/c NFD in 1948;

-    The completion of the building of El-Wak Fort by Grant ('Mac') MacKintosh in 1949.

Songs of the North Frontier District

The Call of the NFD
(To the tune of *Take me back to dear old Blighty*)

> Take me back to Isiolo,
> Put me on the frontier Royal Mail
> Carry me 'way out there, drop me anywhere,
> Mandera, Dif or Marsabit, I don't care.
> I'll see again our dear old 'Uncle',
> To tell him about my lovely mango tree.
> Hi tiddlyiti, travelling day and nightie'
> Up and down the NFD.

* * * * *

Wajir Ballad
(To the tune of *There's something about a Soldier*)

> Oh! there's something about Wajir,
> There's something about Wajir,
> There's something about Wajir
> That gets you down, down, down.
> It may be the Degodia, or even the Ajuran,
> Or may be just fetina from the town, town, town.
> The northern frontier zest
> Is what pleases 'Uncle' best,
> But there's something about Wajir
> That gets you down, down, down.

* * * * * *

Song of the Boma
(To the tune of Sir Harry Lauder's *I Love a Lassie*)

'Oh! I'm the Bimbashi o' the toon of <u>Mudigashi</u>
An' the watu to me they a' bow down.
I may be somewhat littler,
But I'm a kind o' local Hitler,
'Bimbashi Bull's Eye Brown'.

'Oh! I am the Ruler of the toon of <u>Garba Tula</u>.
It's no' the place that I would choose mysel'
There are many places cooler,
Than sweaty Garba Tula,
But as the Ruler it suits me well.

Down in <u>Isiolo</u>, there's not much scope for polo
An' there's little else for which I greatly care.
But when I'm tired of chasing Boran,
Or interpreting the Koran,
To Nanyuki for a party I'll repair.

In <u>Marsabit</u> it's chilly, but still the old Rendille
Are easy, an' they dinna trouble me.
If you want to see the station,
Where there's bags of co-operation
Marsabit's the place to be.

I'm the DC of <u>Moyale</u>, I'm known as Bwana Kali,
The Abyssinians think I'm awfi swell.
But when they try to move the border,
I rule them out of order,
An' I tell them what I think of them as well.

Away up in <u>Mandera</u>, I fly the big bandera,
You will see it wherever you may roam.
But tho' the girls they may be pretty,
I keep singing just one ditty,
Show me the way to go home.

At Garissa on the Tana, the chaps all call me Bwana,
But there's little satisfaction from a' that.
Nairobi's very far,
An' I haven't got a car,
So I wander round beneath my Bwana's hat.

I'm the Bwana Daktari, an' I'm often on safari,
I'm a busy man but seldom do I flap.
I'm loved by Somali an' Rendille,
An' the Boran call me Billie',
An' I'm the idol of the girls with Wajir Clap!

I'm following my career, by the white walls o' Wajir
But it's no' the place that I would choose mysel'.
When I'm feeling no' so happy,
I just take a wee wee drappie.
An' remember I'm the Commodore as well!

by Gordon Hector

* * * * *

Three in Harmony

We three in harmony
Working in the NFD
Gordon Hector, Hector and me (i.e. Bill Barton).

* * * * *

Kilifi, Tana River and Lamu

1950 - 1954

I left Wajir and proceeded on my first home leave, sailing on the BI ship, *Modasa*, with fellow passengers Rolley Stratton of 'Smith Macs', and Reverend Rex and Mrs Kay Jupp.

With all the experience I had had with eye conditions, I thought I would like to become an eye specialist. However, Dr Farnworth Anderson, the DMS, had different ideas, "You'll do your Diploma in Tropical Medicine and Hygiene." Accordingly, I was registered for the course in Edinburgh for 1949/50.

Regrettably, having swum in the pool at the club in Port Sudan, after the recognised incubation period I fell seriously ill with Hepatitis A before we docked at Plymouth and so spent the first six weeks of my leave in Freedom Fields Hospital there, getting out just in time to start my DTM&H course in Edinburgh. Maybe the fact that I was sports officer on the ship and had consumed more gin daily than could ever be good for anyone, resulted in my attack of hepatitis being quite severe. There was nothing left for me to do other than study, and so I won the 1950 DTM&H Class Prize!

After finishing my DTM&H course in Edinburgh, I was booked to return to Kenya on a *Sunderland* flying boat taking off from Southampton. There were stops at Palermo in Sicily and Khartoum before finally landing on Lake Naivasha in Kenya.

On reporting to Medical HQ (then still in Anderson Road), I was posted as MO i/c Kilifi, the posting apparently having been

143

requested by the District Commissioner John Stringer who had been DO Kiambu where I had been posted on my arrival in Kenya in 1946.

I was also informed that I would be gazetted as MO i/c Kipini and Lamu Districts. This meant that I was to be responsible for the care and health of all the people living in the geographical area stretching north of Mombasa from the north side of Mtwapa Creek, thence inland to Mariakani, up the whole of the coast, passing Vipingo and Takaungu to Kilifi, thence to the Mida Creek, Gedi, and Watamu to Malindi. After Wajir, Kilifi was a smaller parish but with a far greater population.

Leaving the Giriama Districts one moved inland and north again through the Galla areas to Garsen, where one reached the Tana River District with the Pokomo tribes. The road then led from Garsen to Witu, thence to Mkoani, where a launch could be boarded to Lamu Island.

The Health Office for Kilifi and Malindi areas was based at Malindi under the charge of Health Inspector Bernard Shaw, with his Giriama Assistant Health Inspector, David Ikumi. They were basically responsible for the cleanliness of the township areas, including refuse disposal of Kilifi and Malindi, as well as food control, mosquito control and, in the case of Malindi, the hygiene of the tourist hotels.

Also, as requested by the relevant DC, they would investigate the cause of any epidemic of communicable diseases which might break out in the rural areas, for example, anthrax, plague or rodent fever etc. All these were in fact epidemics which we experienced during my five years in Kilifi.

They had inadequate trained staff to undertake such responsibilities, and so it was decided that Bernard and David would initiate a request to HQ to establish a 'Training School for Health Assistants' in Malindi with recruitment from the Giriama. The request was approved and so a Training School was set up, and in due course the assistants were available for posting to any health centre or dispensary - all in rural areas. They were to monitor the health situation in such areas and also to supervise

144

specific campaigns for latrine construction and water supplies. Additionally, with health education practices they were to attempt to control the spread of such conditions as bilharzia, leprosy and TB, as well as to educate the public in good nutritional practices.

I was left at Kilifi for a complete tour, 1950-53. I was assisted by African MOs, all having qualified at Makerere University in Uganda.

I had three assistants over the years I was in Kilifi. After two years in the NFD, operating without a Nursing Sister to help, guide and encourage me, it was wonderful to have such support again. I was truly served by three outstanding Sisters, in Genna Parsons, Ruth Botham and Kay Jardine, the latter of whom was in retirement and lovingly known as 'Jard'.

Together with Jard, I established a Preliminary Training School for the young Giriama Form 4 school-leavers to give them an adequate grounding, which would fit them for selection for entry to the Medical Training Centre in Nairobi for training as Hospital Assistants. We succeeded in that and I saw many of them return to serve their District in Kilifi and Malindi hospitals as well as at Mombasa and Lamu.

We tackled the hospital garden and in 1952 won the DMS's annual Garden Cup Competition for the hospital with the most improved garden development. That Cup was won again in 1953 for our work on the garden at the new hospital at Malindi.

With support and financing by the Local Authority we built the first Health Centre in the District at Jibana, with Daniel Johana as the Hospital Assistant i/c. The concept of Health Centres was the brainchild of the then Assistant DMS, Dr John Walker, providing a multi-purpose unit to be staffed with a Hospital Assistant, a dresser, a midwife, health assistant, and the support ancillary staff, for example, cooks, cleaners and gardeners etc.

Jard

Hospital Staff 1950 - 1

Hospital Staff 1952 - 4

147

The centre, which had small wards attached, provided out-patient services for treatment and immunisations, a full range of midwifery services, clinics for leprosy and TB drug distribution, as well as health education.

The Health Assistants had been trained to carry out geographical surveys of the areas, identifying the sources of water supplies and positions of schools.

With the introduction of new drugs for the treatment of leprosy we were able to treat the condition on an out-patient basis. Accordingly, we established the 'Leprosy Tree Dispensary System'. Confirmed cases of leprosy were first treated as in-patients with 'Dapsone' (DADPS) to ensure they suffered from no drug reactions. We divided the District into four sectors and, with the help of the DC, who provided local authority transport, developed a system whereby each sector would be visited once every four weeks. The vehicle completed a circuit of the sector, stopping at pre-arranged trees along the route where the cases would await the arrival of the vehicle and collect their issue of DADPS to last them over the next four weeks.

Prior to discharge from hospital, discussion took place with the patients as to which 'tree dispensary' they would attend, so that proper control of the patients could be established. Once monthly, myself or my Assistant MO would travel with the vehicle to see new cases, referred by the chief or the sub-chief, and to assess the progress or otherwise of every case. In this way each patient was seen monthly by a member of our team, and by myself at least once every four months. New cases would be brought into hospital to have the diagnosis confirmed and treatment established before being returned to the 'tree dispensary' system.

The system helped to involve the chiefs and sub-chiefs with responsibility for identifying cases and controlling the spread of the disease. The success rate from treatment over the years was very good and the register of cases

148

on treatment at these dispensaries rose to over 1,300 by 1955, when I left the District.

A sad episode occurred when one of our Health Assistants who had devotedly involved himself with the system and caring for the cases, himself developed the disease. We were able to have him admitted to the Leprosarium in North Nyanza where, after several years of treatment, he made a complete recovery without any limb deformities.

Before the advent of new chemotherapy for the out-patient treatment for pulmonary TB, such cases were treated surgically by cutting down onto and crushing the phrenic nerve and thus collapsing the diaphragm on the affected side. Artificial pneumothorax was also practised and regular clinics for such treatments were established for such therapy.

With the arrival of streptomycin, PAS, INAH, and other regimens over time, the infection and disease was controlled. After stabilisation, while they were in-patients, out-patient therapy could be introduced and clinics established for the monitoring and distribution of their drugs.

At Malindi the concept of a District Surgeon (DS) was introduced. The DS was essentially a part-time Medical Officer responsible for running the services at the hospital, but permitted to conduct a private practice within the hospital premises. Dr Zoltan Rossinger was the first DS. to take up the appointment in 1950 and he became an almost legendary fixture at the hospital and throughout the township of Malindi. Not only was he an excellent diagnostician and theatre technician but he would always turn out, and nothing was too much trouble for him.

In 1950 it had been decided that the old hospital in Malindi was truly a disgrace and so Commonwealth Development Welfare funding had been provided to build a new one. I was involved with others in the siting of this hospital, and over the next two years watched with more than a little interest in the building thereof. This took us through to 1952 by which time I was married and Libo took it upon herself to design and oversee the landscaping of the whole precincts and garden of the hospital. With a handful of unskilled gardeners (shamba boys) she broke through the coral rock and planted desert roses, bourganvillea, neam trees, and other plants and trees that she knew would survive the coast heat and winds. The end result was quite wonderful... resulting in the DMS's Garden Cup prize for 1953.

The plan of the hospital was similar to the standard design of Kilifi hospital and many others in which I had functioned up country.

The day arrived for the opening. As the Governor of Kenya, Sir Philip Mitchell was to be visiting the Coast Province, he had agreed to open it. The PMO was to be in attendance with his wife accompanying him. All the arrangements for the opening were in the hands of Bob Wilson, the District Officer of Malindi, which was a sub-district of Kilifi.

The line-up for the presentations to the Governor was announced and, naturally, the DO's wife was to be at the head of the line, followed by Dr Rossinger, the MO of the hospital and his wife, and so on down the protocol ranking, finishing at the end of the line with the Health Inspector, Bernard Shaw, and his wife Mary. Just above them in the line for the presentation were to be myself and Libo.

Mrs PMO expressed her objection to the arrangement, announcing that she was senior in rank to the DO's wife and certainly to Dr Rossinger and his wife. Before she remonstrated further the Governor's car and entourage drove up the drive of the hospital and stopped at the end of the line... unfortunately for Mrs PMO, at the wrong end of the line! The Governor got out of his car and immediately walked up to Mary Shaw, shook her hand, moved on to Bernard and talked to them both. He was then introduced by the DO and so moved along the line finishing with Mrs PMO, her husband, and Mrs Wilson, the DO's wife. Though, in fact, it had been a cock-up it was the perfect answer and rebuff to Mrs PMO and her pompous insistence on ranking!

Kilifi and Malindi between them had around thirteen dispensaries which were the focal points for establishing the rural clinics, allowing patients to be seen away from hospital and thus saving them the hardship of travelling to town for their treatments and care. The dispensaries were visited regularly by either myself, the Assistant MO or Sister.

The Giriama were steeped in folk-lore and witchcraft and one experience I had demonstrates this well. One afternoon I was called from my office to see a case of tetanus. The patient had been placed in a corner bed in the general ward with a screen round him. I went along to see him and noticed that when I went round the screen he did not go into a tetanus spasm or convulsion. Rather, I noticed that his eyes followed me as I moved round his bed to sit beside him. He had no sign of 'risus sardonicus' or 'lock-jaw'. After an examination I instructed my staff to take him to the theatre, being convinced that he was not suffering from tetanus, but had been cursed or bewitched. Consternation! The staff followed my instructions.

In the theatre I induced the patient with a minimal dose of pentothal and when he was gently asleep and before he awoke from the drug, I sat him up and crossed his legs and arms. He was in this position when I spoke to him asking him to raise his arms and uncross his legs. "There you are, we have cured you," I remarked when I realised he could understand what I was saying. He smiled. We returned him to the ward, only for him to return to the spinal arched spasm position. I instructed my staff to call his relations and I advised them that the man would not die of tetanus, but that there was nothing really I could do to help him... they would be better advised to take him to their local witch-doctor and have the curse removed.

Two weeks passed and I was conducting a ward round when there was a commotion at the end of the ward. The dresser told me that a man wanted to see me. I sent a message that he should call at my office after rounds. However, he insisted and walked into the ward and remarked, "You don't recognise me? I was the one in that bed and you sent me out to be treated by the witch-doctor. Well, here I am, cured. Thank you for your advice."

My kudos with my staff rose!

While in Kilifi, I truly became aware of the community health issues. I was visiting Jaribuni dispensary and noticed that many women were passing the front door of the dispensary without stopping for any advice or treatment. I was puzzled that, although notice had been given of my regular monthly visits, very few women were attending. I enquired from the dresser for a possible cause and to find out where they were all going? He replied, "They are going to collect water from their nearest watering point."

I decided to follow up this situation and required my health assistants to provide me with a plan of their district area, detailing the sources of water and the position of the villages in relation to the water points. On completion of the survey it became obvious that the average distance walked by women in that area was fifteen miles daily! What hope did I have of expecting them to listen to our health education talks on the need to boil all water before drinking it, or further education on home-care and domestic hygiene? What hope of encouraging the women to attend regularly for ante-natal or well-children clinics when they spent so much time walking many miles for the purpose of collecting water. Discussions with the DC supported his programme for improving the provision of water supplies throughout the district, with dams, bore-holes and piped supplies where feasible etc.

Often, before retiring for the night, if I was on call I would walk round to the hospital to ensure everything was in order. Very often I would find staff asleep on the floor in the ward, ie, after 10.00 or 11.00 pm. A gentle shake was generally enough to awaken the culprit, but on this particular night a good shake had little effect. Finally the dresser turned over and looked me straight in the face.

I enquired, "Wallace, just what are you doing?"
"Sleeping Sir," was the reply.
"Do you know who I am?"
"Oh yes Sir!"
"Well, who am I?"
"You're Dr Barton, Sir! Oh my God!"
It is always difficult to severely discipline a staff member in such a situation.

Doing a ward round one day I was concerned that a case of typhoid was suffering a relapse. I questioned the dresser, "Have you kept him strictly on the diet I prescribed?"
"Yes Sir!"
"You didn't by any chance give him a double helping did you?"
"Oh no Sir! I didn't."
"You didn't what?"
A pause and then, "Do what you said Sir."
"What was that?"
There was another pause, followed by a blank stare, as if awaiting everlasting damnation and then, "What you said Sir!"

In class, when teaching the physiology of the kidney I had drawn on the board the glomerulus with the blood vessels entering, and with the descending and ascending convoluted tubules in position. Having completed the diagram I then wrote against each structure its respective name. I called on 'Charles' to go over the diagram and explain it to the class. He did well until he reached the convoluted tubule... "It then passes into the... the... pause; then, looking at the class he continued, "...what the doctor has written here!" Collapse of the doctor!

I have so many special memories apart from the busy clinics of medical and surgical cases.

Elephantiasis was a plague at the Coast with the culex mosquito and filariasis endemic. Scrota, legs and mammary glands were all attacked. One woman was admitted with large pendulous breasts. Not only were they not functioning on lactation, but they were a drag on her whole system. With her husband's consent, we agreed to carry out a surgical plastic repair. I had taken great care to mark out the flaps and areas for resection and, with humility, at the conclusion of the operation considered I had done a good job! In removing a scrotum or breast we were aware of the amount of fluid being drained at one time and so were always careful to limit the area for removal at one operation. As in this particular case, this could often work against one, for after seeing the result the husband was so delighted with the one repaired breast, that he reckoned there was no need to remove the other. So he took her out with uneven breast balance!

My experience in Wajir over those two years had given me the confidence to tackle most surgical problems but it was always a relief to realise that there was a surgical specialist at Mombasa to whom I could refer a case. Indeed, it was the practice of both the Provincial Medical and Surgical Specialists to visit the district hospitals twice annually to give guidance and, if necessary, remove cases to Mombasa for referral treatment.

Bilharzia was endemic throughout the district and along the Coast. Before modern therapy, the treatment was with intravenous injection of antimony sodium tartrate (AST) over a period of three days. Complete rest and careful dieting was essential to avoid severe poisoning, with heart failure as the possible result. We conducted a series of such treatments, losing one child who sneaked out to play football and who dropped down dead with cardiac failure. The series was my first ever publication; it was accepted by the East African Medical Journal in 1952.

154

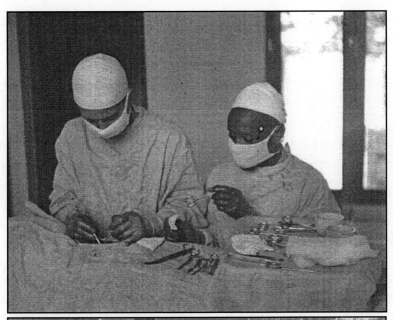

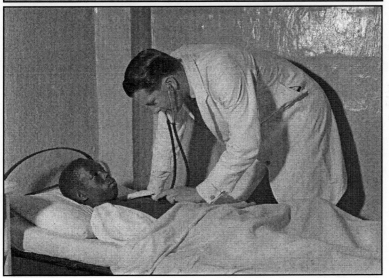

At work in Kilifi

155

My mentors for the article were Dr Ronnie Heisch and Dr Wright, respectively the Kenya Senior Parasitologist and Medical Specialist. The great protagonists of the AST regimen of therapy for bilharzia were Drs Alves and Blair of the Research Centre in Salisbury, South Rhodesia, as it was known then. In due course, nilodar tablets by mouth replaced the dangerous AST intravenous procedure.

In 1952 the Kenya Department of Information decided to make a film on bilharzia, and Kilifi was chosen as the location. I was to be the MO for the production. A whole chapter could be written on so many of the day-to-day problems that the film team encountered in casting local schoolchildren, local farmers and women for the production. A simple everyday matter of issuing them with gloves and 'wellington boots' as a protection against skin contact with the water from the dams etc led to many complications. How do you instruct people in the use of gloves, who have never seen them, far less put them on. Laughter, frustration and time wasting were the rule of the day! Getting the workers to put on wellington boots to allow them to move into the dam edges to rake out the snails responsible for the transmission of the disease, seemed simple enough, until we realised we were filming the workers taking off their boots to empty them of water, for they had waded into the dam over the top of their boots! Again there was laughter, frustration and time wasting, for the shots had to be taken again and a closer watch maintained to obviate a repeat of the occurrence.

Libo was 'continuity girl' to ensure that each day's filming was continuous with the previous day. At the end of the first day she specifically told all the children to appear the next day dressed exactly as they were. Come the following morning all the children turned up in their 'Sunday best' clothes as they knew they were to be photographed. All Libo could do was send them home to change into their old clothes. Again, half a day's filming was wasted.

However, possibly the funniest episode occurred at the end of a day of filming at the local school. Having 'diagnosed' those affected with the condition, the selected children were filmed getting into the ambulance to be taken to hospital in Kilifi. They were told that the ambulance would go to the hospital where they would be filmed getting out of the ambulance and entering the ward for treatment. After filming the chosen cases entering the ambulance, the film team went ahead to set up the cameras for the ambulance arriving at the hospital. Unknown and unseen, about a dozen children had crowded into the ambulance for a lift back to town! The consternation was incredible when the Director called out, "Action! Open the ambulance door... the kids should get out and proceed to the wards." About two dozen children trooped out instead of the chosen six. "Stop! What's going on?" screamed the Director. It all had to be repeated! For us amateurs, it was truly a laugh a minute!

* * * * *

Tana River District

The District was essentially along the Tana River stretching from the Coast up as far as Hola, meeting the boundary of Garissa District in the NFD. Kipini, at the mouth of the river on the coast, was the Administrative HQ of the District, with Tony Palmer as the DC when I was posted to Kilifi in 1950. Tony's wife, Mollie, was the first wife of a DC to agree to be posted to live in Kipini. They were there for two years from 1950 when Tony was succeeded as DC by George Hilton Brown, a bachelor. The Government Boma also had an Agricultural Officer, one Geoff Brown.

To enable the DC to visit his District and all the villages along the river, he had a lorry as well as *The Pelican*. This was a flat-bottomed boat with diesel engine, a cabin and an upper deck with an awning roof. The boat was flat- bottomed to enable it to navigate through shallows and to pass over submerged tree trunks - always a danger to navigation up the river.

157

The Pelican

Tana River

I paid several visits to Kipini boma, especially during the period when we were building, and later commissioning and opening the new minor hospital there. Miss Jardine, the Nursing Sister at Kilifi, was responsible for commissioning the hospital with furniture, drugs, supplies and equipment, and so she also paid occasional visits to Kipini. One such visit was made by her and my then fiancée, Libo Belcher, and Libo's brother Humphrey. In due course the hospital was opened by the Director of Medical Services, Dr Farnworth Anderson, with Dr Bartlett the PMO also present.

The hospital was to be under the charge of a senior Hospital Assistant, a Pokomo named Hillarn Mitchell. He did a wonderful job, not only in running the hospital but also in caring for the sick, often taking his initiative in carrying out minor surgery within his own recognised competence. He always had the back-up of the Lamu hospital, which had an Asian MO, or a Sub-Assistant-Surgeon in charge to whom cases could be referred. For cold surgery he would refer cases to Malindi or Kilifi. I

159

was delighted in later years to see that Hillarn received recognition and promotion and had become Hospital Secretary at the Coast General Hospital in Mombasa.

Several stories can and must be told of various exciting experiences involving myself as MO i/c Lamu and Tana River Districts.

* * * * *

Lamu District

Lamu, with its history of close connections with the Oman and its associated Arabic culture, is often referred to as a miniature Zanzibar; certainly in respect to much of its architecture, its Muslim traditions and, being in the Coastal Strip, flying the Sultan's flag. While under Kenyan Administration, it had Mudirs appointed by the Sultan.

Lamu, an island, had no motorised vehicles. To reach the island one drove to the jetty at Mkoani, where one parked the car and, having notified the DC ahead of time of your likely ETA, one was taken by the Government launch round to Lamu port, a journey of one hour.

The only real hotel was the Lamu Hotel run by Percy Petley, a former 'White Hunter' who carried scars on his body of lion and buffalo maulings. He was a man who had a long history in the area and was a true character amongst the early European settlers. His hotel was unique. On the ground floor was the dining-room, a bar and a small sitting area; the four major bedrooms were upstairs on the first floor, with another two up more stairs to the roof level. All the bedrooms had partition walls made of local matting, so that there was virtually no privacy, with all bodily noises being heard by every resident. The bathroom and loo were along the corridor on the first floor and comprised a bath in which one stood or sat, pouring water from a jug over oneself. The waste water from the bath ran across the floor and down into a drain which linked up with the long-drop loo which fell through the house into the earth below! The loo, in fact, was behind another matting partition and so again there was little privacy as regards noise! There was an additional loo on the ground floor provided for the casual customer who had popped in for a drink or meal.

On arrival at the hotel one was generally met by Percy wearing a kikoi tied round his waist. He was usually shirtless as this was only donned mid-morning. Certainly that was his attire every morning when he appeared at breakfast time or to present you with the bill. He was one of the great characters of Kenya, and one could sit for hours listening to his tales of hunting in earlier days. Much has been written of him in various books and I consider myself honoured to have met him in the 1950s on my several visits to the island.

Lamu attracted numerous interesting men in their retirement, some of whom had taken on the Muslim faith and so felt they belonged in the community. Henri Burnier, a Swiss who acted as Consul for the Coast, was one who had retired to Lamu at Shella beach where he had a delightful house. He was a very well educated and charming man who had known my parents during the war.

The DC during my later visits to Lamu was John Carson, with his wife Dorianne, but earlier there had been Daddy Cornell, who for me was of Wajir fame, having been involved in the building of the hospital there.

One of my visits warrants particular mention. It was with Dr Hugh Watters, the PMO who was escorting the Matron-in-Chief, Kenya, a Miss Mary Griffen, on an inspection visit of health units in the Coastal Province. As I was the MO i/c north of Mombasa, I was expected to accompany them. It was a pleasant safari, except for the fact that early on in the trip it became somewhat obvious to me that the Matron had fallen for me - presumably because I was one of the few remaining young eligible MO bachelors. I spent most of my time manipulating events to ensure that I was never left alone with her!

161

Another trip to Lamu with Dr Watters proved a nightmare. Driving his brand new Fiat car, he arrived in Kilifi to pick me up for the trip. I had a relatively new, short-wheel-based Land Rover, and suggested that we should use that as the weather forecast was for heavy rain - with the monsoon likely to break any time. Dr Watters was so proud of his new Fiat that he insisted we should travel in it.

We set off and spent the night at Malindi. We called in at Kipini to find that Mollie Palmer was on her own, Tony having gone on a short safari in his District by road. We persuaded Mollie to join us on our quick visit to Lamu, where she would stay with her friends John and Doreen Carson. So on we went to Lamu. That night the heavens opened, and at day-break we decided to cancel our inspection visit to the hospital and set off without delay back home. By this time we had another passenger, Captain Lewis - a slightly lame ship's captain and a true but harmless buccaneer. He was well known on the Kenya coast and we had offered him a lift back to Mombasa.

As we travelled towards Kipini the weather seemed to improve. We had to make the detour from the Witu to Garsen road to get Mollie back to Kipini. She insisted on preparing sandwiches for us for the journey back to Malindi, in case we were held up on the way. Before leaving, I decided to phone Malindi hoping to speak with Bernard Shaw. He was on safari so I left a message with his wife to tell him that, if we were not back in Malindi that night when he got back from his safari, he should set off down the Garsen road to look for us.

We set off, only to meet the rain storm again, this time in the middle of the forest crossing the black-cotton soil area approaching Garsen. We slid off the road into the ditch at the side, and were to remain there for the rest of the night. We were about eight miles from Garsen village, the crossing point of the Tana River and where we knew there was a PWD camp. We could not have picked a worse spot for mosquitoes, nor an area more

162

heavily populated with elephants. We were bitten alive by the former and we could hear the latter all around us in the thick trees along the road. No sleep was possible, being devoured by the mossies and from sheer fear of the ellies.

The next morning I suggested that one of us had to walk to Garsen to get help in terms of men and a strong rope to pull us out of the mud. The Captain could not walk that far because he was lame! Certainly I could not allow my PMO, Dr Watters, to do it, so it was down to yours truly. I set off to walk the eight miles, hoping to obtain help and to collect some food and drink. The road was so muddy that I could not keep my shoes on and so had to walk bare foot all the way.

I got to Garsen where the first thing I did was order a meal of fried eggs, toast and a pot of tea. I then located the PWD camp and finally persuaded enough of the road repair gang to walk back with me to help pull the car out. I collected some vital provisions for the two left behind and set off back to the car. We had enough daylight left to have the rope secured round the car, and, thankfully, the first pull got us out into the middle of the road. However, we could not attempt to drive because the road was just thick mud and surely we would have slid back into the ditch. So, with the Captain and Dr Watters sitting in the car, I helped the PWD gang to slowly pull us along the road, out of the forest and onto the open plain towards Garsen. The gang was in good spirit and sang as they pulled us along. Naturally, with failing light, they decided to return to Garsen, promising to come back the next morning. So we settled down for another sleepless night in the car being bitten alive by mossies, but we were now out of the forest and so, hopefully, free from ellies!

In the midnight hours suddenly I was aware of a light over the horizon getting brighter and possibly nearer. Could it be Bernard? Could it possibly be?

The Fiat - Garsen

In time we thought it must be for surely it was the lights of a car, and as Bernard had a small Land Rover only he could possibly get through the mud. Mercifully it was and I went out to greet him. Poor Bernard had not long been in the country and had never been across the Tana at Garsen. He had got the message to come and look for us along the Garsen road, but had unpacked his Land Rover of all supplies of food. All he had set off with was a can of *Coke* and a *Mars bar*. He had imagined that he would find us about twenty miles out of Malindi.

My first question to Bernard was, "What food supplies have you got with you?"
"I have a *Mars bar* and a can of *Coke*," was his reply.

Poor man... he nearly got lynched!

It was not too long till daylight and shortly thereafter the gang from Garsen were seen coming along the road. With the combined efforts of Bernard's Land Rover and the gang pulling the car, with the rope round it to keep it from sliding off the camber of the road, we eventually reached Garsen. Once over the hand-drawn ferry across the Tana we were able, under our own steam, to set off for Malindi and eventually home. The only real casualty of the trip was the car, which bore scratch marks from the rope. Poor Dr Watters, I felt deeply for him and his car, which was no longer brand new... his wife must have had a few words to say on that subject. He did admit that he would never turn down the offer of a Land Rover for any future trip to Lamu!

The other casualty of the episode was Tony who got stuck on his safari and did not get back to Kipini for several days. Poor Mollie was waiting anxiously at Kipini worrying about us and about Tony. Such was life for a DC's wife in a lonely out-station cut off during the rains. In fact the rains on that monsoon were such that Kipini was cut off for a couple of months.

Another memorable experience of Tana River commenced with my receiving a telegram from Tony asking me to come as soon as possible to advise and take action on an epidemic which was raging at Hola - typhoid

165

was suspected. Tony and Mollie were on a *Pelican* trip up the river and were met at Hola by an anxious crowd with stories of children dying.

I quickly organised a trip by road, with a 'dresser' from the hospital to assist me. We set off, and after Garsen ran into flooded roads. We attached a hose pipe onto the exhaust of the car, carrying the pipe above the roof to prevent the water from flooding back into the exhaust.

Setting the car into four-wheel drive mode, slowly we managed to get through the floods, arriving at Hola after quite a hair-raising journey. The whole village was crowded and, as I drove in, I received a cheer from them and a warm welcome from Tony.

I stood still for a moment to review the scene. There were dozens of mothers with their babes in arms, and tiny tots all coughing away with terminal whoops. "So what is it likely to be?" was Tony's question. I had made my diagnosis and replied, "Just listen."
"To what?" was his next question.
"Just listen. Can't you hear the whoop."

It was a self-diagnosing condition for an epidemic of whooping-cough.

We set up two tables, and all children had their temperatures taken. Any with a temperature, I examined physically with my stethoscope. Those with chest signs were given an injection of penicillin and a follow-up dosage of sulpha drugs. Those without temperatures were given aspirin. We stayed the night and next morning examined the crowd again. The penicillin treatment was repeated and a further dosage of sulpha drugs prescribed. The epidemic was controlled; no more deaths were recorded over night and on the third day I returned to Kilifi, the rains and floods having receded.

The scare was reported to Medical HQ and after a short delay I received a query from the then ADMS Health asking how had I diagnosed the condition - had I taken culture plates? My reply was trite! "No culture plates are stored in Kilifi, and in any case they would have melted in the heat of the Tana River District. My diagnosis was made clinically, having had a good medical training at Edinburgh University!" I never heard again from HQ but was thanked by the Administration for my prompt action.

Another story relating to the Tana River features Bernard and Mary Shaw in starring roles. I was introducing Bernard and Mary to the District and we were visiting several of the larger villages on the Tana, travelling by road. We reached Wema to find Tony and Mollie on *The Pelican* tied up at the village. Bernard had not been out long from the UK and Mary had only recently arrived, so this was their first safari.

The three of us were to spend the night in the new DC camp house beside the river; Mary and Bernard in the rest-hut on camp beds under nets; I would sleep on the verandah of the hut. The rest-hut had an earth floor and coconut-leaf thatched roofing. I held up the deitz paraffin lamp and told Mary to go inside, undress and slip on her nightie, then we could come in and change.

Suddenly there was a scream, "Bernard! Come quick, I'm covered all over in pins and needles!"

I went in with the light and there she was standing in the middle of soldier ants on the move. Once disturbed in their travel, or safari as it is called, they scatter and look for the culprit, climb up their legs and pinch bite!

"Quick Mary. Go out to my truck, take off all your clothes and throw them out of the window. This is the only way to stop them biting and to leave you."
"I can't do that!"
"You must! Go quickly and I'll bring you a towel or sheet to wrap round you."

She reluctantly obeyed, got into the cab of the truck, stripped and threw out her clothes. I approached with the sheet and lifted up the light to pass it in to her. She covered herself with her arms across her breasts and exclaimed, "Oh!" Then, dropping her arms she took the sheet, smiled and said, "Of course it's alright! You're a doctor!" - The biggest insult of my life!

The final story of the Tana is probably the most dramatic, and certainly the one that could have ended in disaster.

Tony had arranged that I should join him and his wife Mollie on a safari by *The Pelican*, to visit every village on the whole length of the Tana River up to Hola. I was to hold out-patient clinics at every village, dispensing medicines where required, and when needed and feasible, carrying out minor surgery, for example, removing foreign bodies, small cyst ganglions and suchlike. He would hold barazas - meetings with the villagers to listen to and sort out their problems.

I set off with a dresser and an array of boxes with bottles marked 'Mist. Diarrhoea', 'Mist. Constipation', 'Mist. Cough', 'Mist. Rheumatism' and several others. I also took other boxes full of drugs: the sulpha drugs, aspirin, and others for treating helminthic infections etc. Naturally I had a limited supply of penicillin, which had to be kept on ice.

I had also arranged to vaccinate everyone attending the clinics against smallpox; to take urine and where possible stool samples, to test for bilharzia and helminthic infections, as well as blood slides to test for malaria. The safari was to last four weeks and so I collected some provisions from Fatiallah Dhalla, the Asian grocer's shop in Mombasa. I will never be allowed to forget 'kippers'. Kippers had just arrived from the UK, and so I decided that that would be a real treat for us on the trip. I thought 24 would be enough, so ordered some, forgetting that kippers are sold in pairs. When I met up with Tony and Mollie at Kipini, I handed over the kippers and Mollie's face gave the show away.

"At this rate we'll be eating kippers for every breakfast on the trip," was her justified comment.

Back to the medical clinics. The Tana River winds and twists its way across the flattening countryside as it nears the end of its journey at the coast. Villages are spread out along its banks; some on one side of the river, others on the opposite bank. It proved of great interest when results of the blood-slides were analysed, for the incidence of positive slides was greater in those villages down wind. One could plot out the position of the villages along the twisting river, and then enter the slide results.

There were surely hundreds of villages and at every one we had to unload the tables, chairs and boxes of medicines! Phew what an effort. I then realised why no former MO had ever undertaken such a mammoth medical treatment safari! It was truly fascinating, if at times tiring, but never boring.

At every village along the river we would stop, and while Tony held meetings with the Chiefs I would set up a treatment clinic under a suitable tree, dispensing bottles of mixtures for coughs, diarrhoea, constipation, rheumatism or whatever.

Most of the villagers had never seen a white doctor and so turned up with countless stories, some relating to their sex life and problems with their spouses. There were also children's problems, and of course one unearthed the untreated hair lips, deafness and blindness. One learned to be a great listener.

At lunch on one particular day Tony announced that we would be spending the night at this village for he had many problems to listen to and try to solve! He wondered if I had any possible solution to a certain case. Apparently one of the villagers was terrifying the rest of them, and particularly members of his own family. They reckoned he had the power of the devil and was gradually killing off all his male relatives, whom one imagined were in his way of inheritance for the family land. He was seen to put his right hand on the left shoulder of his 'victim' who duly died

169

within two days! The villagers wanted Tony to arrest him and charge him with murder. No way! Could I help? I'd try!

Everyone had seen me dispensing solutions of medicines from the large mixture bottles. "Well, I'll challenge the suspected man to drink with me from one of the mixtures and test whether or not he is a devil." The villagers were called to meet Tony and myself.

In front of a huge crowd I put two glasses on the table. Into one of these, to be his glass, I had already put a few drops of atropine eye drops. I was cheating, for I knew that atropine dried up the airways and dilated the pupils. Oh so cunning! Then, in front of the crowd, I filled up both glasses with 'medicine' from one of my bottles and challenged the suspect.

"They say you are possessed with devil powers. I don't believe you are and we will test it together. We will drink together from the same bottle of medicine, and if either of us is possessed with the devil then the devil will try to leave our bodies. Our eyes will become dilated and our mouths will dry up. The devil will dry up our souls and he will leave our frames through our eyes. That is if you or I are so possessed. Are you prepared to demonstrate to the villagers with me that neither of us is possessed with the devil?"

He agreed and so we drank together. I duly returned to the launch by the river side.

After an hour or so we heard the sound of villagers approaching. Joy and excitement. "Oh Bwana you should see the devil leaving him just as you said he would if he was possessed. His mouth has dried and he is having heavy breathing; his eyes are like dik-diks, popping out of his head! No longer will he have the power, for the devil is leaving his body as you said."

Wow! what had I done? We rushed up to the village to find him in extremis! Whether this was from fear of losing his power or from an oversensitivity to the atropine, I will never really know. I only know that Tony and I had to administer artificial respiration to him for the next two hours to ensure he would not allow himself to die!

We went further up the river and on our return, about ten days later, we stopped again at the village and the villagers were so happy. "You should see him. He still tries to put his hand on people's right shoulders but we know he has no powers and so no-one has died." I suppose I could feel relieved that maybe I had saved a few lives from being bewitched.

Tony and Mollie were transferred after two years in Kipini, being replaced by George Hilton Brown. I had a few other trips and safaris to Kipini and another short trip with Libo on *The Pelican* with DC Brown, but nothing as fruitful or successful as those with Tony.

My final recollection of Lamu was years later, when with Libo and our two children, Lesley and Ian, we flew there for a short trip when we were all on holiday in Kenya long after Independence. It had changed somewhat... the African DC had introduced a Land Rover onto the island!

The emphasis of the place was on tourism, with daily flights to the island and all manner of holiday and leisure-time attractions. I am always grateful that I was blessed with being left for five years in Kilifi and was able to serve the people on the coastal strip from 1950-55, and that shortly after I was transferred to Zanzibar where His Highness The Sultan was, de jure, the ruler of that area.

Libo

I first met Libo Belcher at a monthly tennis spoon competition at the Kiambu Club in 1946, while on a visit to Nairobi to give professional evidence on a murder case at the High Court in Nairobi. Libo and I were both members of the DC's party, though we did not play as partners. The tennis spoon was followed by a Club Dance and I did have the chance to dance and chat with Libo. I gathered that she was on the eve of leaving for London to train in nursing. She admitted that she was feeling very homesick and was not looking forward to being away from Kenya. Having only recently arrived from the UK myself, I told her I was equally homesick for Edinburgh. I always remember telling Libo that I doubted that she would ever return to Kenya, for she would certainly have many boyfriends and in due course become engaged to, and marry, a young doctor. I have to admit that in truth I fell in love with Libo that night, but realised I would have little chance of ever seeing her again, and certainly would have no hope of marrying her.

In the years that followed, whenever I visited certain homes I was faced with photos of Libo, with statements that their son, grandson, nephew or other near relative was likely to be marrying Libo when she finally returned to Kenya... so what chance did I have! That having been said, I did not even try to contact Libo in London when I was in Edinburgh attending the DTM&H Course during 1949-50.

When I was in Kilifi at the end of 1951, I heard that Libo, still unmarried, was returning to Kenya on the maiden voyage of the *Uganda*. As Kilifi is only 40 miles from Mombasa, I decided that I would go there to see the ship arrive and try to re-introduce myself to Libo, hoping to impress.

I did in fact go into Mombasa, but took fright when I thought that her father, Lt Col Belcher, might be there to meet Libo as her mother was still in the UK. While Colonel Belcher was a real gentleman, he was nevertheless somewhat severe and, to a young Government Official, overwhelming!

As things turned out, I would not have been able to meet Libo anyway, for one of the ship's passengers had fallen ill and required an escort, preferably a nurse, on the journey to Nairobi. Libo had duly volunteered.

In the New Year of 1952 I attended a medical conference in Nairobi and heard that Libo was on a film safari making *The Snows of Kilimanjaro*, and that the unit was filming at Narok. With my friend Gordon Hector, whom I knew from my Wajir days, I set off to Narok, where the DC was John Pinney, former DC Isiolo when I was in the NFD... too late the unit had moved on!

The next development was when Wish Stringer, the wife of John, DC Kilifi, was going up to Nairobi. Before leaving, she asked me whether she should invite Libo, her old friend from Kiambu days, for a holiday with them, so that we might have the chance to meet again. My fate was in the hands of Wish as it all depended on whether she felt that Libo was still the lovely girl she had been before her training in London. I willingly agreed!

Wish returned with news that Libo had accepted the offer, but was not sure when she could make it. We waited for a few weeks before a message came through that Libo would be arriving on the following Monday. Apparently, when Libo had been told she would be meeting Bill Barton, her reply was, "Who's Bill Barton?" At this point Cecily Gavaghan made the comment, "He's the most eligible bachelor in Kenya... and plump and chubby." Whether this was the case or not, clearly I had made no impression on Libo the first time we met!

173

I was due to visit Jibana Health Centre and was crossing the creek on the hand-drawn ferry when it passed the ferry going in the opposite direction. On the deck was a beautiful young woman - it surely had to be Libo. I was invited to dinner at the Stringer's that evening and knew straightaway that I would be marrying Libo. Apparently, Libo had seen me cruising on the ferry, but as I was not plump and chubby she had not identified me.

Libo only had five nights in Kilifi and so Wish arranged for various officers to invite us for dinner each night, without including herself and John, thus allowing me to collect Libo and, in due course, return her home to the DC's guest house where she was staying. As arranged by Wish, on the Friday night Libo and I were invited alone to have dinner with Roger Hoskings and his wife. At 9.30 pm they indicated that they wanted to retire to bed and so we left.

As it was so early, Libo and I went down to the Club and sat on the verandah, before moving down onto the beach below. It was there on the beach, being bitten alive by mosquitoes, that I proposed to Libo and she accepted.

At the time both Libo and I were committed to others. Libo had accepted a proposal of marriage from a young, recently qualified doctor at the Middlesex Hospital, but fortunately she had not accepted an engagement ring, having suggested that they should formally announce their plans on her return from Kenya. As for myself, I had to tell Libo about Katharine, a widow with two children. I had been friendly with Katherine for several years and had just written offering her money to come to Kenya with her two children, to decide whether they could happily settle with me there. In other words it was a proposal of marriage. Libo and I both agreed that we would write to our respective partners telling them of our engagement to each other.

Libo - 1951

Libo's fiancé was naturally shattered, while Katharine replied that she was relieved to have my letter for she had recently met Gordon Adair, a solicitor on leave from India, who was anxious to marry her and she reciprocated. He was five years older than herself and so well able to be father to her two children. Indeed, Libo and Katharine later became great friends and I was delighted to be asked to propose the toast at Katharine and Gordon's wedding.

Libo's mother had returned from the UK and so Libo was able to break the news to her parents after her return from Kilifi. They had arranged for a holiday trip to Uganda, the Belgian Congo, Ruanda and Burundi after the visit of Princess Elizabeth. They agreed to include me in the holiday and so plans were set for the trip which was to include Cliff and Peggy Ellis, mutual friends from Kiambu, as our chaperons.

History records that when Princess Elizabeth and Prince Philip arrived in Nairobi, they held a Garden Party at Government House, to which Libo and her mother were invited. The Royal visitors were to spend a few days at Sigana Lodge, the wedding present from the people of Kenya, before moving to the Coast to hold a further Garden Party at Government House in Mombasa. The day before they were due to travel to Mombasa we had arranged a farewell party for our chief cook at Kilifi Hospital. Libo had already arrived down at Kilifi to drive up with me to start the holiday to the Congo etc. While at the party Roger Hoskings, the DO, arrived from Mombasa to tell us that King George VI had died that morning and that Princess Elizabeth, now our Queen, was returning to London and therefore all arrangements for their visit to Mombasa were naturally cancelled.

One never forgets such moments of history as they affect one personally.

In due course Libo and I set off at 3.00 am for Kiambu in my short-wheel based Land Rover to meet her parents. We arrived there early afternoon. Getting out of the car, Libo's parents came out to greet us. Colonel Belcher turned to Eileen and remarked, "There you are, I told you I had

176

never met him before." Who was I to argue that we had met several times over the past five years in the Club at Kiambu!

With Peggy and Cliff, we set off in two cars, my Land Rover and the Ellis' Citroën, heading for Uganda, spending the first night at Soy Country Club. Naturally, the sleeping arrangements were that I shared a room with Libo's father, Ted, whilst she shared with her mother, Eileen; Cliff and Peggy had their own room. Libo and Eileen would talk about events and developments, while Ted was obviously searching for my intentions and any risks surrounding me. The outcomes were swapped next day as Libo and I travelled together. Peggy and Cliff would pass on daily discussions with Ted and Eileen.

We moved on from Soy to Kampala before we headed for Kabale on the frontier with Ruanda. The days that followed took us into the Congo, with fascinating places to visit, including Lake Kivu, Kabale, Butere, Matimbo and the pygmies in the Ituri Forrest, before we moved back to the Mountains of the Moon in the Ruwenzori Mountain Range, Uganda.

During this period, I think it was in Kivu, Ted told Libo and I to go for a long walk and return to Eileen's room around 6.30 pm. How could I ever forget the date - February 14th... in a leap year.

When we duly returned, on entering the room we noticed that there were two bottles of 'bubbly' with six glasses, and plates of toasties, including caviare. When the Ellis' arrived, Ted started with the words, "Friends! It is my very great pleasure to announce the betrothal of our darling daughter Elizabeth to Bill." They had not warned us, nor told us of their agreement to our engagement, but they must have heard that I had in fact proposed to Libo and that she had accepted.

After the Ruwenzoris, we sidetracked to Lake Edward for game watching from the camp and along the Lake and connecting river. As we drove on, for the first time I saw the now famous sign, 'Elephants have right of way!'

177

Crossing back into Kenya, Libo and I were allowed to branch off to visit friends and family on our way back to Kiambu, where we found that Ted and Eileen had inserted the notice of our engagement in the *East African Standard* on 29th February; an appropriate date after they had announced our engagement on Valentine's Day, the 14th!

Two massive drinks parties followed on successive days at Torito Estate, where Ted was Manager of Mrs Dent's coffee estate.

One of the 'conditions' to which I had agreed on our engagement was for Libo to visit her Uncle Donald in Singapore, where he was about to retire as Chief Executive of *Shell Oil*. So off she set, to my deep concern and self-pity at her absence, but she duly returned, not having been stolen from me by one of the many young ADCs or other administrative officers around in Singapore.

Libo spent a little more time in Kilifi finalising things regarding our wedding, which we planned for 30th August. The service was to be at the church in Kiambu, followed by a reception at the Club. We had around 300 guests, of all ages, coming from all over Kenya: Officials and Settlers, and many friends from the coffee farms of Kiambu and from the golfing fraternity, Eileen being President of the Ladies' Golf Union.

My best-man was Bobby Winser, with whom I had served in Kisii. He had previously married Anne Carrick, who had travelled out on the *SS Alcantara*. Bobby had asked me to be his best-man, but unfortunately I was on study leave in March 1950 when they were married.

Libo's bridesmaids were Judith Stringer, her cousin Susan Palmer, and Sarah Ellis. We were married by Rex Jupp, who had travelled up from Mombasa on the Friday night train, returning the following evening for the Service on Sunday at Mombasa Cathedral. Dr Farnworth Anderson, the DMS Kenya, proposed the toast to the Bride and Groom.

178

30th August 1952

My parents travelled up from Mombasa and returned with Rex Jupp. Ted and Eileen had insisted that my parents should stand in line to greet the guests. After all the guests had passed, Dad went up to one of the Club servants and shook his hand, telling him he must have missed him in the line!

Until now, Ted had insisted on paying for everything, but as I was waiting for Libo to come down for us to set off on our honeymoon, Ted came up to me and remarked, "You pay from here on Bill."

We drove Ted's car to the Ellis' home, where I had left the Land Rover. Arriving at the Ellis' I realised I had driven the several miles with the hand-brake on... that was before the days of the drink-drive laws!

Our first night was to be spent at the *Blue Post Hotel*, Thika. We settled in and went through to the dining room for dinner. Just as we did so, the African night-watchman ran into the dining room with his gun at the ready and shouted, "I'm going to shoot all you Europeans." My immediate thought was, 'Oh no! Not now, not tonight of all nights!'

Fortunately the hotel manager came in and quietly led the night-watchman away... Phew!

The next morning we set off for the *Mawingo Hotel*, near Nanyuki; this had been the home of a wealthy lady and her French husband. On booking the room I had sent a telegram from Kilifi requesting the 'honeymoon suite'. We arrived at the hotel early afternoon hoping it would be quiet and so no fuss would result from our arrival. Walking up to the reception desk, I stated that I had made a reservation.

While they were checking the reservation they had turned round the register, but just before I signed it the receptionist said, "I am sorry, you must sign the other register," and she produced a white book stating that it was the one for the Honeymoon Suite. So my identity was made public.

180

As I was about to register I turned round to Libo and asked, "Shall I sign first, or would you like to?"

The receptionist intervened with, "May I suggest that you get into the habit of signing Dr and Mrs, Sir." I gulped and signed!

We had booked in for four nights, staying in the blue suite. We had a large bedroom with an XXL bed. There was a separate lounge with balcony and, of course, a large bathroom with mother-of-pearl fittings... including the toilet seat.

Every afternoon while resting, there was a knock on the door and a group of three hotel boys entered. One carried a tea pot, milk and sugar on a tray; another had a selection of tiny sandwiches, while the third was carrying the hotel cake of the day. As we were in the prime suite, it was our privilege to select our sandwiches, cut the cake and take out our slices. The sandwiches and cake were then taken down to the lounge for the other residents! This was a privilege I could well have surrendered to allow undisturbed sleep in the afternoons after a substantial lunch, especially on one's honeymoon.

Two interesting episodes require recording. On our fourth evening, sitting in our lounge waiting for drinks to be delivered, the boy entered, set down the drinks and ice and instead of withdrawing as was his custom, he just stood there. "Yes?" I enquired. "Sir, I have served many people in this room. They usually stay for one night or possibly two, but I have never known anyone spending four nights in this room." I suddenly realised that I had never asked about the cost of the room.

I made my way down to the reception desk and stated that I would be leaving after breakfast and would like my account ready in the morning. I also took the chance to enquire discretely about the room charge. "Five pounds a day full board." So what was the fuss?... I could afford £20 for our honeymoon stay.

181

The other story relates to when one of the residents recognised Libo as we entered the dining room one evening. She and Libo had travelled out together on the *Uganda* late in 1951. Libo turned and introduced me. The reply was encouraging, "Oh yes, I read of your engagement in the *Standard*. How long have you been married?" Libo swallowed and stuttered, "Four days." The reply was, "Only four days, you look as if you have been married at least two weeks!" We waited till we had been married for two weeks and then studied our images in the mirror.

Our next destination was to be Meru, but we stopped over in Isiolo to see Hector Douglas (Douggie), the Development Officer at Wajir, and his wife, Joan. We chatted, drank and ate and were persuaded to stay overnight with them in their guest house. That was an effort, for the guest house was sparsely furnished by the PWD, with two metal beds at separate ends of the room, and few other comforts. When the time came to retire, Joan and Douggie accompanied us to the room. To our horror, the houseboy, Douggie's servant in Wajir, had only made up one bed. We persuaded Joan to let us have sheets etc for the second bed, and when asked why he had only made up the one bed, the houseboy replied that in Wajir the boys never made up more than one bed. I did not require an interpretation, only hoping that Libo would not jump to the wrong conclusion.

Our next stop was to be Fort Hall, where again we were booked into the local hostelry, but were prevailed upon by Frank and Kathy Loyd to spend the night in a tent in the garden. This time at least there were two beds made up in the tent... but they were at different levels. One was an officer's regulation bed and the other a collapsible low-lying bed. Thoughtfully, the beds had been pulled together and made up with double sheets, however, in view of the Fort Hall temperatures, it was quite drafty to say the least!

We arrived back in Nairobi in time to attend the wedding of a school friend of Libo's, Isobel McRae to Richard Winnington-Ingram. The service was held in the Presbyterian Church in Nairobi and so I knew all the hymns well. For the 23rd Psalm I broke out in tenor descant, only to be told by Libo, "Try to sing in tune."

Heading back to the Coast we called on Tony and Mollie Palmer at Machakos, where Tony was DO. On hearing of our tale of woe, they generously sacrificed their double mattress for us to sleep in front of the sitting room fire!

Our final honeymoon stop was the *Sinbad Hotel* in Malindi, where unfortunately Libo fell ill, so she was happy to get back to Kilifi and our matrimonial home. We found that in our absence John Stringer had built a new guest house in our garden as an unofficial wedding present from the Administration.

Upon return from our honeymoon we gave a reception for our boma friends on the drive in front of our house. We arranged a Scottish country dancing evening and provided champagne cocktail (champagne and brandy). Well into the evening, Ken Smith, Mr Lillywhite's manager at Kizimbani, came up to the drinks table. I told him we had finished the champagne, but I could offer him a brandy and ginger ale. He looked straight at me and, in his delightful Scots accent, remarked, "I don't think I should have any more, for I have just experienced the first ecstasy of an alcoholic shudder!"

After our first year of marriage Libo and I sailed to the UK for study leave at home in August 1953. I had accepted that my future career in Africa lay in Community and Public Health and, as I had been granted a year of study leave I decided that I should return to Edinburgh to take my Diploma in Public Health (DPH). We travelled home on the Union Castle ship *Kenya Castle*.

Auntie Whyte was still alive and running her home at 131 WPR, so it was natural that we should head for there. Before we set off for home we realised that Libo was pregnant. Poor darling what a prospect - me out all day at classes and studying in the evenings, while she gradually got larger

183

and larger having to put up with old Auntie's Victorian and rather austere ways. One example was that in Kenya we were used to bathing daily, but in Scotland the habit was still a weekly event. There was never enough hot water for poor Libo's daily bath, but fortunately, as she had become close friends with Katharine who lived nearby, Libo was able to have the occasional bath at her home! As I was playing rugger and squash again I was able to shower almost every other day at least, so I was fine.

Libo was a great supporter of my rugger exploits and turned up generally as the only spectator at every match; she always says it was to collect my small denture set before I rushed on to play! I became Captain of the 5th Watsonians, having played for their 1st XV during the war. I played my last game of rugger the day Lesley was born on 27th February 1954. Libo had started labour on Thursday 25th and went into the Simpson Maternity Hospital, but after her pains ceased she returned home, starting again lunch time on 27th. After taking her in I went down to Myreside, the rugger fields and turned out to play, to take my mind off things. In those days, thank goodness, husbands were not allowed into the delivery room. During the match, while going into a ruck I called one of the forwards and told him to get his head down and to get stuck in! He turned round and replied, "Yes Sir!" That did it, to be called 'Sir' on the rugger field was too much, and so with my new responsibilities of fatherhood, I gave up playing the game that day. Libo had been in labour on and off for over fifty-six hours and Lesley was finally delivered by high forceps. Lesley's Godmother was Mollie Palmer of Kenya association, with Rev Dr Gus McKnight and John Henderson of school and Edinburgh connections as her Godfathers. So Lesley's first six months of life were spent in my old home at 131 WPR.

I successfully completed my DPH and, as related elsewhere, came top of the class. There was no Class Prize for the DPH course, however, Professor Crewe, the Head of Department, wrote to say that as I had completed an outstanding performance in the examination, it had been

184

agreed by the Senate that I should be awarded a University Medal - a precious memento I still possess.

In time we travelled to London and stayed at the Middlesex Residential hostel for nurses and staff. We had several days in London with built-in baby sitters. What a ball it was, going to such shows as *The King and I* and Norman Wisdom at the *Palladium* among others. We embarked at Tilbury on the Union Castle ship *Durban Castle*, and had an amusing interlude with the customs as we boarded the ship. We had a great deal of luggage which had been loaded on board and, in addition to our cabin luggage, we had Lesley in her carrycot. The Customs Officer asked us if we had anything to declare? Anything new which we had not brought into the country? We replied, "Well, yes... but all personal items."
"What about that?", he asked pointing to Lesley in her basket.
"You didn't have her when you arrived a year ago! I am not sure we can allow you to take such a precious item out of the country!"
Our faces must have dropped for he paused and, with a twinkle in his eye, added, "You promise to bring her back again?"

Fellow passengers with us were Bridget Wainwright and Sue Richards, the latter being Peggy Ellis' sister. We had a fright in the Red Sea when the head wind was being cancelled by the following wind so the ship got hotter and hotter. There were no air-conditioners in those days, so, in order to cool the ship, the Captain used to turn the ship right round 360 degrees to get the wind blowing through the whole ship. Phew!

We stopped at Port Sudan and, while there, a sandstorm blew up. All portholes were shut and ventilation blowers stopped. Lesley began to boil with rising skin temperature. We rushed to the galley and grabbed an ice bucket, filled it and placed it in the basin and plonked Lesley on to the ice to cool her down. In due course her temperature began to fall, but not before time.

Lesley's first home in Kenya was Kilifi, where she had been conceived and where we started our married life in 1952.

Lesley - 1954

Our home in Kilifi

and

the view from the window

Mau Mau and Manyani Prison Camp - 1954

Libo and I had first become aware of the potential danger of the Mau Mau on the first night of our honeymoon at the *Blue Post Hotel* at Thika, when our dinner had been interrupted by a drunken night-watchman threatening to 'shoot all you Europeans!'

Later that year, in October 1952, after the arrival of the new Governor Sir Evelyn Baring, a state of emergency was declared, followed by the arrest of Jomo Kenyatta and several other leaders of the Mau Mau movement. Since his return to Kenya in 1946 on the *Alcantara*, Kenyatta had set about creating a state of anarchy to destroy the stability of the country under Colonial Administration.

The Mau Mau activities were basically restricted to the Central and Rift Valley Provinces, affecting the Kikuyu and related tribes including the Meru, Embu and the Wakamba on the fringe. The rest of the country for the most part lived in peace. This was true of us living at the Coast Province. It must also be realised that, while many Europeans were murdered and brutally attacked, the main sufferers were the Africans themselves who were either opposed to the Mau Mau rising or suspected of being informers.

At the Coast we lived with no fear of brutal attack, however, if visiting Nairobi and the surrounding provinces, we always took our pistols with us in order to be ready to defend ourselves if necessary. The Belcher's, my in-laws, lived in Kiambu, a very active area for Mau Mau activities. Their wooden house was built on stilts and during the emergency, a gang of the Mau Mau were discovered living under the house. They were finally shot.

While playing bridge with Libo's parents, we would all place our pistols on the table, with a bullet up the nozzle but with the safety-catch on. Ted and I would be placed to cover a door or window lest a gang should suddenly burst in to attack. In that event, we would shoot immediately.

When we stayed with the Belcher's we usually had the use of a local guest house. This was near to where Mrs Dorothy Dent lived - the owner of the estate which Ted Belcher managed. Mrs Dent's large wooden bungalow was surrounded by a high expanded-wire fence for her safety from the Mau Mau.

On one visit, we were making our way back to our room when Libo and I noticed a glow in the sky and could smell burning. We realised it must be Dorothy's house so quickly raised the alarm for the Police and Fire Brigade. We rushed over to find her standing on the steps from her bedroom with the house ablaze behind her. She was very fond of whisky and seemed to be rather oblivious to what was going on! We had been out for dinner earlier that evening and I was wearing one of my favourite drip-dry suits. I was confronted by the high fence and realised that I would tear my clothes if I tried to climb it, but I had to get over. So without much thought, I stripped off my suit and, in my socks, vest and underpants, I climbed over and rushed to pick her up from the steps.

I decided to take Dorothy to the fence and as I did so, the Police and Fire Brigade arrived with headlights blazing, shining straight at me in my pants, vest and socks! The house was totally burnt down, and next morning strict security was set up to search through the ash to retrieve melted gold, silver, jewellery and other precious items.

Those of us living at the Coast played a useful role in offering breaks away to friends living constantly in danger. The emergency ended with the release of Jomo Kenyatta from his confinement at Lokitong in the Turkana District of the NFD.

188

Much has been published about the Mau Mau, the state of emergency and its effects on the country and its economy, and reference should be made to these publications for any details.

We returned to Kenya in August 1954 and were delighted to be re-posted to Kilifi Hospital in the Coast Province. We had no sooner settled back into our home when one evening we had a phone call from the Director of Medical Services, Dr Farnworth Anderson, telling me to get to Manyani as soon as possible, in fact sooner than that, for I was to report within 24 hours! This was around mid-September, if I remember correctly.

On politely requesting an explanation for the sudden transfer I was advised that there had been a major outbreak of typhoid fever at the Mau Mau detention camp at Manyani.
"Where is Manyani?"
"Just get there!"

I was to be answerable to Dr Bill Stott in HQ who was responsible for Medical Services in all Mau Mau prisons. Though Manyani was in the Coast Province, I was to deal directly with Dr Stott and Dr John Walker, the ADMS Health. So next morning I arranged everything with the Sister i/c, Miss Jardine, and the African MO posted at Kilifi, advising them how to handle any emergencies. I took my leave from Libo and our five-month old daughter and set off for the unknown.

It appeared that the outbreak of typhoid had been raging for quite a time; my predecessor unfortunately had 'taken to the bottle', diagnosing the condition prevalent in the camp as dysentery and sunburn. It was only when the number of deaths reported from the camp were seen to be rising dramatically that Medical HQ took action to check on what was taking place.

The 'dysentery' was obviously typhoid and the 'sunburn' was pellagra due to Vitamin B deficiency following the acute typhoid and a breakdown in

189

digestion and absorption of essential elements from food. After a detailed analysis of case records and an examination of all cases, it became evident that various other signs and symptoms of element deficiencies existed, including protein deficiency and other vitamin deficiency syndromes. Added to this were the many complications of typhoid. It has always been reported in literature that typhoid fever could have complications, with every system of the body being affected with inflammation. We detected iritis, colitis with accompanying bowel perforation and peritonitis, and osteomyelitis, to name but a few of the complications of the disease. A real task lay ahead.

I found that we truly had an epidemic on our hands with over 400 cases of typhoid in a camp of 18,000 detainees. I had one Hospital Assistant posted to the camp to help me, with about six dressers, all of course non-Kikuyus. All these staff were housed within the hospital compound. I was housed in the Prison Officers' Mess, which proved to be quite a problem, for as the only non prison officer I came under a degree of harassment, insults and isolation. The trouble was that my attitude to those with typhoid was in sharp contrast to that of the others who considered that the more detainees who died from typhoid, the better! On several occasions I was called to certify a death from 'malaria', which had occurred in one of the huts during the night. They were surprised when I refused to 'blindly' sign!

If there was an attempted escape, when the poor detainee was caught, he would be whipped and on occasions almost beaten to death. I was called in hopefully to testify that the tears in the flesh were due to him crawling through the barbed-wire perimeter fencing, while it was obvious that they were due to lashes from canes or whips. I stood my ground and generally stated that unless the detainee was moved immediately to the hospital I would not be responsible for his death nor sign any certificate. Such action did not improve my position within the Officers' Mess, but they eventually realised that I could not be persuaded to sign a death certificate against my professional judgement.

An early problem I had was to persuade the Prison Camp Commandant that I required more medical staff to assist me. Surely, I felt, there were bound to be several Kikuyu staff of the Medical Department who had been rounded up with 'Operation Jock Scott' and were among those housed in the huts. He agreed for me to tour the various huts to see if I could recognise staff with whom I had previously served in the NFD or at other stations, and invite them to join me in the hospital, and to call for others who were members of the Medical Department also to join us. I recognised several of my former staff and they, with all others who had served in the Department, agreed to join us working in the hospital - Amos Gatwache of Wajir days was one of them.

Our next task was to get agreement for them to be housed in huts to be built within the hospital compound, which of course was well within the camp perimeter and itself was surrounded by its own barbed wire fencing and gates.

Because I had to refer such requests to Nairobi, over the head of the Officer i/c, I quickly became unpopular with all the Prison Officer staff. I soon realised that they were almost, without exception, recruited from those who had served in such insurgent situations in other colonies: Palestine, Malaysia, Cyprus and others. They all had a hardened approach to their charges; many of them had their own Alsatian dogs with whom they conducted their patrols, generally also carrying a long whip with them.

After organising the staff and their sleeping arrangements within the compound, we were able to organise how to handle the cases and to try to work out the epidemiology of the epidemic.

I was fortunate to have had posted to the camp a Health Inspector, Leslie Lewis, with whom I had worked in Kiambu, in my first posting after my arrival in Kenya in 1946. Leslie Lewis was later promoted to Senior Health Inspector in the Uganda Health Service. He was a tower of strength with a good practical approach to problem-solving when it came to health and hygiene. We set up an intelligence service through our medical staff whom we had recruited to work with us in the medical compound. From this we learned that the practice of Mau Mau oath-taking was being conducted in the huts. The prisoners were shut up in their huts around 4.30 pm. Their food rations for their evening meals were placed inside the huts before they were locked in, while two night soil buckets were placed at the end of the hut as latrines.

It transpired that during the evening, after sunset, the Mau Mau leaders in the huts set up an oath-taking ceremony. This usually entailed food, generally pieces of meat, being dipped in the soil buckets and then eaten. Detainees who had not been initiated, or who were suspected as not having already taken an oath, were forced to participate in the procedure. Gradually even those who had taken the oath were made to reinforce their commitment to the Mau Mau by taking the oath again. It was quite clear from this information just how the epidemic had started and was spreading with intensity.

New cases were being diagnosed on a daily basis and patients were admitted to the compound for treatment. The death toll was rising, while the Colonial Secretary, Alan Lennox-Boyd, later Lord Boyd of Merton, was getting more and more impatient. Things were getting desperate.

The first priority was to change the system so that the detainees would have no food left in the huts for such oath-taking and in turn reduce the transmission of the disease from infected faeces. They were fed before they entered their huts, all food was then removed from the compound and each detainee was searched for food to ensure they had nothing with which to conduct the oath-taking. All soil buckets were removed early each morning and the contents buried in trenches some distance from the hut compounds.

We hoped that these two initial procedures would help to reduce the exposure of the detainees to infection. This was confirmed in time, with the gradual reduction of new cases being reported.

As luck would have it, at that time (September 1954) we received notice in Kenya that the first true antibiotic Chloromycetin (Chloramphenicol) was available for human treatment. It was reputed to be particularly effective against typhoid fever. The Governor of Kenya, Sir Evelyn Baring (later Lord Howick), gave special permission for the drug to be purchased and used at Manyani for the typhoid cases. We were all convinced that this directive had come from London, for the epidemic was truly political dynamite and had to be stopped. The Department soon obtained the drug and we received it for discretionary use. By that it was meant that I, the Medical Officer, had to use the drug to treat those whom I considered would benefit from its use and so be cured by the treatment. This would have the effect of reducing the death rate for the disease.

The cost of the drug at that time was US $2 per capsule, and as the treatment was eight capsules a day for five days, it meant the cost was $80 per patient. The Medical Department annual budget at that time only provided £2 per capita per year, so we had to use great discretion in electing cases suitable for treatment. Cases of longer standing, i.e. those who had been in hospital under the old palliative regime of treatment and were responding to same, naturally did not receive the new wonder drug Chloromycetin.

New cases confirmed clinically as typhoid were put on treatment, with a strict regime of control. They were closely watched for half an hour immediately after being given the drug. If any vomiting took place during that time, the vomit was collected, then camouflaged with concentrated

193

orange juice or other fruit juice and spoon-fed back to the patient. It was impossible to allow the drug to be wasted through a vomit! We took no risks that the case was purposely vomiting the drug as an indication of rejection of treatment! It sounds a non-ethical practice, but in such circumstances we had no alternative, other than to ensure the drug was properly utilised in the body. Treatment with Chloromycetin was supplemented by intravenous transfusion with saline and other electrolyte salts, along with vitamin supplements.

Time was the great healer! The epidemic dramatically started to recede; there were fewer new cases and fewer deaths. It had taken a month of non-stop effort, with little sleep, to achieve. I was so grateful for the support and encouragement I received from Leslie Lewis, as well as Dr Stott.

At this time a relief Doctor, Oscar Killen, had been posted to help and after about six weeks I was able to withdraw and return to my own station in Kilifi, but not before a visit from the Colonial Secretary, Alan Lennox-Boyd. He came to visit the camp along with The Governor, Sir Evelyn Baring and the DMS, Dr Farnworth Anderson. Lennox-Boyd told the other two that they could wait in the Mess and have tea, for he wanted me to be with him as he toured the camp, to take him round the medical compound and provide answers to a series of difficult questions, which would enable him to face the House of Commons the following week and respond to questions raised about the epidemic. At the end of our tour he thanked me and told me it had been a great relief for him, knowing he would now be able to stand up in the House and answer the Opposition's attacks and criticisms.

The story has a follow-up about fourteen years after that visit, when I was a Reader in The London School of Hygiene and Tropical Medicine and Lord Boyd was then the Chairman of the Board of Governors at The School. The occasion was the opening of an extension to The School by

Her Majesty The Queen Mother, with Lord Boyd escorting her. Staff had been invited to the library to share tea with Her Majesty, and as her entourage entered the library with the very tall Lord Boyd beside her, he was looking around the room and caught my eye and smiled politely. Later, while drinking tea, again our eyes met across the room. Lord Boyd slowly crossed over to Libo and me and remarked, "We have met before haven't we? What is your name?"

"Yes Sir, Barton," I replied.

"Which Colony?" was the next question.

"Kenya Sir."

"Yes, of course, I remember, Manyani Prison Camp! Thank you for what you did to help."

What a man, what a memory! How many officers had he met in the field during his many years as Colonial Secretary. The Colony was all he had to be told!

Dr Killen and I wrote up extensive case notes covering the epidemiology of the outbreak and showing the wide range of its clinical complications, while also showing the dramatic effect of Chloromycetin, the new wonder drug, on the cure and control of the disease. We submitted our report for permission to publish in medical journals, but were refused on the grounds that details of the epidemic had been placed under a tight political embargo, which remained in force up till Kenya Independence. After such time medical reporting on the epidemic would hold little interest to the profession, when so many other research reports on the drug would have been published.

Kakamega and Kisumu 1955-1956

Kakamega District

Perhaps because of my success in controlling the epidemic of typhoid at Manyani Prison Camp, or whatever, at the beginning of January 1955 I was transferred to Kakamega, to be MO in charge of the hospital and MOH of the District of North Nyanza, considered to be the most progressive Medical District in the country.

Rex Fendall had been the MO in charge for a few years and had done a great job in introducing the new policy of the Medical Department, namely establishing health centres throughout the districts. The health centre policy was to decentralise the delivery of medical care, by bringing the 'out-patient services' of the District Hospitals nearer to the people in rural areas. Newly-built buildings, custom designed for the new concept, provided units for the diagnosis and treatment of a wide range of medical cases as well as minor injuries and surgical conditions which could be treated as out-patients. Examination, treatment and injection rooms were part of the clinical unit.

Office accommodation was also provided for a health assistant and, where required, back-up health office staff. They would advise on the health situation of the area as well as undertake necessary surveys to plot out sources of water supplies, conduct health education, and organise necessary vaccination campaigns and the out-patient treatment of TB and Leprosy. Provision for ante-natal and post-natal clinics, with office accommodation for a midwife, was also included in the centre.

Most centres had small wards of up to four beds for overnight stays for patients awaiting transfer to hospital, and a separate ward for maternity cases. Dispensaries and laboratories with trained staff were also provided, while many centres were supported with an ambulance and driver. Ancillary staff and buildings for such services as cleaning, gardening, cooking, etc, as well as staff quarters, completed the health centre.

Hospital assistants were therefore in charge of the centre and responsible for providing out-patient dispensary care in the clinic units. They were supported by male and female dressers, trained midwives and midwifery nurses, pharmacy and laboratory staff, health assistants and auxiliary health staff, drivers and ancillary subordinate staff.

The concept of health centres had been introduced by Dr John Walker, the ADMS, under the direction of Dr Farnworth Anderson, the DMS. They were to be financed mainly by the African District Councils, with basic infrastructure costs provided by Central Government. Wealthy District Councils could move forward rapidly while others had to develop centres more gradually.

While at Kilifi I was able to persuade the Council to provide a centre at Jibana. At Kakamega, a wealthy District, Dr Fendall persuaded the Council to build around thirteen centres, which were fully staffed and provided a wide range of treatment and care along with health prevention and promotion. The Kakamega hospital was large with a staff of three medical officers, three European nursing sisters, a health inspector and supportive dressers, health assistants, clerical and administrative staff, along with a wide range of auxiliary and ancillary staff.

As MO i/c I took responsibility for infectious diseases including the TB ward, supervising OP treatment of leprosy, and the hospital administration. The two other MOs took responsibility for the medical and surgical wards. The three of us took it in turn to be on call after hours for all emergencies, medical, surgical or obstetrical, if necessary calling on the support of a colleague when required. To ensure that we were all aware of the District's health conditions, we were all involved with the regular visits to the health centres to give second opinions on any cases referred to us and

197

by the hospital assistant or midwife, and to provide general support to the staff and their endeavours.

Dr Fendall had set up several systems of reporting, referrals, clinical cards etc. These we were able to implement and analyse, and report on their value for introduction in other Districts.

The two MOs who were with me at Kakamega were Dr Colm O'Colmain and Dr Otysula. The former was a brilliant surgeon though he had never taken his higher surgical qualification. Dr Otysula came from the Province and was an excellent general physician. He had served with me in Kilifi during my stay there.

In 1955 Bungoma was a sub-district of North Nyanza, and so the hospital there was under my supervision. As MO they had Dr Brian McShane, but the three health centres in that area remained under the control of the District Centre. Kakamega was probably the largest, richest and most developed District in Kenya; the hospital was certainly one of the busiest, with its 300 plus beds.

The experience I had as MO i/c certainly provided me with the opportunity to implement my new-found interest in community and preventive medicine.

In Wajir in the NFD I had exposure to treating eye conditions and decided that I wanted to be an eye specialist. It was Dr Farnworth Anderson, the DMS who insisted that I study for the DTM&H before making any final decisions on the speciality I wished to follow.

Kilifi followed and at the end of that tour my interest had changed to one in community medicine, hence my study leave for the DPH. I was quite convinced that I could accomplish more serving the people of Kenya if I specialised in community care and preventive medicine rather than concentrating my efforts to seeing around 2,000 eye cases a year.

In the 1930s Kakamega had been the centre for the gold rush and so the township had expanded with several European businesses established. The sports club, with tennis and squash courts and a golf course, was a legacy of those earlier days. Kakamega and its golf course was like a 'mecca' for all leading Kenya golfers. The Brian Stitt Cup and the Goldfields Trophy were the two major tournaments which attracted the big names. I myself took up golf quite seriously after my introduction to the game during my short spell in Kiambu, at one stage having a handicap of 11. The Goldfields was a handicap tournament and I well remember my collapse in chasing the best handicap medal. I was leading by three strokes with two holes to play, but two drives out-of-bounds on the 17th tee was the end of my effort. Sheer nerves!

Dr Tom Mathews from Kisii was the winner of both cups while I was in Kakamega and he later went on to win the Kenya Open Golf Championship and title at Kitale the same year. What a party that was with a smoker sing-song led by Neil Loudon of the Administration, and myself. I don't suppose I will ever live down my attempt to encourage The Duke of Portland, or was it Manchester, not knowing who he was, to join in with actions, singing the round *Down in the Station Early in the Morning*!

Incidentally, Neil Loudon was a District Commissioner and a great golfer. When he left Kenya at their Independence he became Secretary of the famous St Andrews Golf Club.

A feature of Kakamega always to be remembered was the weather. Almost every afternoon it started to pour with rain when one was on the golf course, so the decision had to be made whether to start and, having started, whether to continue and get soaked through. It was when the lightning flashed that discretion was the better part of valour, for it certainly flashed!

After the experience at Manyani Camp I was offered this great opportunity to put into practice the organisation of community health services. I learnt so much during my time in Kakamega. It was only ten months, because in mid-September I was temporarily posted to Medical HQ in Nairobi as Acting ADMS because the substantive ADMS was due leave. Dr Fendall had left Kakamega to become Provincial Medical Officer of the Rift Valley in Nakuru. Similarly the PMO at Kisumu, Dr Jack Taylor, had only been posted to Nyanza Province a few months earlier and should not be moved so soon. It was decided that my temporary posting for three months to HQ would cause the least disturbance.

I will always remember my three months in Medical HQ in Nairobi for three major events. The first of these was the birth of Ian. Libo was nearing full term and when on 7th October she started her pains, we went to the Princess Elizabeth Maternity Hospital, where Dr Van Someron was the Obstetrician i/c the confinement. After only an hour back home I got a call to say I had a son! Whoopee!

Libo's brother Humphrey was with me when I got the news. He had just arrived for a spell of leave from his life living rough in the Aberdare forests, following the Mau Mau gangs and discovering their hideouts. As part of the operation, he had not been allowed to wash or clean his teeth so was pretty grubby and smelly. We opened the whisky and, having been told to wait half an hour before coming round to the hospital, we started to celebrate. This was, of course, before the days of no drinking and driving!

When I got to the labour area I was told I could not see Libo as she had suffered a post-partum haemorrhage, having had a precipitated delivery. In time Dr Ken Van Someren, who delivered Ian, came out and said I could see Libo but could not stay long because she needed a transfusion. I truly got a fright for Libo was so drained and weak. It was all very worrying, but thankfully finished well.

When I finally got back home Humphrey and I finished the bottle of whisky!

Libo and I had always wanted to have four children, but after the trouble Libo had had delivering both Lesley and Ian I decided I would rather have two children and their mother, than four children with no mother! We were lucky to have had a girl and a boy.

The Family - 1956

The second event was being invited out to lunch at the DMS's home. Just as we were about to set off the ayah came out in great distress with fear in her face. She called us in to see our daughter Lesley, who was now 19 months old. There was Lesley sitting on her potty passing a squirming round worm! Consternation, but in reality nothing too serious and easily treated!

201

Ian and Libo with a first day cover
Salisbury, Southern Rhodesia
[This picture was featured in the press]

The third event of consequence for me was a lesson in decision-making and, I suppose, pragmatism. An epidemic of poliomyelitis had broken out in Nairobi affecting several boys in the Prince of Wales Boys' School. Several were paralysed, requiring treatment in an iron lung, which was the life saving treatment at that time. Thankfully, Nairobi suffered few electricity power failures, although one occurred during this epidemic which had the effect of turning off the iron lungs. Fortunately these lungs had all been fitted with alternative switch-over generators for use in the event of such power failures. This necessitated manual intervention to start them operating. All staff had been trained and instructed in such action, and so when the power cuts occurred, staff acted quickly, with the result that there was no real interruption in the functioning of the lungs and no life was lost. The Chief of Infectious Diseases, Dr Harries, and the Senior Anaesthetist, Dr Laws, were however naturally concerned lest there be such a loss, and approached the then Acting DMS, Dr John Walker, requesting that an automatic switch-over to the generator be fitted to replace the manual one presently operating.

Dr Walker asked me as the Acting ADMS (Health) to investigate the alternative choices available in Nairobi and their costings. The cheapest was something in the region of £1,500, which in 1955 was quite a sum. A meeting was called with the two specialists to review the situation and come to a decision. Despite a further power failure, the transfer to the manual generators had again occurred and no death had resulted.

Dr Walker's final response was to the effect that the decision finally rested with him and that was that. With £1,500 he would be able to treat and cure several hundred TB cases with domiciliary therapy as against saving one life, in the unlikely event that the manual transfer to the generator failed to maintain the functioning of the iron lung. In his view the balance in expenditure was unequal and so he refused the request of the specialists. For a time there was considerable ill-feeling between the specialists in the department and those 'administrators' in HQ. This gradually faded when the schoolboys were finally all discharged, albeit one or two with residual paralysis. This dilemma regarding finite resources left a lasting impression with me, one which I had to follow later in my career.

While at HQ I first made personal contact with the programmes of the World Health Organisation (WHO) and UNICEF. While UNICEF had been established immediately after the end of the Second World War, WHO was not established until 7th April 1948. Being in the NFD I had heard of both UN Agencies but had had no direct contact. In HQ we had various visits from their regional officers. Dr Charles Egger was the Regional Representative for UNICEF based in Paris, and he was trying to establish the needs of Kenya. I later met him in Kakamega after my return there and we negotiated supplies for our various health centres, which included Land Rovers, along with a wide range of equipment. UNICEF's supply officer, Perry Hanson, was based in Uganda.

While in HQ I was encouraged to consider an application for a study fellowship for a post-graduate degree. In due course I did apply and was selected for one of the fellowships allocated to Kenya for study in the USA.

After my three months sojourn in Nairobi I was moved back to Kakamega, but only for a short spell, during which time we entertained Dr Egger and I escorted him round the District, before being transferred to Kisumu as Acting Provincial Medical Officer (PMO) and MO i/c of the Provincial Hospital.

* * * * *

PMO - Kisumu

Our stay in Kisumu was a very happy time with several interesting events. Sir Eric Pridie, the Chief Medical Officer at the Colonial Office, stayed with us and I had the privilege of taking him round the Province. He was a true gentleman and certainly very knowledgeable about Kenya and its medical problems. During his stay in the Colonial Office he had had the chance to visit all the Colonies as well as many other countries round the world. He was a bachelor with no difficulties regarding constant travel.

Another highlight was the day visit of Princess Margaret accompanied by the Governor, Sir Evelyn, and Lady Baring. We were not involved with any of the Princess' official functions, but Sir Evelyn and Lady Baring visited the Provincial Hospital, so I had the honour of escorting them.

After my experience at Manyani Prison Camp I suppose I was the obvious choice to carry out an exercise involving 'black' Mau Mau detainees, who had been transferred from Manyani to an island in Lake Victoria. This was two years after my sojourn at Manyani and great strides had been made in rehabilitating most of the original detainees. They had been categorised into black, grey and white groups, according to their willingness and desire to be 'cleansed' from their earlier oath taking. There was a small but very recalcitrant group of detainees who were refusing to confess to anything and had been transferred out of Manyani and put on the isolated island from which there would be little, if any, chance of escape. The detainees had decided to go on a hunger strike, but accepted fluids. They had been on strike for many days before the Commissioner of Prisons, Taxi Lewis, had decided he should personally visit the island to assess whether to take any specific action to break the strike. He needed a medical opinion and that is where I came into the act. I had the message from Medical HQ, and in due course joined the Commissioner on a flight to visit the camp. I was taken into the hut where the strikers were housed. They were lying listless on the floor, obviously having lost weight but with no signs of dehydration, having been taking fluids.

I entered the hut and slowly walked its length, stopping to examine each detainee to assess his condition. When I reached the end of the hut I turned back to face my only point of escape, the door where the Commissioner and his minions were standing. I realised I had to walk the gauntlet through the lines of detainees to join my colleagues. My heart missed a beat, for I realised that if any of the detainees wished to attack or cause a riot I would be cut off. I held my head high, looked straight ahead, and ignoring the searing eyes obviously fixed on me, made it to the door.

"What do you think?" asked the Commissioner in a loud voice.

I took another deep breath and said, in a voice loud enough for those detainees who understood English to hear, "I think they are fine and could safely continue their hunger strike for another two weeks a least!"

I quickly turned round and walked out. There has never been bravery in my heart, except possibly when faced with a crisis at the operating table! I heard later that the detainees decided after our visit to break their fast! That episode was my last interface with the Mau Mau and detainees.

A particularly enjoyable aspect of my time in Kisumu was being able to renew my love of the stage for the first time since university days. I appeared in the Kisumu Amateur Dramatic Society production of Ben Travis' play *Rookery Nook*, and later in the play *Escapade*.

As PMO I officiated on occasions at the weddings of several nursing sisters, giving the bride away in the case of Ruth Botham who had been at Kilifi; proposing toasts for the bride/groom etc.

I always enjoyed my official visits to the District Hospitals, Kisii, Kericho, Bungoma and, of course, Kakamega, attending PMO meetings in HQ, and running our MO meetings in Kisumu. They were all experiences which served me well in my future career.

We had only ten months in Kisumu, for in October I received an offer from the Colonial Office in London to be Assistant Director of Medical Services in Zanzibar (ADMS).

I contacted our DMS, Dr Farnworth Anderson, to have his reaction. He told me he did not want me to move for he felt I would have a better career in Kenya. I asked if there was any immediate possibility of being established as PMO Nyanza. Dr Anderson's response was that there were several MOs senior to me on the establishment and he would find it difficult to promote me above them. I made the point that since our return from leave in 1954 we had lived in five different homes and I had noticed that my daughter was becoming withdrawn, finding it difficult to make friends, for no sooner had she made them than she lost them on our transfers. The DMS also made the point that if I moved from Kenya I would lose my fellowship for study leave from the Kenya allocation. Arm twisting!

At the time when I was considering the offer, Miss Rena Angus, the Acting Matron i/c Kenya, was paying an official visit to the Nyanza Province and I was greatly influenced by her advice and decided to accept the Colonial Office offer. After a short period I paid a visit to Zanzibar to meet the DMS, David Baird, to discuss the job, terms of service and of course to give him the opportunity of interviewing me to accept the Colonial Office selection.

All went well and in November we started our move to Zanzibar, stopping off in Mombasa to see my parents, before travelling to Zanzibar in the *Seyyid Khalifa*, one of the official ships of His Highness's Government.

While we were in Mombasa we noticed that our beloved dog, Punch, had developed a growth in his nose. It was diagnosed as a cancer and we had to allow him to be put down before we left. Punch had been born in Wajir, one of twins born to Judy, the bitch of Hector Douglas, the Development Officer. She was a cross between a French bulldog and a bull terrier and had been crossed by another bull terrier. Unfortunately Judy died giving birth and it was left to me to feed the pups till they could be weaned from a pure milk diet. Dougie naturally wanted to keep the little bitch and he named her Judy. I could not part with Punch and so he was our pet from 1948 till 1956, loved by all the family.

Governor's Visits

Of course, the story of my time in Kenya would not be complete without reference to several Governors' visits which took place.

Maybe times have changed, but certainly on joining the Colonial Service I never received any instruction or training on the protocol pertaining to the visit of HE The Governor to the boma. I gathered that if the visit was a formal one then HE would arrive generally with his wife, but always with a full retinue, ADC and servants. The latter would take over the household, serve the drinks and all meals; the DC's staff would be the support group. The visit would be supplied with the necessary drinks! If the visit was to be informal then Government House staff would not arrive and the DC's staff would do the honours. The drinks however would still be supplied!

Formal or informal, as the representative of the Queen, HE always took precedence over all others. He would therefore sit at the head of the dining table taking the DC's or the host's place. The DC would sit at the other end normally taken by his wife. While this might seem of little significance, during informal visits it could lead to confusion even embarrassment.

My first encounter with a Governor was with HE Sir Philip Mitchell when he visited Wajir in August 1949 to attend the celebration of Id-ul-Fitr at the end of the Holy Fast of Ramadhan. This was attended by his ADC, an Army detachment, the PC Dick Turnbull and the Police Superintendent of the frontier FC Brookes (Brookie).

All went well till the reception in the house of the DC, Gordon Hector. HE had known my parents while he was The Governor of Uganda and my father was Skipper of *S W Lugard*. HE called me over to sit with him to bring him up-to-date about my parents. During our talk, HE summoned his ADC requesting a gin. As stated, all drinks had been provided from Government House and this included HE's favourite *Plymouth London Gin*. The DC's servants had taken in the supplies and placed them on the drinks table that had been set up. Unfortunately they had not removed the decanters containing the DC's whisky and gin!

The ADC, no doubt rightly, supposed the decanter contained *Plymouth Gin* as it stood beside the *Plymouth London Gin* bottles. Wrong! The decanter contained Italian Somaliland *Chofi* gin, which we obtained from across the border in exchange for Kenya butter: one pound of butter for a bottle of *Chofi*. The ADC returned with the gin and handed it to HE. After taking the glass, HE swept it under his nose and after inhaling the fumes exclaimed, to the great astonishment of all, and to the total embarrassment of the DC "David, I asked for a gin, not boot polish!" There was a moment's silence before HE broke the ice with animated chat. What a nose! What a connoisseur!

I went on home-study leave after that episode and on my return was posted to Kilifi under the DC, John Stringer, and his lovely wife Elizabeth (Wish). Before long a visit from the acting Governor, John Rankine, was announced. He was the Chief Secretary and later became the British Resident in Zanzibar, after Sir Vincent Glenday and before Sir Henry Potter. It was a formal visit with Government House servants in attendance. Without fuss, they went round the dinner table, filling up glasses as they emptied and as the courses changed. I was really quite unfamiliar with such protocol and unaccustomed to wines, but still held my own, till after the dessert and cheese was served and removed. At last I thought I can now have a cigarette! I proudly produced my silver cigarette case and was on the point of offering them around when I received a sharp kick under the table from Wish, who gave me a sweet smile and a negative shake of the head. It had been a near thing, but worse was to come. The servants had removed all the glasses and produced sherry glasses. How odd, I thought. When they were filled up I immediately took a sip, and another, and yet another! HE suddenly rose to propose the Loyal Toast to Her Majesty. I had drunk all my sherry and had an empty glass from which to toast The Queen. Only Wish had noticed my faux pas! I had learned two lessons which lasted for always.

Our next Governor's visit in Kilifi was HE Sir Evelyn Baring, the new Governor. It was an informal visit in that no GH staff were in attendance. Dennis and Barbara Hall were our DC and wife. Barbara had been advised that HE was allergic to shell fish. Oh dear, she had prepared a starter of lobster vol-au-vent. No matter, she would prepare a fresh fish vol-au-vent and place it on the top of the serving for HE to take first. As usual he was sitting in the master's chair, but Anne had carefully primed her staff that this night they would not serve the senior lady first, but HE, and thereafter the ladies before the rest of the men.

I was near enough to Anne to hear her say to HE, "I understand that you are allergic to shell fish, so I have prepared a fresh fish serving for yourself and it will be on the top of the dish when it is brought in." All was well till, seated at table, the servant entered with the bowl of lobster vol-au-vent with, unknown to the rest of us, the fresh one sitting on top. The servant panicked and started with the senior lady. By the time he reached HE the fresh fish had obviously gone and there was HE tossing up the helpings, digging in and looking for the fresh serving. No luck!

Anne turned and looked down the table and said, pathetically, "I'm sorry, but HE is allergic to shell fish. I had prepared a fresh fish helping for him. Has anyone by mistake taken the fresh fish helping?"
"Yes! I have" said the senior lady!"
"Well, I am sorry, but HE is allergic to shell fish!"
Pause!
"So am I" replied the lady!

The plate moved back and forth till HE took it and said in a tone to relax the situation, "I'll take it to relieve the embarrassment. You know, in

210

Government House we never have a dinner party without a crisis such as we've seen tonight. I think it really helps to make a party go!"

When we moved to Kisumu there was a visit by HRH The Princess Margaret. It did not affect us directly, but a story related to it is worth recalling. The PC was 'Ngombe' Williams. Before the visit the PWD met the PC's wife, Joy, to discuss the redecoration of their house for the visit, in particular the loo which was to be made available for The Princess. What colour would Joy desire?

"Buff" was the reply.

"Buff?" in a questioning tone.

"Yes! Buff. We've been in service for the last twenty years and we've always been decorated with buff by the PWD for all our homes. Buff it has been for us and buff it will be for The Princess!"

And so it was. The irony we understand is that The Princess did not have occasion to use the facility!

Zanzibar was a service station with full protocol, having not only The Queen's representative by way of The British Resident and his Lady, but also the Ruler HH The Sultan Seyyid Sir Khalifa bin Harub bin Thweni. You can imagine just what could go wrong for the uninitiated, whether an acting DMS, a visit of The Indian Navy, or even The Royal Navy itself with its Royal Naval Band.

We learned through experience, that at any Residency function, for example, drinks or dinner party, the Senior Officer and his wife had to leave first before any others could take their leave of HE and his Lady. We had been invited to a drinks party at the Residency and on such occasions my policy was to drink as much as needed to be sociable and to circulate and be entertaining! So it was this evening, till the Private Secretary approached me and said, "Have you thought of retiring? As Senior Officer present I think you should, for no-one can leave before you do!" Wow... What a pity, but we had to leave!

The Colonial Service

Zanzibar 1956 - 1964

Zanzibar

We sailed to Zanzibar on the *Seyyid Khalifa*, one of HH's Government ships, in November 1956. I finally left after the Revolution in April 1964, though as a family we left on 23rd December 1963 and were on leave when the revolution took place. For all of us they were seven very happy years. They turned out to be the climax of eighteen wonderful years of service in Her Majesty's Overseas Service, and without doubt proved to be the most fulfilling of my medical career. Zanzibar offered so much and gave us a depth of experience in so many spheres of life. It is difficult to accurately and adequately review the years in Zanzibar for so much happened in so many aspects.

* * * * *

The Work Experience

As ADMS I realised that my clinical days were over. No longer would I have the 'hands on' involvement with patients. My duties were to be in the field of administration, organisation and management. While I had learned a great deal about administration as PMO Nyanza, it was all self-taught.

In Zanzibar I had a great teacher in Dr David Baird, my DMS. We shared some basic values as we were both Scots, but it was his leadership, as demonstrated by his example, and his gift of being able to communicate at all levels which made him stand above the rest. He held high personal and professional standards and had an expectation of the same from his staff, especially from those in his close team. He had a gift for clear thinking and persistence in pursuing the policies he outlined for the Department. He was small in stature but tall in his standing, respected by His Highness

215

The Sultan, The British Resident and by all the senior echelons of Government. His wife, Isobel, was paralysed from the waist, and so confined to a wheelchair. David was so patient, attentive and caring to her, which allowed both of them to fulfil their social roles as head of a major department of Government. They were both very musical, while David enjoyed a personal hobby of ornithology, sharing authorship of a book on the birds of Zanzibar.

When I arrived in Zanzibar, the Medical Department HQ was housed in a small office block separate from the Department's health office building. Plans had been completed for the construction of a new two-storeyed HQ block to be attached to the health office building, completing the fourth side of a square of offices. In the new building the central pharmacy and stores unit were on the ground level, while upstairs were the new offices for the DMS and secretary, the ADMS, the main office for personnel, and general administration and filing. The accounts office and the office of the MOH Zanzibar township remained, as before, upstairs in the old health office block, with the health inspectors and ancillary staff in offices downstairs. David had qualified in Engineering before studying Medicine, so had had quite an input into the design of the new HQ, specifying certain standards for the fittings etc. Fortunately, it was completed in time to allow him to function from it for over two years before, in 1959, he was transferred to be DMS Sarawak.

David had also planned, before my arrival, for WHO and UNICEF to assist Zanzibar in the training of staff in parasitology and entomology, and to organise a Malaria Eradication Programme (MEP) for the Protectorate. At the same time, in another project, WHO was to provide a tutor to develop a programme for the Training of Rural Health Workers (RHWs) and in due course some as health inspectors, with UNICEF providing the necessary tools and equipment for the programme.

I was appointed the Government Liaison Officer to both programmes, to help draw up the final details and to supervise their adminstration and conduct. Such work brought me into close personal contact with WHO staff from their Regional Office in Brazzaville as well as from their HQ in Geneva.

The MEP entailed the organisation of the operation, which before its introduction required the training of staff, research with regard to the entomological and parasitological environment, testing of the various pesticides and their sensitivities to the vectors, and later the phenomenon of parasite and vector resistance. The WHO staff posted to Zanzibar in 1957 included Project Leader Dr W Stoker, a Dutchman. He had been on the Dutch Delegation to the New York meeting when WHO was established in 1948. The entomologist was Dr Iyengar from India, the son of a renowned entomologist. Gerry Shute, the parasitologist, came from the UK. He was the son of a renowned parasitologist from the London School of Hygiene and Tropical Medicine who had worked with the famous Professor of Parasitology PCC Garnham on his research work into the discovery of the exo-erythrocytic cycle of the human malaria parasite. Mr Cecil Showman, an Australian, was the sanitarian in charge of the pesticide spraying programme of eradication.

The Government had to provide housing and office accommodation for the WHO staff, as well as the provision of local staff which included the trainees, pesticide spraying teams, drivers, clerks and other auxiliary staff as required. In addition, the Department was responsible for petrol, offices, supplies, stationery, postal charges and various other items, for example, local travel costs. While WHO provided staff, UNICEF provided all transport vehicles, laboratory equipment and supplies, drugs, pesticides and many other items needed for the smooth running of the programme. All this required good adminstration and organisation, with myself as the Government Liaison Officer.

For the other WHO/UNICEF supported programme, namely the 'Training of Rural Health Workers' the WHO educator/trainer was sanitarian George Jinks from the UK He had been in the Organisation for several years and had considerable experience. This programme was designed to train staff working in rural dispensaries in the simple diagnosis and treatment of out-patient conditions. They were to replace the hospital trained nurses who would return to their original functions for which they had been trained. In addition the RHWs would carry out community surveys to locate villages, the location of their water supplies and schools. In this way accurate geographical surveys could be completed to identify the location of the population which was broken down into families and individuals. This would later facilitate the work of the MEP pesticide spraying teams, as well as helping to plot the distribution of disease patterns.

After the first phase of the RHW training programme a few students would be selected for further training to allow them to enter the examination for the East African Health Inspectors' Certificate. UNICEF's contribution to this programme was, again, transport, all formal training equipment and supplies. They also provided the necessary materials for field training, for example, bore-hole equipment for pit latrines and water supplies etc.

Both training programmes were successfully completed so allowing for the MEP to be implemented. In due course, as the WHO staff left the Protectorate, local staff took over the entomological and parasitological responsibilities. When the RHW's programme provided health inspectors, these took over the supervision of the field spraying teams. The final tragedy was that the revolution in 1964 brought an end to the MEP programme and many of the RHWs were removed from their centres of operation.

An innovation that we introduced when we built the new extension to Medical HQ was the installation of an office intercom-system, with all senior officers being able to call each other instead of having to visit them in their offices. The DMS had a set in his office which allowed him to conduct a conference with two or more offices at one time.

Later, when I was DMS, I had the occasion to call up our accountant Mr Aladina. He was just finishing a conversation with his assistant Mr Joe De Sousa. He closed his conversation saying, "Well Joe, let me have the figures this afternoon for the DMS is chasing me for them. OK?"

Joe rang off and just before Aladina did so, I interrupted him saying, "Mr Aladina could you possibly come along to my office, I'd like to discuss the budget submission."
There was a pause and Aladina replied, "Say that again Joe. It is beautiful, you must have been practising for you have his voice perfectly."
"Whose voice?" I interjected.
"Joe! His voice... the DMS. It is perfect Joe. Say it again, I love to hear it - it is beautiful."
I felt I should put him out of his agony, so I replied, "This is the DMS speaking Aladina."
Another pause, as if working it out, then, "Oh my God! Sorry Sir!"
"Mention not!" I responded, for this was the expression that my Asian staff always used in such situations!

In 1957 when the DMS was on overseas leave I attended the WHO African Regional Committee Meeting in Brazzaville as one of the UK Delegation. The African Region at that time comprised UK, France, Belgium, Holland, Portugal, Spain, South Africa and Liberia, with Nigeria and Ghana as Associate Members, for while they had their own internal self government they had not achieved full status as independent states. It was my first experience at international meetings and an introduction to political intrigue. As the years passed and the 'wind of change' in Africa took force, fewer of the delegates to the Regional Office Meetings were from a medical professional background, with more and more from the field of politics. So one saw the beginning of political positioning in

219

health matters. This trend quickly followed in the delegations attending the WHO Annual Assemblies in Geneva.

I had the privilege of attending several AFRO Annual Meetings in Brazzaville, Nairobi and other centres as one of the UK Delegation. In 1963 I was appointed Chief of the UK Delegation to the Annual AFRO Meeting, which had been planned for Brazzaville. By this time the independent African states outnumbered the former European colonial powers, and so they advised the Regional Director that they would refuse to attend any meeting to be held in Africa if South Africa were to be present, in view of the latter's apartheid policy. If the African countries were not present there could be no quorum for a meeting!

The Director General of WHO, Dr Candau, attempted a compromise and suggested the meeting be held in Geneva at the Palais de Nations, the United Nations HQ. I attended a briefing at the Foreign Office in London and then in the UK. I was advised of the delicacy of the situation and told that the head of the Mission in Geneva would attend the opening session with me, in case any political situations arose.

My big moment as chief of the UK Delegation had arrived. Dr Candau opened the proceedings and various African delegates made their opening statements, all with a political twist. All seemed to be well. The delegate from South Africa requested the floor, at which point all the African delegations collected their papers, placed them in their brief cases and walked out of the hall, leaving the delegations from the UK, France, Belgium, Holland, Portugal, South Africa, Spain and Liberia still sitting. As there was no quorum the Director General closed the meeting sine die. My moment of glory had passed without me opening my mouth. Never let it be said that Barton was without words... but he was!

To many, the words 'administration', 'organisation' and 'management' are synonymous, but to me they identified my various responsibilities.

'Administration' involved me in personnel, fiscal and office affairs. These divisions meant dealing with selections, promotions, training and development of staff; providing the draft budgets for expenditure and accounting of such, as well as presenting such budgets in due course to the Legislature Council; providing systems for tidy and meaningful filing of correspondence, minutes of meetings etc, all with adequate communication to ensure that staff were well informed about decisions taken affecting the working of the Department.

'Organisation' is concerned with providing the staff, stores and supplies, and space, that is, all accommodation, necessary to run the various activities of the Department.

While 'Administration' and 'Organisation' form the infrastructure for implementing the policy decisions of the Government and the Department, 'Management' is the process by which the Department's goals are set and met, and involves the infrastructure outlined above, all directed by the policies and leadership given. Management is therefore involved with 'getting things done through people', in other words, managing the use of motivation of staff, the clear delegation of tasks to staff, and proper time management. It follows that managerial responsibilities are directed at the clear identification of the tasks to be accomplished and the development of the individual members of the team to ensure that the teams operate effectively and efficiently.

In all this I realised that the final responsibility of an ADMS must surely be to provide the DMS with all the support needed to allow for proper leadership.

Dr Baird had a clarity of what was needed to improve the operation of the Medical Department, and of the administrative process and management required to ensure implementation of the decisions taken. So I profited from him and his experience, and I reckon that I owe a great deal to him for all I learned while I was his ADMS.

221

Zanzibar Hospital

The Hassanali Karimjee Jivanjee family provided the funds for the Zanzibar Hospital which was handed over to HH Government in 1955 and provided a very high grade of medical service to the Protectorate.

The Hospital was staffed with a full compliment of medical and nursing staff, with specialists in various fields: Medical, Dr Wilf Kenyon; Surgical, Mr Donnah Hurley; with the Dental Specialist being Mr Arthur Pollard. There were also Zanzibaris in specialist posts: Dr Kingwaba, TB Specialist; Dr Mafudh, Radiologist and Dr Farsi, Ophthalmologist. The Medical Superintendent was Dr Teddy Derola who had numerous medical officers on his staff, some recruited from the UK, but most were locals who had qualified at Makerere University in Uganda, several taking post-graduate studies in the UK including Dr Awadh and Dr Jabir who took their DPH qualification in Public Health.

The Hassanali Karimjee Jivanjee Hospital

It was the policy of the Department to select local staff - doctors, nurses, laboratory assistants and others - for post-graduate studies and to equip them in due course to take over senior positions, thus replacing overseas staff. During my period in Zanzibar several were sent to train as surgeons and medical specialists including psychiatry, mental nursing, laboratory technology, pharmacy and other fields.

The Matron of the hospital, Miss Pam Kinnear, was from the UK. She was supported by senior nursing staff including sister tutors for the Nurses' Training School. While many nursing sisters had quite extensive experience in other Colonies, and included Miss Sheila Murphy, Margaret Fitzgerald and Dorothy Cooper, several were on first appointments though all fully qualified in general nursing as well as midwifery. There were several local nursing sisters on the establishment who had trained overseas or had supplemented their initial local nursing training at the hospital with overseas advanced training.

The pharmacy services were under the charge of a qualified pharmacist from the UK who was replaced by a local pharmacist, Barakat Barwani, after his return from training in the UK.

Dr Baird planned the extension to the hospital which comprised a new out-patient department on the ground level with a modern fully-equipped laboratory on the upper floor. He was closely involved with the plans of the building and saw its completion in 1959. To ensure the proper running of the new laboratory the Department recruited a pathologist, Dr Barnes from the UK, who established a comprehensive laboratory service including a blood-transfusion unit. It was a lasting credit to the name of Dr Baird.

In due course Dr Baird was replaced by Dr Mackichan as DMS. He had been ADMS in Tanganyika, prior to his promotion.

The Health Services in the township were under the control of Health Inspector Mr Drummond from the UK, who had a team of several Indian and Goan Health Inspectors recruited for the service from India - Messrs Rhemtula, Aguiar, Ashadali and J and C Periera to name a few. In addition there were several local staff who had been trained on-the-job over the years and who had achieved positions as Health Inspectors on merit. This Health Department team was responsible for the cleanliness of the town which was undertaken by a squad of street sweepers and cleaners who operated twice daily in collecting rubbish from the markets, port and streets. The rubbish was dumped, under control, into the tidal creek which ran through the back of the town. Gradually over many years the creek was filled in and at first the area was turned into playing fields, while later, after settlement, the street along the creek was widened and in time allowed for shop building development.

Mosquito breeding control was also undertaken by the health staff until the MEP was put into operation, while the fly breeding nuisance demanded constant monitoring.

The DMS Zanzibar was a member of the East African Research Council, which met and decided on the areas of research to be undertaken in the four territories of East Africa. Funding for the research projects was shared by contributions from the four governments and the Medical Research Council (MRC) of the UK. Accordingly, along with their secretary, the MRC sent three senior scientists representing the various fields of interest for the research to meet with the four DMSs annually. They considered the research proposals submitted by the various Research Centres in East Africa, selected those for approval and then allocated the funding for the separate projects. The main Research Centres in East Africa were The Yellow Fever Centre in Entebbe, Trypanosomiasis Centre in Tororo, Malaria Centre in Amani and the Leprosy Centre in Uganda. Scientists, included Professors George MacDonald and Alan Woodruff from the London School of Hygiene & Tropical Medicine, as well as several other clinical specialists. It was a great experience to be involved with detailed discussions and decision making on the various research proposals submitted.

Zanzibar was also privileged from time to time with visits from senior medical personnel from the UK who were visiting other territories in East Africa. Professor Wilfred Sheldon, the Queen's Paediatrician, Lord and Lady Limerick from the British Red Cross, Professor Edward R Cullinan, Professor Frank Crockett and Dr Dill-Russell from the Colonial Office, to name a few.

In preparation for the training of the RHWs and their later postings to the Health Centres, I was given responsibility for drafting a manual for The Diagnosis and Treatment of Simple Conditions in Health Units. The manual had two parts: those conditions which could be treated at the Units and those conditions which could be diagnosed at the Units but were to be referred to the hospital for treatment. In this way the RHWs were given certain authority in the eyes of the public for they could not only safely diagnose and treat certain conditions on the spot, but they could also provide the patient with a diagnosis of their condition requiring transfer to hospital for treatment. Such manuals had already been developed by Dr Baird when he was in Nyasaland, which was the model I could follow. They were later taken up and developed in several other Colonies.

As ADMS I was chairman of numerous committees in the Department which gave me considerable experience in handling meetings, and the skill of developing group consensus in arriving at recommendations which often had to be referred to the DMS for his final decision regarding action. I learnt the art of being a number two, with the responsibility of providing the DMS with argued alternatives from which he could make a considered decision. It was then my responsibility to implement that decision. All this helped me greatly when I became DMS myself and was faced with making such decisions. I learned that as number two one got the blame from junior staff for obstructing proposals they may have submitted, although the DMS might have made the decision based on argued alternatives. As DMS one, of course, could over-rule recommendations made by the ADMS or other senior staff! The distinction between these roles was always an element of leadership.

Dr Mackichan was at the end of his Colonial career and for him the task was one of maintaining the status quo and keeping the peace. This did allow the rest of us to drive ahead with specific projects and programmes without too much interference as long as we did not rock the boat. Dr Mackichan finally retired at the end of 1962 when I was promoted to DMS.

* * * * *

Royal and Official Occasions

The Ruler of Zanzibar in 1956 was His Highness The Sultan Seyyid Sir Khalifa bin Harub bin Thweni. The Thweni Dynasty originated from the Royal Family of Muscat and Oman. In 1804 Seyyid Said bin Sultan was the Ruler of Zanzibar and Oman and made frequent visits to Zanzibar. In 1832 he established his capital there and later, in 1861, he advised his brother that he would remain in Zanzibar permanently and that he would establish a new dynasty as Sultan of Zanzibar, with his brother the Sultan of Muscat.

Seyyid Sir Khalifa bin Harub acceded on 9th December 1911 while he was in London and attended the Coronation there of His Majesty King George V and Queen Mary. He also attended the Coronation of our present Queen Elizabeth II in 1953. Seyyid Sir Khalifa bin Harub died aged 80, on 17th October 1960, only one year short of his Golden Jubilee, and was succeeded by his son Seyyid Sir Abdulla bin Khalifa bin Harub.

226

His Highness The Sultan Seyyid Sir Khalifa bin Harub bin Thweni

227

Each year on the Sultan's birthday there was a parade on the Mnazi Moja Ground, with the Sultan taking the salute at a 'March Past' of a contingent of the East African Navy and the Zanzibar Police Force. In 1957 and 1958 Zanzibar celebrated The Sultan's 79th and 80th birthdays. We were privileged to be present at these special birthday parades. For the latter I was acting DMS and therefore we were seated in the VIP tent or 'shamiana' behind the saluting base. A truly Royal occasion with pageantry.

A similar parade took place each year on Mnazi Moja with HE The British Resident taking the Salute to celebrate the Queen's official birthday.

Libo and I had the great personal privilege to be invited to a luncheon at the Sultan's Summer Palace at Kibweni on 15th October 1959 at a farewell luncheon for the departing British Resident Sir Henry and Lady Ruth Potter. We also enjoyed several invitations by HE to formal dinners at The Residency; these latter occasions were for the official visits of warships from the UK, India and Pakistan, as well as VIPs, for example, WHO or other UN officials, CPA members from Parliament, medical specialists and others. On special occasions HH The Sultan and The Sultana would be present.

The fleet of Royal cars were all crimson red, the colour of the Zanzibar flag. No-one else was allowed to have a red car, and so the Royal cars were very conspicuous. Every afternoon The Sultan with The Sultana sitting beside him, would set out from the Palace and drive slowly into the countryside, everyday in a different direction. The car was always driven at about fifteen miles an hour. It was accepted, in acknowledgment to HH, that no-one ever overtake his car, and if the car was seen approaching, to drive off the road and stop. If there was time, you could get out of your car and stand beside it and bow or wave to HH. Our first house in Zanzibar was on the harbour front, just along from the Palace, so we often saw the Royal car departing from or returning to the Palace for the daily drive. The children loved to wave as HH and the Sultana always returned the waves.

Our first home - on the left with the black balustrade
- next to the Sultan's Palace and Beit el-Ajaib

The beach in front of our third home

Ian playing with Honey on Mangapwani Beach

In 1960 Dr Derryberry stayed with us. He was from Chattanooga in the USA and had a very deep Southern accent. We set off for an afternoon drive and warned him that we might see the Sultan. If we saw the car approaching us we would stop, thus allowing Derry to get out with his camera. He would then have the chance to see HH while at the same time he could snap them as they passed. The kids often got out to wave to the Royals, so they probably would not see our guest taking a picture. Sure enough, we saw the car a long way off approaching us. Derry got out and as planned snapped the camera discretely while bowing. He was thrilled to have seen the Royals. It was only when we got home that the whole experience struck him. He remarked, "I did enjoy that, but how am I going to tell the folk back home that I actually got out of the car and bowed to a coloured boy!" In 1960 there was still strict racial discrimination in the Southern States of the USA, which we experienced during our visit there in 1958.

Another amusing story relating to the visit of Dr Derryberry concerned our daughter, Lesley, who was six at the time. As Derry's accent was so broad, often Lesley could not understand what he was saying and had to ask, "Pardon?" Derry had to repeat what he had said and Lesley generally repeated the statement in an English accent. As he was about to leave for the airport she remarked, "I am sorry you are leaving us just as you were beginning to speak English properly." Wow!

The Sultan occasionally made official visits to Pemba, which were very formal occasions demanding the presence of members of the Legislative Council at the wharf on His departure and return on His Ship *The Seyyid Khalifa*. His last overseas visit was to the UK in 1960, a few months before his 80th birthday and later in that year, his death in October.

* * * * *

Legislative Council

The Sultan opened the Legislative Council every year, copying the pageantry of the Queen's Opening of Parliament. His Excellency The British Resident was the Chairman of the Meetings of the Council, a position similar to the Speaker in Parliament. The Sultan would arrive at the Gardens of the Victoria Hall, be met by HE, and with him inspect a Police Guard of Honour before entering the Victoria Hall to open the Council.

In 1957 the meeting of Legislative Council followed the first election of six unofficial members who sat, along with another six nominated members, opposite the fourteen official government members. In the Council were the three leaders of the new political parties: Abeid Karume, Ali Muhsin and Mohammed Shamte.

The Opening of the Legislative Council

In 1957 Dr Baird was on leave, so I was a member of the Legislative Council as well as of the Executive Council. I well remember that in the debate on the Sultan's speech, Ali Muhsin and Abeid Karume became involved in clear confrontation. HH interrupted the discussion to call the two to order, remarking, "I should tell you two that I remember your fathers well, in fact, we used to play football together and so I have known you both since you were youngsters. If you continue to confront each other as you are doing, I will have no hesitation but to come down and bang your two heads together." Silence reigned, but everyone present realised the high respect in which HH was held. He was probably the only one who could have spoken in such a manner. It was the first public indication of the political problems which were likely to affect the future of the Protectorate. This was finally demonstrated with the riots which broke out at the first open elections in June 1961.

My experience of sitting on Legislative Council, having the responsibility of presenting and defending the Medical Department's budget etc, was unique; it introduced me to the parliamentary system operating in London and provided personal knowledge on which to base future lectures at the London School of Tropical Hygiene and Medicine.

As Acting DMS and a member of Executive Council, I had the rather frightening responsibility of advising HE, in the event of the commutation of a death sentence. Such an experience only arose once and fortunately it was easy to advise on the commutation of the sentence, which HE accepted.

One benefit of the privilege of being a member of Legislative and Executive Councils was that I was eligible to become an Associate Member of the Commonwealth Parliamentary Association (CPA), which granted me entry to the Houses of Parliament. A direct benefit I enjoyed was on the occasion of the death of Sir Winston Churchill in January 1965. At that time I was teaching in the LSH&TM, and contacted the CPA offices in the House of Commons to ask if there was any chance of viewing the Lying-in-State of Sir Winston. I was allowed entry to the CPA offices and taken directly to Westminster Hall to view the coffin with the crowds walking round the cortége. Later I was invited, as a representative of the Colonial Medical Service, to the funeral service in St Paul's Cathedral. It was very moving and a great privilege, not only to be present at the ceremony, but also to see all the leading dignitaries on the world stage passing down the aisle before The Queen and Prince Philip arrived. These included, General de Gaulle, President of France, President Eisenhower of USA, as well as several monarchs and heads of state and other world leaders.

An innovation at that time were the TV screens fitted to every pillar in the Cathedral, so that those invited to the ceremony were able to follow the whole procession through the streets of London, as well as the arrival of all

233

the VIPs. After the service I spotted the Colonel of the 2nd Battalion Coldstream Guards, who was in charge of all the arrangements for the funeral. I had met him in Zanzibar during the riots in 1961, and after introducing myself I congratulated him on the excellence of the arrangements. His response was, "Typical of Sir Winston, he had left detailed instructions for his funeral and took ten days to die so we had ample time to practise well."

* * * * *

Id-ul-Fitr

A major event was the annual Celebration of Id-ul-Fitr, at the Seyyid Khalifa Hall, at which HE would attend in full morning suit (and full sweat) in the presence of the Royal Princes, the Diplomatic Corps, members of Legislative Council and other leading citizens of Zanzibar and Pemba. While we were in Zanzibar this celebration occurred while dhows from the Gulf of Arabia and India were in port preparing for the change of the monsoon. So scenes of their crews parading through the streets and performing their dances in front of the Sultan's Palace were an annual event. The crews looked like a bunch of ragamuffins. Today, with the discovery of oil in the Gulf area, they probably all own their own businesses, four-wheel-drive cars and yachts. The sea trade with Zanzibar has, of course, ceased since the Revolution, but Arabs are returning to the Islands for general trade.

* * * * *

Sport

The different communities including Arabs, Goans, Comorians, Hindus, English and others, all had their own sport and social clubs and entered into all sports competitions. The English Club provided hockey, cricket, tennis, squash and golf, but no football. For the Africans football was the major sport, but several of the community played for the Comorians in

234

their cricket and hockey teams. Considerable rivalry existed between all the teams but there were no leagues.

Prior to Zanzibar, I had never played hockey but became very involved with it and, in due course, became Chairman of the Zanzibar Hockey Association. I later established the Zanzibar Hockey Umpires' Association and ran training programmes to try and improve the standard of umpiring. Hockey was certainly the most popular inter-club 'competition' and we had a 'Four Countries Tournament' which involved teams from the four East African Territories. The Tournament was held in rotation in the different Territories, and the Hockey Association was responsible for organising and running it when it became Zanzibar's turn.

The Zanzibar team included players from all the clubs who played the game. The Hockey Association Committee ran training sessions for those chosen for possible selection and was responsible for housing all the visiting teams. This was not so difficult, for every community offered to house those of their community. In 1960 the Olympic Games were to be held in Rome. I heard that the Pakistan Team was travelling to Rome through Kenya to have several practice games in Nairobi. I approached the Kenya Association and requested their advice and support in inviting the Pakistan team to visit and play in Zanzibar.

After it was agreed, work on the organisation really started for we had to raise funds to pay for their travel expenses to Zanzibar, as well as arranging accommodation for the players and reserves, their chairman, coach, physiotherapist and others. To raise the funds we ran a dance which was well supported by all communities. We also published an official programme for the event, raising funds from advertising charges, again well supported by the trading community. Offers of accommodation came from all corners, from The Residency to private households. Everyone was fitted in. After the event we had another social evening with presentations. Zanzibar residents paid to participate, but all players

235

and their hosts were guests for the evening. The event was a successful sporting and social occasion, even though our team lost! Later we all enjoyed the reflected glory of Pakistan's victory in winning the Olympic gold medal.

Whenever we had a visit from a Naval ship, whether HMS, Indian or Pakistani, a welcoming committee with representatives from all communities arranged various social and sporting events for the visitors.

Many of the clubs had excellent cricket teams, and matches were played between them. The English Club had a good selection of players which was reinforced by boys home for school holidays during the summer from the UK, Kenya or South Africa. During the years we were in Zanzibar the highlight was an MCC touring team to East Africa, under the management of Freddie Brown, former English Captain, and the Captaincy of Colin Ingleby-Mackenzie of Hampshire (more recently President of the MCC). Regrettably the visit coincided with heavy rain and so little cricket was played... but plenty fluid flowed. We were lucky to have Colin Ingleby-Mackenzie as our guest, whilst Freddie Brown, staying at the Residency, found himself locked out after the late party... but all ended well!

The Zanzibar Sailing Club had been established for many years and a programme of races for monthly cups, all aimed at the Annual Championship, was arranged. We had a Club Commodore and Sailing Secretary, with a supporting Committee to supervise the sailing and social programmes. Special programmes were also arranged for inter-club competitions with teams from Tanga, Dar-es-Salaam and Mombasa as well as sailing contests with crews for visiting Naval ships. The Club was run by its members without any paid staff, other than the boat boys who assisted with launching and beaching boats on trolleys.

In 1963 I was the Sailing Secretary of the Club with responsibility for setting the championship course to be sailed on each race day. I was also

236

responsible for making arrangements for the visits of other sailing clubs from the mainland and setting the programme for those events.

Each month there were generally eight races with a monthly cup to be won, along with a mug as a memento. Points were awarded for positions in each race, which were then added towards the Club Championship at the end of the season. The Champion for the 1963 season was Libo, who at the end-of-season dance collected her trophy. When the time came for me to pack up our belongings in March 1964 and leave Zanzibar, I packed away the trophy and so Libo has retained the cup ever since.

* * * * *

On the Boards

Having been reacquainted with my love of the theatre in Kisumu I was pleased to be able to indulge my passion for acting in Zanzibar. I appeared in several plays, the first being in 1957, when, as the Captain in *Captain Carvallo*, I played opposite and had an assignation with Libo, under the direction of Brian Eccles!

This was followed in 1958 by *Sport of Kings* by Ian Hay, playing Algernon Sprige, before again playing opposite Libo in RC Sherrif's play *Home at Seven*, when we played David and Mrs Preston.

In 1959 I played Lord Pym in *The Chiltern Hundreds*, by William Douglas Home. My 'father' was played by Clarence Buxton. It has to be related that Acts II and III both start with a breakfast set. Unfortunately, at the start of Act II, Clarence began with the opening words for Act III. I quickly interrupted and, apologising to my 'mother', turned to Clarence and said, "Father, I have something to tell you. It must be as a surprise to mother, so can we go on to the patio for a moment or two?" I got up and led him out, his face having dropped several feet! "Clarence, you have taken us straight into Act III. Let's go back and start again, this time in Act II."

237

Back on stage I turned to my 'mother' and said, "I'll tell you the secret at the appropriate time."

Only the director realised what had happened and we had fooled the audience!

That year also saw me as Peter Marriot in *The Sound of Murder* by William Fairchild. However, the following year probably saw my greatest success in Zanzibar, playing Tony Wendice in *Dial M for Murder* by Frederick Knott. I played opposite Marjorie Peart and Tony Parfitt. I have often been told since then how alike I am to Ray Milland, who played Tony Wendice in the film version! I cannot be accused of copying his performance of 'Tony' for I only saw his film portrayal years later.

Those who know the play will remember that the final scene is set with everyone in the room waiting for 'Tony' to enter using the key to the door, thus revealing himself as the murderer, for only the murderer would know the whereabouts of the key. In the production, the spare key for Tony's entrance was to be left under the stair carpet. On approaching the door, imagine my shock when I searched for the key under the carpet only to find it was missing, so preventing me from opening the door and entering the room! As it was the dress rehearsal, I rang the front door bell! Consternation! Silence! I rang again and called out in a Scottish accent, "I canna get in for the key's no there!" Thereafter, extra keys were made and spares were placed in many spots outside the door!

In 1961 and 1962 I decided to enter the world of direction myself and produced *Count Your Blessings* and *The Happiest Days Of Your Life*, by Roland Jeans and John Deighton respectively. In the latter play I cast Henry Hawker and his wife Peggy as the Headmaster and the Sports Mistress, and for the first time in any Zanzibar production, I cast a non-European in a part, one Pramesh Mehta (Dik-Dik).

Probably the greatest fun on stage in Zanzibar was when the European Community decided to entertain themselves with a satire to a very restricted audience. It had to be restricted for we had decided to satirise the political situation in Zanzibar with the impending elections. No local staff, or friends were allowed into the premises of the Victoria Gardens Hall, where we had decided to have a 'Café Kazungu' evening.

It was a series of satirical sketches, songs and parodies, all written by a small panel of us and acted by a select group of trusted friends. All scripts were to be closely guarded and not photocopied for fear of leakage. One of the leading parodies was adapting the songs of *My Fair Lady* to 'My Dark Arab'. Titles like 'Just You Wait Ali Muhsin, Just You Wait!' and 'Why Can't an Arab be More Like Us' were examples.

The Revolution in 1964 interrupted our further theatrical efforts in Zanzibar.

Some Special Events

Visit of HH Aga Khan

Prince Karim was named as Aga Khan IV on 12th July 1957 on the death of his grandfather, Aga Khan III. He made an official visit to Zanzibar in October 1959, during a tour of East Africa, ostensibly to be accepted and crowned by His followers in the various East African Territories. During His short stay we were asked by the British Residency to arrange for HH to be taken for a goggling trip to Prison Island prior to a major open-air reception at which he would meet 'his people', and to which we were invited. Accordingly, Libo along with John and Lorna Cameron, arranged the trip to include a picnic with a swim and goggle. The four of them set off from the Sailing Club for the Island in John's speed boat, with me joining them later in my sailing boat. We found it difficult to get HH to stop goggling and were worried about having enough time to get him back to the Residency to prepare for the official function that evening. Eventually, he came out of the water and suddenly saw that his gold 'coronation' ring from Kenya had slipped off his finger while goggling! We all returned to the water to try and search for the ring - a rather forlorn hope as indeed it proved. HH finally called off the search, announcing that it was really of no consequence for he was sure to be given another ring that evening. We decided that, as we were so late, John would take the Aga Khan straight back to the Residency while the rest of us would sail back to the Club. As he set off, HH said that we were excused from attending the function that evening, much to our great relief!

The following evening The Resident gave an official dinner for the Aga Khan to which Libo and I were invited. Libo was seated next to HH, which was a great thrill for her.

The Aga Khan paid another visit to the Island while Sir George Mooring was The Resident. As before, we were invited to the official dinner on that occasion.

* * * * *

Colonel John Glenn - Man in Space

At the end of 1961 a large number of Americans started to arrive in Zanzibar to develop Project Mercury. This was to be a tracking station, initially to monitor the flight of the USA's mission of sending Colonel John H Glenn (in his capsule Mercury, Friendship 7) to be the first American into an orbital flight in space. Later the project functioned as a satellite-tracking base. America's first man in space was in fact Alan B Shepard on 5th May 1961, but that flight was sub-orbital lasting only fifteen minutes.

Colonel Glenn's flight was to be orbital and the first responsibility for Project Mercury was to be ready for monitoring his flight as the astronaut flew over Zanzibar while orbiting the earth. For us in the medical world it was an exciting time, because Dr Sam Fox III from Washington was posted to set up the equipment and lead the team which would monitor the heart-beat, blood pressure and other aspects of Glenn's health as he flew over. The team would be able to talk with Glenn as well as register all his various physiological measurements thus monitoring his body's reactions, as well as ensuring that he was performing normally, health-wise. Senior Medical Department staff were allowed access to the centre and we were shown all the equipment for following this historic event. Excitement grew as the time to the countdown neared and the day of 'take-off' dawned on 20th February 1962. We later heard on the tapes of the conversations with Glenn, his heart beating as he flew over thrice to complete the mission. I will ever remember the anxiety as we waited to listen to the wireless reports on the successful touchdown into the sea at the conclusion of the mission. We had all been part of a moment in history, only to be capped by Neil Armstrong's first step on the moon from Apollo 11 on 21st July 1969 ('one small step for a man, one giant leap for mankind').

* * * * *

Death of President Kennedy

Most adults alive on 22nd November 1963 will remember just where they were and what they were doing on that fateful day when President Kennedy was assassinated. I certainly do, and think a short sentence should be included here, for that event is associated with the Sailing Club. Club Members took it in turns to run the Club bar each night so avoiding outside paid staff. On that evening I was on duty at the bar. It was quiet and only a few of us were present, so I turned on our radio for company. The BBC World Service suddenly broke the incredible news. It was truly a shock for those present. We were stunned and I for one quite unashamedly shed several tears. The 'young leader of the world' who had offered such hope for the future was gone.

* * * * *

Seyid Khalifa's Funeral

The Sultan's death evoked great mourning in Zanzibar, not only because he had reigned for just a few months short of 60 years, but also because he was loved by all, and everyone felt that while he lived there could be no political unrest. Following Islam tradition his coffin was carried through the streets of Zanzibar from the Palace to the Royal Mosque behind. The coffin was draped in the plain red flag of Zanzibar, and was passed from person to person over the heads of the crowd. He was buried in the garden of the Palace.

* * * * *

Seyyid Sir Abdulla bin Khalifa

Again following tradition, the new Sultan was presented to His subjects from the verandah of His Palace, by the British Resident; this was a simple ceremony but one which drew crowds along the sea-front. Seyyid Sir Abdulla had a short reign from October 1960 till July 1963. He was a heavy smoker and a diabetic, both conditions placing him at risk for the hardening of his arteries. Unfortunately in 1963 he developed signs of gangrene in his right leg. Our Surgical Specialist, Mr Donnah Hurley, called on me at my office with his concern that the leg would require amputation. The Resident had to be advised and a request made for a Specialist to be flown out from the UK to perform the operation. I was involved in contacting the Colonial Office. They acted with speed and the next day Mr Frank Crockett from St Thomas' Hospital was flown out on a Royal Air Force plane. Preparation was made for the operation, and in due course Mr Crockett had to amputate mid-thigh. He suspected a similar condition in the left leg and decided he should open up and have a look. He found gangrene had also progressed into the left leg and required an amputation, which he performed.

242

As DMS I had the responsibility to meet the Sultan, with Mr Hurley and Mr Crockett, after HH recovered from the operation. I had to discuss public relations with regard to him advising his subjects as to his position. He told us it was up to me to tell his subjects what had happened. His son, Seyyid Jamshid Abdulla, heir to the throne, entered the room while I was talking with his father and was furious, telling me that the Muslim faith could not allow anyone to be buried in hallowed ground if his body was not complete. He refused permission for me to advise the public of the Sultan's amputations. I reflected with him that surely the theatre staff would have seen the operation and so it could be no secret. Seyyid Jamshid was obviously very angry and asked us to leave the room. Mr Crockett unfortunately had to return to the UK, and so left Mr Hurley and myself to handle the situation. Seyyid Abdulla was clearly upset by Seyyid Jamshid's intervention and gave up any real will to live. He died later that day. Seyyid Jamshid thereafter blamed me for his father's death. So I earned the stigma, notoriety or fame of being the man who was responsible for the death of the Sultan of Zanzibar.

* * * * *

Minimum Wage Committee

During the period of political evolution in Zanzibar the concept of Trade Unionism was strongly developed and every department of Government was allowed to establish its own Trade Union. We in the Medical Department were no exception, and I became the departmental liaison officer, responsible for meeting and, where necessary, negotiating with the Union representatives on issues relating to terms and conditions of service, including such issues as uniforms for the different staff groups, rota systems and other items. Any decisions had to be framed in terms of recommendations to be presented to the DMS for his final approval. As ADMS it then became my responsibility to ensure that any decisions were implemented. If the DMS did not approve any recommendations I had to

243

advise the Union accordingly and where possible arrange a workable compromise! I became known to the Union as the one who said 'no'. All this was, of course, before the establishment of the Ministerial System, when the responsibility for negotiation fell to the Permanent Secretaries and finally to the Minister.

Many employees of the Government were casual labourers and were paid daily rates. In time the demand for revised terms from casual labour became a threat to the Government. Again, before the Ministerial System, it was the Secretariat who had to handle the demands with accompanying threats of strikes etc. The Chief Secretary decided there should be a review of all the terms and conditions of work, including pay, and set up a Review Body or Select Committee to carry out the survey and report back to him with relevant findings and recommendations. I was selected to be one of three members of the review group, the others being Administrative Officers, John Reid and Clarence Buxton. I'll never know why I was chosen to be one of the group, but I was told that I had a reputation for being a good listener! In later months my presence on the Review Body weighed against me with the 'Revolutionary Council'. After long and protracted discussions we finally came up with our recommendations for a minimum daily rate of pay. While quite an increase on the old rate, it did not match the demands of the Unions. But as in all such situations a compromise was reached.

* * * * *

Zanzibar - Political Development

The first stage in Zanzibar's political development occurred in 1957 with elections on 21st July for six seats on the Legislative Council. Before the elections, the Council was made up of officials of HH's Government with unofficials nominated by the Government representing the various ethnic groups in the population. There was an official majority in both the Executive and Legislative Councils. The Coutts Report in 1956 proposed that membership of both Councils be increased. The Executive Council was to consist of seven officials and three unofficials, while the Legislative Council was to be made up of fourteen officials and twelve unofficials, of which six members were to be elected on a common role basis.

There were three main political parties in position: the Afro-Shirazi Party (ASP) under the leadership of Abeid Karume; the Zanzibar Nationalist Party (ZNP) under Sheikh Ali Muhsin Barwani, and the Zanzibar Pemba People's Party (ZPPP) with Mohammed Shamte as leader. These first elections resulted in the ASP winning five of the seats with an independent Muslim winning the sixth. The ZNP, who had expected to sweep to victory, suffered a major defeat.

The next development was in 1959 with the decision to appoint five Ministers from the unofficial members in Legislative Council. Three were to be from the elected members and two from those nominated members. The Medical Department was to have its first Minister, Ameri Tajo, appointed Minister for Social Services. I well remember his first visit to the Department offices. He was sitting in what had been the DMS's desk, before offices were made available for him in Beit-el Ajaib, which housed the central offices of the Government's Administration.

While talking with him I suddenly noticed that a bed-bug was running along the collar of his kanzu. The challenge was whether to draw his attention to it, thus suggesting that his personal hygiene left something to be desired, or to ignore it and worry about an infestation of the bug! I took the latter course.

Following the Blood Report in 1960 plans were laid for the next stage, progressing hopefully to internal self-government and finally complete Independence. In November 1960, the British Government announced that the Legislative Council would consist of three ex-officio members, twenty-two elected members and up to five appointed members. The Executive Council was to consist of the British Resident as President, three ex-officio members and five unofficial Ministers, one to be designated Chief Minister. Considerable political activity occurred in the months ahead, with even the USA Project Mercury, mentioned elsewhere, becoming affected by opposing views. While for nearly six decades during his reign Seyyid Khalifa was regarded as a unifying institution, Seyyid Abdulla had forfeited his father's universal respect and approbation. The ASP accused him of partiality to the ZNP, basing their suspicion on the pro-nationalist activities of his son Seyyid Jamshid, who later became Sultan.

Eventually, on 17th January 1961, the people of Zanzibar went to the polls. The election gave the ASP the narrowest possible victory, gaining a majority of one seat, secured by a single vote. Of the three ZPPP seats two joined forces with ZNP and one with ASP - a dead heat. A coalition caretaker government resulted, with the Civil Secretary to act as Chief Minister, and the further agreement that a second election should follow as soon as possible.

* * * * *

Election Riots - 1st June 1961

The result of the 1st June election was that ASP and ZNP obtained ten seats each, with ZPPP the remaining three seats. ZPPP had a pre-election commitment to support ZNP and so the two parties were able to coalesce to form a government, with ASP as the opposition. In all there was a turnout for voting of 96.15% of which ASP won 49.9% of the poll, ZNP 35% and ZPPP 13.7%

The election however touched off an unprecedented degree of violence and rioting. The disturbances started early and continued throughout the day. They were in full swing until the arrival of units of the British Army flown in from the mainland to help the local police restore law and order. The troops were from the 2nd Battalion Coldstream Guards. The riots continued over the next day and in all 68 people were killed, 64 being Manga Arabs living in the rural areas, with several hundred severely injured. The world press had turned up to witness what was expected to be a tense election and so tremendous pressure was placed upon the Medical Department, not only to handle the situation of the wounded but also to maintain close relationships with the press to keep them informed of the situation regarding casualties. Our small mortuary was soon full to overflowing with dozens of corpses being brought in, especially from the rural areas. Obviously there was a major massacre going on in those areas with hoards of Arab refugees flooding into Zanzibar town.

As ADMS it fell to me to organise and handle the logistics of the affair, and many gory sights were witnessed and distressing stories could be told. Three events out of the many deserve mention.

Standing outside the main hospital I recognised the Camerons' car drive up. As soon as it stopped, Lorna (Mrs Cameron) jumped out and asked for help as an African woman was in the process of child-birth. On opening the back door of the car, I saw the delivery was imminent and indeed the child was delivered there and then. There was just enough time to remove the woman onto a stretcher for the after-birth.

Later, a truck drove up to the main entrance with an Arab standing up and screaming his head off asking us to hurry. I supervised its reversing to the main door, calling on the Arab to pull himself together and shut up. With the truck in position and stretchers ready I opened the tailgate to be met by a scene never to be forgotten. Lying on the floor were four adult women, two with their stomachs slashed open and a foetus being visible from one. There were also three little children with their legs slashed and virtually hanging loose. I felt such shame at having told the Arab to pull himself together, while at the same time feeling quite sick at the sight of the horrific and dreadful crime. It appeared that the father had left their house to go to the local shop to buy some cigarettes when the Africans arrived. They set the makuti roof (coconut palm) alight and waited for the women and children to come out. As they did so they were slashed apart, leaving the carnage.

The final story relates to a telephone call I received from the maternity home, Mwembilado, in the middle of the African quarter of the township, Ngambo. The midwife was very agitated, telling us that there was a mob of Africans fighting, beating up and slashing out at others. The women awaiting delivery were terrified and they wanted rescuing. We had an eleven-seater long-base Land Rover in our yard so I called the driver and set off to the home. As I entered Ngambo I met up with the rioting mob, who were blocking my way. I got out of the cab and standing on the running board I called out in Swahili, "Doktari! Give way! I need to get to the Maternity Hospital." The crowd seemed to stop fighting and separated enough to allow us through. We got the women and midwifes into the truck and set off back home, only again to face the unruly mob. I repeated my call for a free passage and again they stood back, stopped fighting and let us through only to resume their rioting as soon as we had passed.

The Arab refugees pouring in from the rural areas numbered several thousand and would soon pose a dangerous problem, not only with overcrowding, but also the spread of infectious disease including chest conditions, dysentery, polio and diphtheria to name a few.

We decided there was a need to vaccinate all those from the rural areas against polio and diphtheria, so I contacted Dar-es-Salaam for the necessary vaccines. We also set up temporary dispensaries at various schools throughout the stone town to treat any minor conditions. This would obviate the purdah and prevent frightened Arab women from having to walk through the streets to the hospital. At the same time it would relieve the main hospital's out-patient department to handle major conditions. We recruited women from the European community whom we knew had been in the nursing profession, along with any other volunteers from the other communities. Such actions did result in the prevention of any epidemics in the town and so allowed us to visit the Arab homes to assess the overcrowding situation and make any adjustments where necessary.

Following the riots and unrest we had a visit from a USA warship which was on a 'goodwill tour' of the African Region. They requested to visit with the offer of 'supplies'. We were delighted and were hoping for supplies of flour, rice, tinned foods, milk and suchlike. They arrived with supplies of sugar, sweets, magazines and old editions of *Encyclopaedia Americana*! The Americans enjoyed driving through the streets throwing out handfuls of sweets to the kids as they drove along. We suggested that as few of the public spoke English the Encyclopaedia should remain on board. One had to say that the visit did little to enhance public relations regarding the Americans.

* * * * *

M.B.E.

Before I flew back to Zanzibar in April 1962 after my WHO Travel Fellowship, I stayed in London at the East Africa House in Cumberland Avenue just off Marble Arch. The House was a like a club for officials and visitors from East Africa.

The morning after I arrived I was called downstairs to the phone in the hall where the following conversation took place.

"Is that Dr Barton?"

"Yes."

"This is the Prime Minister's Office and we have been trying to contact you as you have been travelling round the world. We need an almost immediate reply to this question. Your name has been submitted for recommendation to The Queen for the award of the MBE in Her Birthday Honours list, for organising the medical care and welfare of the people of Zanzibar, during and following the riots of 1st June. We have to finalise the names for submission this week, so I am glad that I got hold of you before you set off back to Zanzibar."

Pause!

"This is Dr Barton from Zanzibar. I really think you must have got the wrong person, for I truly don't understand what you are saying!"

"I know I have the right Dr Barton, the DMS of Zanzibar. Correct?"

"Yes."

"I know it is a bit of a surprise and normally we would not have been phoning about the matter but it became urgent, hence this call. Are you willing to accept that the PM submits your name to the Queen for her acceptance?"

Meekly, I replied, "Yes."

"You must understand that this is a strictly secret matter and you must not mention it to anyone, not even your wife, until it is officially announced in the Gazette on Her Majesty's Official Birthday."

Stunned and dumbfounded I flew back to Zanzibar to maintain my complete silence, keeping the secret even from Libo. The British Resident Sir George Mooring did contact me after my return to ask if I had been contacted in London and to request my total silence till June. It was then April!

The night before the Parade for the Queen's Birthday Sir George phoned to inform me that the Gazette was out and that I could now tell Libo! I did so with tears in my eyes.

I was offered the opportunity to accept the award personally from the Queen in Buckingham Palace, or have it presented by Sir George in the British Residency in Zanzibar. I felt I wanted my staff in the Department to enjoy the honour, for without them I could have done nothing to deserve such recognition, so in due course with my beloved Libo, Lesley and Ian supporting me, along with my Secretary from the Department, I received the medal at The Residency.

There was joyous celebration throughout the Department and many parties were held, all recorded by the many photos taken at the various events. What an emotional time it was! Never in my wildest dreams had I ever suspected such an occasion. My graduation, my marriage, the birth of our two children and now this honour from The Queen.

* * * * *

M.B.E. Investiture at The Residency

Pre-Independence 1963

Following the elections the Ministerial System was formalised and I became Permanent Secretary to the Ministry of Health as well as DMS. In due course it was decided to appoint an administrative officer to be the Permanent Secretary, thus leaving myself to function as the Chief Technical Officer of the Ministry, which delighted me.

At the 1962 Constitutional Conference in London, it was agreed that elections would be held between 8th-11th July 1963, with the number of constituencies increasing from twenty-three to thirty-one; seventeen from Zanzibar and the rest from Pemba. The election results gave the ZNP/ZPPP coalition eighteen out of the thirty-one seats and the ASP thirteen seats. The 1963 Constitutional Conference to arrange for self-governing Zanzibar was held in September when the date for Zanzibar Independence was fixed as 10th December 1963.

With Independence approaching and the Afro-Shirazi Party in opposition, the African community became restless and the casual labourers began to threaten the Government with strike action involving a boycott of the Independence Ceremony and Celebrations. This would have seriously embarrassed the whole process, postponed the event and threatened the visit of HRH Prince Philip. It was apparent that the Labour Office and Chief Labour Officer had failed to win over the Unions, resulting in a stalemate in the discussions. I was suddenly summoned by the British Resident and was requested to act as his personal representative to meet with the Unions to attempt to calm the situation and so avert strike action. Many of their representatives were keen sportsmen whom I had known in the various fields of sport. It was with great trepidation that I approached the Union representatives, realising that if I did not succeed HE would be faced with major problems and decisions to take regarding the Independence Ceremony. It was with the greatest relief that I managed to obtain the Unions' agreement to withdraw their threat of strike action and so allow the whole process of Independence to be followed through.

253

Again, my role of negotiator with the Unions stood me in poor stead with the later Revolutionary Council.

Seyyid Abdulla died in July 1963 and was succeeded by his eldest son Seyyid Jamshid bin Abdulla.

Prior to the date of Independence the European Community decided to have a final 'Band Night' evening in the English Club. It was the custom for the Police Band to play under flood-lighting, in front of the English Club every Wednesday evening for an hour. The band played in several other places in town during the week, but the Wednesday evening 'band night' attracted many club members to sit on the verandah of the club while having a sundowner. So it was that on the last Wednesday evening before Independence most of the European Community turned up in formal dress for what turned out to be the very last public performance by the band. I had had the presence of mind to take along my 35mm reflex camera and took a full reel of 36 transparencies recording all our dear friends and colleagues of our happy years in Zanzibar. It has turned out to be a truly wonderful, treasured and unique collection.

Another pre-Independence function was a party which our neighbours, Robin and Geoffrey Horsfall planned. We shared a large old Arab house which had been divided down the middle, giving each of us a three-storeyed home while we shared the same garden. We planned the party to be held in the garden which provided a beautiful setting overlooking the sea. Guests were to wear 'local' style dress kanzus, kikois, kangas etc. We played several stupid but fun team games, for example, passing the apple down the line from chin to chin, and passing the string up the back and down the front of each team member in the line. We also had pillow fights balancing on a pole placed between two chairs - feet were tucked up under the pole for balance and then the fight ensued. Again, I had my camera and recorded some great shots, including HE being toppled off the pole by the Dutch Consul, who was manager of a local company.

As the first HMS Cruiser had arrived in port for Independence functions, we had several Officers join the party. One uninvited guest brought along by someone with an official invite approached me during the evening and offered me ,50 for the privilege of developing my film and the right to retain any of the negatives. I refused his offer telling him he was at a private party! I later discovered he was a reporter from an English paper and read his account of our party as part of his major article on the Independence celebrations.

All our guests were European colleagues and friends, except 'Dik Dik' Ramesh Mehta, an Indian Hindu who had become like a younger brother to us and a big brother to the children. I recall that the Chief Medical Adviser to the Colonial Office, Dr Dill Russell, had arranged a formal tour of the East African Territories which coincided with the Independence celebrations in both Zanzibar and Kenya. The tour turned out to be very informal and he was at our party in his kikoi!

* * * * *

Independence Celebrations and Ceremony

The ceremony and other celebrations were attended by many VIPs including The Colonial Secretary, Duncan Sandys, HH The Aga Khan, while the Queen's representative for the Independence Ceremony and Celebrations was HRH The Duke of Edinburgh. The day before Independence HRH toured the hall where the various Government Departments had set up their exhibits demonstrating their work. HRH approached our exhibit and it was for me to accompany him. He looked at the various graphs showing the incidence of various diseases over the recent years. The Duke remarked, "You seem to have had an increase in the incidence of typhoid, dysentery, diphtheria, and measles in 1959." Without a pause, but turning to me he asked, "Were you on leave Barton?"

255

The actual transfer of power took place at Mnazi Moja, with HH The Sultan and His party and other VIPs seated on a flood-lit dais. The rest of the officials and the public were seated in rows all facing the dais. The flag pole was floodlit and at the stroke of midnight when all other lights were extinguished a search-light picked out the Union Jack as it was lowered, and then illuminated the new Zanzibar flag as it was raised.

HRH Prince Philip formally pronounced Zanzibar's Independence at midnight. It was a moving moment for all members of Her Majesty's Overseas Service present to watch the Union Jack being lowered and replaced by the new flag of Zanzibar.

The next day HRH left, followed by HE The British Resident, Sir George and Lady Mooring. It was the end of an era, the end of the British Protected Government which had lasted for 73 years from 1890.

* * * * *

Post-Independence

Our children Lesley and Ian were with us for the Ceremony of Independence and we thereafter prepared for our UK leave which was to start on 23rd December. We were booked to sail on the Lloyd Trestino Ship *Europa* which was to call in at Mombasa to pick up Sir George and Lady Patricia Mooring, who had already left Zanzibar on the evening of 10th December. We had a great send-off and were expecting to be on leave for only six weeks, returning for a two year tour at the request of the new Independent Government.

We landed at Venice and made our way to our first family skiing holiday in Austria. We stayed in the village of Swendt near Kössen, not far from Kufstein, Kitzbuhl and Innsbruck. We had intended to ski for two weeks, but on our first morning in Kössen we heard the news on *Voice of America* of the Revolution in Zanzibar on 9th January 1964. The same morning we also received news from my father in Mombasa that Mother had been operated on for a cancer of the bowel.

256

Seldom, if ever, had Kössen seen such excitement for we tried hard to phone through to Kenya. That failed so we spent the rest of the day sending telegrams to Zanzibar and Mombasa. All contact with Zanzibar had been cut off, while contact with my father proved extremely difficult. The whole village buzzed and our family became like VIPs overnight, being greeted by all the village. It must be remembered that in 1964, after the Christmas and New Year season was over, a small village in Austria became empty of visitors. We finally received word that I was not to return to Zanzibar until further advised. At the same time news of Mother's good progress relieved our anxiety and we were told there was no need to fly out. So we stayed in Kössen for four weeks, becoming really quite expert on the ski slopes. At that time the exchange rate was 17 Austrian Shillings to ,1, so life was reasonably cheap!

We finally took off for the UK and made for Nottingham, to be put up by the Stringer family who were our friends from Kiambu, Kilifi and Zanzibar days. The Stringers had retired from Zanzibar in 1961 so were well established in the UK. In due course I received instructions to return to Zanzibar alone, to pack up my personal possessions.

As far as the Department was concerned, I had become 'the one who brought the bad news'; as a member of the Review Body I had 'taken sides with the Government against the Unions'; as HE's representative I had again 'fought' the Unions in preventing their strike! When the Revolutionary Council took control, I was the person selected to demonstrate their power and became the first senior Head of a Department of the former Government to be dismissed and officially declared 'persona-non-grata'.

On arrival in Zanzibar the following week I was instructed to pack up my possessions and get them on the BI ship *Mombasa* which was sailing in five days' time! I was also advised that I would receive no help from the Government regarding assistance with packing, or transporting my possessions. All my papers, notes and stationery items from my desk, and books from the shelves in my office were dumped on the lawn of our house, having been sent round from my office in a wheel-barrow. I contacted an African carpenter whom I had known and asked him to help me put together a few crates so that I could pack up my things. He worked for one day then reported he could not continue for the Revolutionary Council had warned him that if he was seen to be working for me, he and his family would suffer the consequences.

I contacted the Revolutionary Council to ask their advice as to how I should proceed with my packing etc. I would need a whole chapter to describe the procedure I had to follow; suffice to say I followed their instructions to the letter. I would have achieved nothing but for the fact that the wives of our European colleagues and friends volunteered to help pack up our crockery, ornaments and other breakable possessions. Fortunately, over a few years we had collected several 44 gallon metal drums, which had originally contained the insecticides used on our Malaria Eradication Programme, and again, fortunately, we had kept several crates and boxes for storage when we went on long overseas leaves in earlier years, for example, when we were in the USA in 1958 for six months for post-graduate studies. A few of my male colleagues turned up and together we were able to crate and pack up all the possessions I was prepared to take back to the UK. Many things, including bicycles, toys, some sports gear etc, I gave away to Asian, Arab and other community friends who also were willing to help me.

It was a traumatic five days, with sleepless nights, but in the end I got my possessions on the ship and finally left Zanzibar and my Colonial career behind me. It was to be 34 years before I was to step ashore again on Zanzibar.

WHO Fellowships

1958

I mentioned earlier that on my transfer to Zanzibar I forfeited the WHO Fellowship to study in the USA. The Fellowship had been granted to Kenya and so I could not take it with me on transfer to Zanzibar in 1956. By 1957 I had completed my normal three year tour and was entitled to 'home' leave in the UK. I agreed to stay on a further six months to allow the DMS to have his leave, and meanwhile Zanzibar had requested WHO to grant me a Fellowship to allow me to do some post-graduate study in the USA. Earlier I had read WHO Expert Committee Report No. 83 'The Methodology of Planning an Integrated Health Programme for Rural Areas', under the Chairmanship of Professor Hugh Leavell of the Harvard School of Public Health. My interest was aroused and I applied to Harvard to study under Professor Leavell. Unfortunately, Harvard would not accept me unless I officially registered for their MPH Course, which meant a year of study. As I had taken my DPH in Edinburgh in 1953-54 I saw no benefit of taking a further degree. I really wanted to 'audit' certain courses, for example, Applied Anthropology, Medical Sociology, Community Organisation for Health Education, as well as Public Health Administration methods. Fortunately, Dean McGavran of the University of North Carolina at Chapel Hill agreed for me to be attached to his School and to design a programme to suit my request.

My tutor and course supervisor was Professor John Cassel from South Africa, whose speciality was Epidemiology. My other major mentors were Professors John Wright in Public Health Administration, Lucy Morgan in Health Education and Community Development, and Dr Laura Thompson in Applied Anthropology, besides Dean McGavran himself. I had a wonderful six months' experience and study. After twelve years in the Colonial Service, all in East Africa, I was able to step outside my environs and culture and question just where and why I had succeeded in some projects and failed in others. I came to understand the importance of appreciating other cultures and the different approaches of motivating and communicating with them. It truly opened my eyes on how to communicate with people and plan public health programmes to avoid opposition or conflict.

My participation in the Applied Anthropology course created great interest, in that I was the only medical graduate on the programme; all the others being post-graduate anthropologists. Each of us was expected to give a presentation to the class as part of our programme on a subject decided by Professor Thompson, and I soon realised my disadvantage in not being an anthropologist when she handed me the title of my dissertation: 'The Lineal and Non-lineal use of Language in the Codification of Reality for Primitive Cultures, with particular reference to the Trobriand Islands.'

On reading the title I gulped and had to ask Professor Thompson to translate it and give me some idea as to where I should start. "I would suggest that you read Malinowski!" was her reply. I did and enjoyed the task.

I studied at the School for one semester, 28th January to 17th May 1958, and then set off on a field trip which took me to Puerto Rico, New Orleans, Jackson Mississippi, Atlanta Georgia, Knoxville and Chatanooga Tennessee, Washington DC, Boston Massachusettes and New York... all in ten weeks! I met a host of renowned scholars in the many fields I covered and felt very privileged to have met and been influenced by them. I wrote a comprehensive report on this vital study period in my life which is available among my papers for reference.

1960

In 1960 I was awarded a Travel Fellowship to visit several countries in West Africa in differing geographical conditions and climates, operating Malaria Eradication Programmes in various stages. The countries and places I visited were the Regional Office in Brazzaville for my briefing, thence to Bangui in the Central African Republic, Fort Lamy in Chad, before flying on to Marua, Yaounde and Dualla in the Cameroons and then moving onto Maseru in Basutoland thence by air to Mauritius. There the British Governor was Sir Deverell Ray, whom I had known when he was Development Secretary in Kenya and who was a close friend of Libo's parents.

1962

In 1962 I was awarded a WHO Travel Fellowship to allow me to visit several other countries in Africa, Asia and the Middle East where their MEPs had reached a stage of surveillance, ie, they were in a situation where monitoring of the continued success of the programme had been introduced. In Zanzibar we were hoping that by 1963 we would have reached a similar stage in our MEP. So it was that I set off in January on the Fellowship. My first visit was to Salisbury in Southern Rhodesia, on which Libo and Ian accompanied me. After three days, they returned to Nairobi while I continued to Bulawayo and thence to Bechuanaland to study surveillance techniques.

I was advised that certain countries in Asia were a few years ahead of Africa in their MEPs so after Rhodesia and Bechuanaland I headed for India, stopping over in Bombay en route for Delhi. There I had discussions with the Malaria Programme Officers at the Regional Office for South East Asia (SEARO) and the national malaria team operating throughout India.

My field visits really started in Ceylon where I had a fascinating trip visiting many of the ancient, historic centres of Buddhist culture, while at the same time carrying out my survey of the country's MEP. These ancient centres included Sigiriya, Anuradhapura, Polonnaruwa, Kunuregala and Kandy. Sigiriya is famous as the city built on the top of a small mountain which was the fortress of an early ruler. To visit the city one had to rise very early, because of the heat of the day, and climb up the steep path hewn out of the mountainside. On the way up, beautiful coloured murals and engravings on the walls were seen. The view from the city on the top of the hill was breath-taking, with a 360 degree panorama of the countryside. Special memories of the visit to Ceylon include the sight of working elephants, which after coming from Africa was an awesome sight, and the gold and jewellers' shops in Colombo, full of precious stones, sapphires, emeralds, rubies, opals and others. They were all so cheap (for sterling currency) that I went to town buying rings, bracelets, brooches etc, for Libo, my daughter and Mother. The festivals of elephant parades through Kandy while I was there were true pageantry. The fascinating Buddhist temples throughout the country almost rival those of Thailand which I was to see in later years. I visited the temple of the collar bone, where supposedly the Buddha's bone was buried, as well as the tree associated with the Buddha's first vision.

With regard to the MEP in Ceylon it should be recorded that in 1936, as a result of a horrific epidemic of malaria, there were reputedly one million deaths from the disease. By 1962, the year I visited, only four cases were recorded, while by the late 1970s, due to laxity in the surveillance practices and a developing resistance to insecticides and drugs by the vectors and parasites respectively, the disease had returned to epidemic proportions, and remains a major threat today.

On my field trips I was accommodated in Government rest houses, which were of great comfort compared with many on the African mainland.

262

From one such abode I was taken on a long and tiring trek into dense forest to look for an aboriginal tribe which was reputed to have become isolated and had never been included in the Malaria Eradication Programme. The surveillance team had not found the tribe and so the search promised to be of interest, if possibly fraught with apprehension and even a degree of danger. We did find the tribesmen and, sure enough, we found from blood tests that four were positive to *P vivax*, the parasite of benign tertian malaria. The dominant malaria in Ceylon was *P falciparum*, the parasite of malignant tertian malaria. The problem associated with the vivax parasite is that it has an exo-erythrocytic cycle in the liver in its development in the human, and so can lie dormant and erupt from time to time into the blood, causing a recurrence of malaria, which not being lethal is therefore not noticed in such isolated groups of the population. It was a lesson to me that one could never be complacent, believing that the surveillance programme was total in its success.

My next move was a stop-over in Singapore en route to Kuching, the capital of Sarawak. I had known before I set off that my former DMS in Zanzibar, Dr Baird, was now the DMS in Sarawak. I was therefore warmly welcomed and housed for my stay in Kuching. It may be remembered that Sarawak was given to Rajah Brooke by the rulers of Borneo for successfully overcoming tribal risings before the outbreak of the Second World War. Kuching town is on a river, across from which is the old palace of the Rajah, which by 1962 lacked the coat of paint and the pristine look it had worn before the war. Sarawak was handed back to the British after the Japanese surrender in 1945 and later became part of Malaysia at the time of its Independence in 1963. Rajah Brooke's daughter married Harry Roy, a renowned Band Leader in the 1930s. His signature tune 'Sarawaki' became equally famous for it was named after his wife! The trip to Sarawak was possibly the most fascinating and interesting of all my travels, for I was taken from Kuching by truck into the forests of the Land Dyaks, living in their long houses and watching spraying operations as well as surveillance methods.

The Land Dyak houses are built on stilts because of the heavy rainfall. Their homes (called 'long houses') are joined together, each with its own door opening from a common verandah. Guests sleep here on very uncomfortable bamboo cane flooring. When one retires at night one is 'protected from evil spirits' by members from various homes. They take turns to sit up all night to ensure you are safe! It is embarrassing to wake up in the morning to find people all around you, especially if the call of nature needs to be answered! When I asked about ablutions and toilet facilities, I was taken into the back room of the home where they pointed to a hole in the floor through which one was required to aim! I felt so embarrassed about this, that after the first morning I retired to the bush to carry out my functions. Unfortunately, I had not realised that under every long house they kept their pigs, whose task, and no doubt pleasure, it was to devour all household rubbish and human excreta. Accordingly, on my first venture into the bush I was followed by the pigs, no doubt interested in some new menu. While squatting, I found I was soon surrounded, and the pigs, rather like hyenas in Africa, ventured closer and closer. On future sorties into the bush I always took a long pole with me which I swung around while attempting to perform. It certainly kept the pigs at more than arm's length.

In some villages separate guest houses away from the long house verandah had been built. There was a long-drop through the floor in the corner of the room, but it was obvious from the stains down the side of the house from the main window that most of the guests, if called by nature at night, had urinated through the window!

We had several days living with the Land Dyaks and I found it truly fascinating. I flew up to the 3rd Division in Sarawak where all transport was by river and where the tribesmen were 'Sea Dyaks'. Again their homes were long houses, but they were all built along the edge of the rivers, still on stilts because of river risings at times of floods. As we moved down the river from one long house to the next I saw people seemingly squatting in the river who often waved as we passed along. I discovered the explanation for this when I went ashore and again enquired about toilet facilities. "Just walk down the plank and as you do so it will gradually, under your weight, lower you into the river. When below the water level you can do what you desire." I found myself waving to the passers by as I had seen the others do! The bush round the houses was so dense one could not disappear into it as with the Land Dyaks.

I had heard that the Dyaks had developed a technique of shrinking the skulls of their deceased or enemies, and I now witnessed these hanging down from the ceiling in many of the long houses... fortunately I don't believe in ghosts.

I learned a great deal about carrying out an MEP under such situations and among such tribesmen. I thoroughly enjoyed my stay in the country and was sad to say farewell to the Bairds and the Dyaks.

I moved on to the WHO Western Pacific Regional Office in Manila where I met Dr Francisco Dy and the Malaria Advisor Dr Postiglione. This was a transit stop-over en route to Taipei in Taiwan. In 1962 Taiwan was very undeveloped, for General Chiang Kai-shek had only moved from mainland China three years earlier and no true USA financed development had started. There were no cars, only bicycles, no factories and everything was so very cheap with very low salaries. Taiwan, previously known as Formosa, had been occupied by the Japanese for many years and their culture was still very dominant.

After arriving in Taipei, an overnight train journey was made to Kao-chung to visit TAMRI HQ at Chao-Chow to meet up with Dr Wan I Chen. Field visits were also made to Tai Chun and Wu Fong with rural visits to Tao Lin and Lin Nai to study the field malaria work.

From Taiwan I made stop-overs at Hong-Kong and Calcutta on my way to New Delhi, before moving on to Lebanon. I was based at Beirut, but with field trips to Zable, Jib-Janine, Baalbeck, Tripoli and neighbouring villages. I was expecting to travel to Alepo in Syria, but on the day of my flight there was a coup in Damascus and so I moved on to Amman in Jordan, and was able to visit Jerusalem, Bethlehem, the Red Sea and other places of interest. All this of course was before Israel invaded the West Bank and took over Jerusalem.

My next stop was Turkey with visits to Istanbul and Ankara, before setting off on a field trip of approx 1500 miles visiting rural areas in the eastern and southern regions of Turkey including Konya, Antalya, Mangaret, Afyon and Esakehir. The malaria programme was of enormous size with dozens of MOs in charge of the field teams.

My Fellowship travel programme finished in WHO HQ, Geneva, where I held lengthy discussions with the Malaria Unit's team of malariologists, which included Dr Bruce-Chwatt and Leonard Charles, both of whom I was to meet later in my career at the LSH&TM and while in Zanzibar.

Academia

1964 - 1972

Settling in England

Our Return to UK

After escaping the trauma of my last few days in Zanzibar I flew to Mombasa to see Mum and Dad at their home in Likoni, before flying on to Heathrow. Reaching there I saw Libo waving from the arrival platform. I was thrilled and delighted, if a little puzzled, for I knew that she was staying with John and Wish Stringer at Beeston, near Nottingham.

It turned out that while I was away in Zanzibar, Libo had seen a house, *The Bells*, advertised in the *Daily Telegraph* in a little village, Hemingford Grey, in Huntingdon, on the River Ouse just outside the small town of St Ives. John, who had been a student at Cambridge, knew the village and had driven Libo down to see the house. The owners were an elderly couple who obviously wanted Libo to have the house and promised to reserve any decision on the sale until after my return from Zanzibar. Libo had hired a car so that she could drive me to Beeston via Hemingford. Before this, we stayed the night with Pat and Penny Robertson, who had returned to London after Zanzibar Independence. They knew a surveyor in Cambridge who could do the survey for us and so next day we headed north to see the property.

The house had been built 200 years before, and early in the 20th century it had been *The Six Bells* village pub. It opened directly onto the village street which led down to the River Ouse; the present pub was just fifty yards further down the street from the house!

Libo remarked, "Don't worry about how it looks now and its present decoration. I can see what the house will be like." I could appreciate her enthusiasm and we agreed to go ahead. The old couple, the Clarks, were delighted.

We contacted the surveyor on the Monday and his report arrived by the end of the week. WOW! For me it was full of problems and I could not see how anyone would buy such a place. However, Libo persuaded me not to lose heart and when I contacted our solicitor and estate agent it was agreed that, with such a survey, we could safely offer £500 less than the asking price. The offer was accepted and so it was that we bought our first house - four bedrooms and two bathrooms and a granny-cottage in the garden for £6,000. I have to say at this point that I had received no salary from the Zanzibar Government since December 1963 and it was now April 1964. However, I knew that, in time, I would be receiving a 'golden handshake' from the UK Government for my loss of career, and so on the strength of this I was able to convince my banker to allow us a bridging loan.

I shall never forget waking up the next morning, Saturday, turning to Libo and saying, "We have no job, no salary and we have bought a house 65 miles north of London." The *BMJ* arrived that morning and I quickly opened it remarking, "Let's see if our trades union magazine has anything to offer." I couldn't believe my eyes when I read: "Vacancy for Assistant MOH Huntingdon" - just five miles from where we had bought our house! I dashed off a letter of application. The following Tuesday I received a telegram asking me if I could attend an interview that Thursday. Surely!

At the interview I was asked how many staff I had under me as DMS Zanzibar. When I replied, "Around 1,000" I was told, "You realise you won't even have a secretary in this job?"

In due course I was asked if I could wait outside while they discussed whether they might have more questions to ask me.

Waiting outside in the car, Libo looked at me and questioned, "Well?"
I told her that I thought I was the only applicant! I was called back and offered the job. On being asked when I could start I replied, "The first of May."
"Done."

The house we had bought had a granny-cottage in the garden with its own kitchen and bathroom. The Clarks kindly offered to rent us the cottage until mid-May when it officially became ours! Has anyone ever had such luck and kindness shown them in life?

The cottage in time became a haven for Mum and Dad when, in 1966, they both came to the UK because Dad had a skin ulcer removed. Whilst this operation was successful, sadly he was later diagnosed as suffering from pulmonary TB. Unfortunately, Mum had developed secondaries from her earlier cancer and died of heart failure in late summer 1966. Dad died in 1968 having lost all desire to live after Mum's death.

After a busy life in Africa my new job was an absolute sinecure, with short hours, lunch breaks for which I received an allowance if I could not get back home for lunch, and of course a mileage allowance. I had warned them at my interview that I may be offered an appointment at the London School of Hygiene and Tropical Medicine in the autumn. They understood and were happy to employ me on that basis!

So it was that I spent a happy and relaxed summer travelling round the county of Huntingdon, listening to test matches on the car radio while eating my sandwiches parked in country lanes. The only major lasting impression retained from those few months was the revelation as to the extent of incest among the families across the 'fenlands'. The people were still very insular, referring to those from neighbouring villages as 'foreigners'. It was quite frightening to behold.

271

The Bells

Mum and Dad

273

The Barton Family ~ 1966

The call for an interview in London came in early September 1964. It was for the post of Senior Lecturer in the Department of Tropical Hygiene under Professor George MacDonald, whom I had met several times during his visits to East Africa as a member of the MRC team. It was he who told me to contact him if ever I found myself declared redundant after Independence.

The Barton Family ~ 1966 - 1668

We had fun settling into our new home over the summer period, and the family loved the house and the punt that went with it. We had to make decisions regarding the education of the children. We finally settled on Hawnes Girls' School for Lesley, a boarding school very near Bedford, about a one and a quarter hour drive from home. St Andrew's Preparatory School for boys near Pangbourne in Berkshire had been recommended to us and, after reviewing it ourselves, this was where we enrolled Ian. He subsequently went on to the Leys School in Cambridge. Both children were settled in before I started the academic year at LSH&TM, commuting by train from Huntingdon to King's Cross with a walk to the School of fifteen minutes. The morning journey by train was one and a quarter hours, while the evening journey was under the hour. The drive to the station was only fifteen minutes, so travelling was not too arduous.

Having been involved in the Guiding movement all of her life, Libo was asked to sit on the Overseas Committee at Girl Guide HQ in London. This dealt with the problems of Guide Associations in still dependent countries of the Commonwealth, known as Branch Associations. She was later appointed Commissioner for the Branch Associations, and in this capacity chaired a Conference of Commissioners of the Pacific Islands held in Fiji in 1971. She also visited their Associations before continuing round the world to attend the Caribbean Link Conference and visiting ten Island Associations.

Being in HQ, Libo was involved in the Girl Guide Diamond Jubilee in 1970, some of the last functions attended by the World Chief Guide, Lady Olave Baden Powell.

PORTRAIT GALLERY

Mrs. W.L. Barton is Commissioner for Branch Associations. In her post-bag at C.H.Q. she receives letters from many parts of the Commonwealth and you can read more about this in 'Far and Wide' on page 4.

In Kenya, where Mrs. Barton used to live, she was a Brownie and won her Gold Cords as a Guide; she loved the outdoor side of Guiding and used to camp on the shores of Lake Victoria. Later, she was a Guider in Kenya and Zanzibar. Just after the Second World War, Mrs. Barton trained as a nurse. When she married, one of the Guide badges she found most useful was Handywoman!

Mrs. Barton enjoys sailing and swimming and playing tennis and squash: indoor interests include embroidery and knitting and her keenness in shell collecting goes back to the days when she lived in Kenya and Zanzibar.

277

As I was working in London and Libo also needed to be there for two or three days a week, after Dad's death in 1968 we decided to buy a house which we could rent out, retaining one room as a pied-à-terre for ourselves. We found a property in 1969, already divided into little flatlets, which we started to lease out on the day of purchase. This meant that I travelled to London on Monday mornings, returning to Hemingford Grey on Fridays. Libo came to town on Tuesday and returned home on Thursday, so we had a wonderful pied-à-terre and shared so much time together. Our accountant soon told us to buy another flat, take a mortgage and so save income tax. This we did, and in 1971 bought a small flat in Bidborough Street near King's Cross.

I confess I was surprised and quite frightened at the thought of entering the academic world. I discussed my fears with Professor MacDonald, stating that I had no proper post-graduate degree, eg MRCP or MD, and that I had never done any real research. His reply was quite reassuring. "We are starting a new post-graduate diploma course to be called the Diploma in Tropical Public Health - DTPH. It is designed for medical staff holding middle or senior posts in the administration of Departments of Public Health in the developing world. You have been working successfully in this field for over 18 years, doing the job, and I want someone on my staff who has done it to teach about it, not someone who can read about it and so learn to teach from the book. I took my MD 30 years ago. Yes I have the initials, but my thesis is now so out of date as not to be of any value. Your value to us is that you have done it. When I took my MRCP, again, 30 years ago, the clinical medicine I learned and practised is now so out of date as to be almost dangerous. Forget about degrees - your value is your experience." I felt relieved and confident.

On another occasion I asked George MacDonald if he had any tips to offer a new entrant to the academic world. He thought and replied, "Don't clutter your mind up with unessential details or unimportant things. Too many people in the academic world try to remember everything. They think they will impress people if they can quickly trot out the answers to trivia. No! Don't try to remember things which are unimportant, but develop some quick retrieval system from which you can readily find the answer - a personal card index or other such system. You don't need to remember everything but you must be able to know where you can find the answer!" This was an excellent piece of reassuring advice for someone like myself, likely to be overcome by the minutiae and details to be remembered. It came back to roost with me...

The next summer as I turned up for the beginning of the new session I met George MacDonald in the corridor. "Oh good to see you're back. I have just been talking to Dr Waddy about the curriculum of studies for the new term. Let's go along and see him." On entering Dr Waddy's office he said, "Waddy, look who has conveniently turned up." He then turned to me and paused. "What is your name?" A quick flashback came to me - never remember unessential details, things unimportant to you! I got the message.

I learned a lot more from George MacDonald, for example, one day he said, "You have spent all your career to date in a service where loyalty is truly paramount. Loyalty to your seniors and finally to the Queen. I respect that, but it is different in our world. Everyone is for himself! I would hate to think that you gave up any chance of progress because of loyalty to me, this department, or the School. It would give me tremendous pleasure to see you promoted in another university, department or wherever. I would revel in the reflected glory of your promotion. Your loyalty is to yourself in this new world you have entered." So, eight years later, when I was offered an appointment in the WHO I accepted it and knew George would have been proud of me.

I was given the awesome task of designing a course programme for the new diploma course to be called 'Public Health Administration in the

Developing Situation'. I designed a programme of 28 sessions of two hours each, in a syllabus which stretched over the 30 weeks of the academic year, providing comprehensive printed notes for each session to facilitate the students' learning, rather than them having to spend effort on note-taking in a language foreign to most of them.

In 1968 Professor MacDonald died and a year later Dr Leonard Bruce-Chwatt was appointed. He was a staff member of WHO in the Unit of Malaria whom I had met in Zanzibar when he visited our Malaria Eradication Programme on several occasions. A Pole by birth, he was fluent in languages. Dr Waddy was very disappointed that he did not get the Chair, and after a short while resigned and joined Save the Children Fund. He was a great loss to the Department and to the Royal Society of Tropical Medicine & Hygiene, of which he had been Secretary for many years, having first had a renowned career in what was then the Gold Coast.

After Leonard's appointment I became Deputy Director of the Ross Institute which was incorporated in the Department of Tropical Hygiene, for Ronald Ross was the creator of the Department after establishing the Institute. In 1898, Ronald Ross had established the fact that the anopheles mosquito was the vector responsible for the transmission of Malaria. It was a great honour for me to hold the post of Deputy Director of the Institute.

In the eight years during which I taught on the DTPH I saw over 200 students pass through the programme as well as many more on the DTM&H, Diploma Tropical Medicine and Diploma Parasitology & Entomology courses. Most of them were from the developing world, and I have felt very proud over the years to watch many of my former students become Ministers of Health, Directors of Departments and even Professors of Public Health in their home countries.

The great advantage of having an academic career is the long, summer holiday, during which one can conduct research and act as a consultant adviser for the UK Government or WHO. So it was for me. In 1965 I was asked by the ODA of the UK Government to act as a Consultant in Afghanistan, writing and preparing an Enabling Act in Public Health for them. I spent two months there, returning to London to start the new academic session and to prepare the Act.

To provide myself with the necessary information and to help understand the problems of the various areas of the country, I travelled extensively over Afghanistan. The most impressive area I visited was the Bamyan Valley and the Lakes of Bandamir - truly one of the wonders of the world. I also had the never-to-be-forgotten experience of travelling through the Khyber Pass to Jalalabad in Pakistan.

Having completed the Act, I was requested to return in the summer of 1966 to prepare the Subsidiary Legislation. This I did, finally handing over the completed Act and Legislation to the then Minister of Health at a reception in the presence of the British Ambassador.

As an initial 'reward' for my efforts, on my first visit to Afghanistan in 1965 I was taken to a Karakul shop to select a traditional hat made of Karakul (Astrakhan) fur as a present for myself and to select a camel fur coat for my wife. This I duly did and wore my hat with pride for many years during the winter months back in the UK. With regard to the coat, I chose a full length one with the usual hand-sewn coloured embroidery designed by the maker. This was a traditional coat which was truly attractive and very fashionable in the UK at that time and I knew Libo would be thrilled with it on my return home. I had to pack it to carry as hand-luggage on the plane as I knew I would be over my weight limit otherwise.

I had decided to return to the UK via Kenya to give me the chance to visit Mother who had been so ill the previous year, and so I flew to Karachi on my first stage of the journey for a night stop. The next morning, having checked in at the airport, I was aware that the package I was carrying, namely the coat, was emitting the smell of a rotting carcase. I laid it on the seat beside me and within a few minutes I swear that every fly in Karachi International Airport was hovering around me and settling on the package. I removed the coat, which stank terribly, and laid it away from me on the couch where I was sitting. I really was terribly embarrassed, but fortunately I did not have to wait long before my flight was called. The hostess looked at me on entering and I asked her if she could place the coat in a freezer cupboard. At the height of Kabul, with its very rarefied dry atmosphere, there was no need to cure the skins, however, on descending down to sea-level, combined with the high humidity, the raw state of the skin exposed itself.

Once in Nairobi, I took the coat straight to a taxidermist renowned for curing skins for the hunters and tourist trade. When I collected it to take it back home to the UK, I discovered that in the curing the coat had shrunk quite considerably. My daughter, then aged eleven, was the beneficiary for it fitted her well - she truly was in fashion and the envy of her many school associates!

The second story relates to another present I was given, this time in 1966 at the end of my second mission, when I finally handed over my completed work of the 'Enabling Public Act for Afghanistan'. The British Ambassador had arranged an official luncheon for the presentation to the Minister of Health. The Act, with its Subsidiary Legislation, had been nicely bound in red leather and was duly presented to the Minister. She indicated to a junior staff member to produce a large package which she presented to me. It was a beautiful, medium-sized Afghan carpet... I was thrilled. As I had to drive almost directly to the airport, the carpet was roped up conveniently for hand carriage. On departure I had to pay £80 in excess luggage charges. I had a voucher allowing me payment for such charges so I was not unduly worried, and I was overwhelmed with the present.

At London Airport in 1966, one didn't walk through the 'nothing to declare' channel, but presented luggage at the customs desk and either tried to convince the customs officer or declare any purchases. I declared my duty free allowance of alcohol and then said, "I don't suppose I could walk through with this?" pointing to the carpet all tied up in a roll.

"What is it?" enquired the officer.

"A carpet, a present from the Minister of Health in Afghanistan for the work I completed for the Foreign Office, on their behalf."

"You realise that all gifts, whether official or otherwise are charged custom duty," replied the officer. "What is it worth?" he added.

"I have no idea, I only know that I paid £80 on excess luggage charges."

That did the trick, for the officer replied, "Blimey! I think you've been stung enough for the present whether official or not. Go through Sir!" He didn't know that I would be claiming back the £80 charge!

On my 1965 trip to Afghanistan I stayed in the *Kabul Hotel*, but the following year I was accommodated in the British Embassy, a great experience and privilege. On both trips I had a night stop in Teheran and on both occasions I was wakened by the noise of rushing water. Fearing flooding, I got up only to see the storm water drains being flooded with water, washing them clean of rubbish and human faeces after the previous day's residues. Certainly the flooding cleared the atmosphere.

During my time at the London School I made several visits to Teheran, twice as the UK Delegate to CENTO Meetings to discuss health matters (The Central European Treaty Organisation countries included Iran, Turkey, USA, UK and Pakistan). Another visit to Teheran was in 1968 to attend the International Conference of Malaria and Tropical Medicine, at which I presented a paper and acted as Secretary of the UK official delegation, organising the travel and other arrangements. I also made visits in Iran to Isfahan, Persepolis and Shiraz to attend various meetings while in WHO.

283

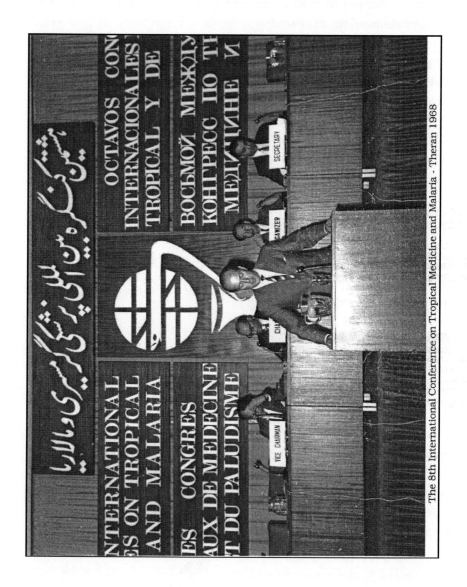

The 8th International Conference on Tropical Medicine and Malaria - Theran 1968

284

During the summer of 1967 I was Director of a WHO training course in The Administration of Parasitic Disease Programmes, in Makerere University, Kampala. In 1968, before attending the Conference in Teheran, I conducted research in Kenya for designing a computer programme to forecast medical auxiliary staff needs and the required accommodation for training schools. I presented the results at a meeting of the Royal Society of Tropical Medicine and Hygiene in 1969. That same year I was invited by WHO to visit their HQ in Geneva to conduct a study to advise on a pattern of the integration of auxiliary staff in multi-purpose field programmes.

I was then appointed as a short-term consultant to visit Indonesia to advise on their Third Development Plan and to conduct a training programme for District Medical Officers in the Administration and Management of Rural Health Services. I travelled extensively over Java including Bandung, Jogjakarta, Surabaya and Bali and saw many rural health centres. I enjoyed working with the people and government officials of Indonesia and I think gained their confidence for I was invited back to continue training programmes in 1970 and '71 in Surabaya and Jakarta.

It would be wrong to comment on my very happy years teaching at LSH&TM without some reference to the colleagues with whom I worked and the great experiences I gained from my years working with them.

I have already referred to Professor MacDonald, the Head of the Department of Tropical Public Health and Director of the Ross Institute and also to Dr 'BB' Waddy, his Deputy. George Davidson, Michael Colbourne, Brian Southgate and Chris Draper were my professional colleagues involved with the heavy load of teaching, and we were supported by a team of researchers, technicians and secretarial staff.

We worked in close harmony with colleagues in most of the other Departments in the School: Public Health, Professor Morris; Nutrition, Professor Waterlow; Epidemiology, Professor Read; Statistics, Professor

285

Armitage, and Demography, Professor Brass, as well as the more closely related scientific Departments of Entomology, Professor Bertram; Parasitology, Professor Garnham, and Helminthology, Professor Nelson. We assisted with support teaching in their academic programmes of Diploma of Applied Parasitology and Entomology (DAPE), and Diploma in Clinical Tropical Medicine (DCTM), all later to become MSc programmes.

I was nominated Secretary for the development of syllabi for the teaching of our subjects in their various curricula as well as Secretary for the curriculum for the combined DTM&H Diploma programme. This provided great experience in the skills of communication, compromise and tact as well as attention to detail, in order to produce a final curriculum, acceptable to all the Departments.

Professor Donald Read of Epidemiology, a fellow Scot, taught me the art of running meetings from all aspects, convening, producing agenda and working papers, as well as conducting and controlling them. He was quite brilliant. He was Chairman of the Board of Studies for the Teaching of Public Health and Community Medicine in the twelve schools of Medicine attached to London University and I was his chosen Secretary. The Board comprised around fifty academic staff of the University, so the enormity of his responsibility in conducting the meetings can be understood if they were to be completed in a 'reasonable' time. His skills and technique in running meetings allowed all this to happen and I benefitted from it. We used to meet before the meetings to finalise the topics; I would prepare cards with the title of the subject, purpose of topic (information, discussion, decision making etc) along with the expected outcome. I would pass the card for each item to him, and after discussions etc he would read out the conclusion and have it agreed. He handed the card back to me with the outcome written on it, and this became the substance for compiling the minutes. I have practised this formula ever since with great success.

Suffice to say that I thoroughly enjoyed my eight years in academia and they certainly helped to qualify me for my later appointment of being in charge of WHO 'Staff Development and Training' (SDT).

On the lighter side, in 1965 when I was at the London School of Hygiene and Tropical Medicine, I was involved with writing and producing a revue presented by staff and a few students which we called *Channel No. 4 : Not so much a Programme; Just a Way of Life.* It was a take-off of the David Frost and colleagues famous TV programme at that time.

The following year I undertook to produce RG Sherrif's play *Home at Seven*, which Libo and I had played in together in Zanzibar. Looking at the cast of that production it is interesting to realise just how many of them have had successful academic careers... nothing to do with their acting experience I hasten to add! It was all just good fun.

My involvement with the Channel 4 production encouraged the Secretary of the Senior Common Room, of which I was a member, to ask me to provide the entertainment for their annual dinner. I was to receive a free dinner for my wife and self in return for a twenty minute stand-up comic routine.

On the Monday following the dinner the Secretary approached me and asked if I would consider repeating the performance the following year. He explained that they had enjoyed the show and also that it saved the Senior Common Room money. "How come?" I asked. "Well, last year we had an entertainer and had to give him £10 as well as his dinner." The entertainer had been David Frost. I could not help reflecting a few years later just where he had got to and where I am now!

In fact, the following year I did provide the entertainment, along with a student, Dr Peter Christie, who was studying for his DPH. He had been actively involved with student productions at St Thomas' Hospital and was trying to raise funds for his education by singing and strumming his guitar at well known cafés around London's West End. Later, with two other St Thomas doctors and the editor of *Punch* they set up the group *Instant Sunshine*, which became, and still is, well known on radio, TV and in theatre.

In our Senior LSH&TM Common Room entertainment, Peter and I used as our introductory song, *Smile! Smile! You have got to Smile!* which became one of the *Instant Sunshine* repertoire. Among the diners was Sir George Godber, the Chief MO of the Ministry of Health. When we started the performance I noticed that Sir George did not join in the smiling we had called for. We withdrew and started the show again. Again no smile! I approached Sir George and showed him how to smile, calling on him to try. I had no idea who he was, but soon found out when, after the show, a colleague remarked, "Well I hope you never need to apply for a job at the Ministry. Your fall-guy happens to be the CMO!"

This was a lesson well learned - never tease your audience unless you know who he/she is and whether they are capable of taking a joke!

International Health
1972 - 1987

World Health Organisation

In the last chapter I mentioned that, while I was a Reader in the Department of Tropical Hygiene at the LSH&TM, I was invited on several occasions to be a consultant for WHO. Between 1967 and 1971 I worked in WHO HQ in Geneva with the Divisions of Parasitic Diseases, Public Health Administration and also for the South East Regional Office (SEARO) in Uganda, Indonesia and Thailand. In my assignment in HQ in 1967 I met Dr Halfdan Mahler for the first time. He was then MO i/c of the TB Unit and we worked well together. He was later appointed head of the Programme Systems Analysis (PSA) and invited me to be one of his advisory consultants working on the outline of the new thinking in planning and evaluation of health service delivery.

In 1969 I was invited to be consultant adviser to a Scientific Working Group in HQ Geneva. The topic was 'The Role of Health in Family Planning Services', which was organised by the Division of Family Health.

Two years later, Dr Jungawala, the Director of the Division, invited me to apply for the post of Chief of the Unit of Health Administration in the Division of Planning Health Services. Before the selection for the post could take place, Dr Jungawala was appointed Director of Health in WHO SEARO in New Delhi.

In Spring 1972 I was invited by the then ADG, Dr Mahler, to apply for the post of Senior Medical Officer in the Division of Family Health, to be number two to the Director of the Division, Dr Albert Zahra. I tried to argue with Dr Mahler that I was probably of more value to WHO as a teacher of senior health administrators, acting occasionally as a consultant, rather than as a staff member of the Organisation. His response was rather on the line of 'maybe I can judge that more objectively from within the Organisation!'

When I was asked to attend a meeting in WHO HQ I suggested that Libo come with me to look around Geneva to see where she might like to live in the event of my selection. She saw an apartment in Chemin de Taverney, in Grand Sacconnex, within walking distance of WHO HQ. Having been selected, I had to give the London School six months' notice. In the meantime, we heard that the apartment which Libo had visited was still on the market, so I flew over to Geneva and bought it in May, three months before I was due to join the Organisation. In June, a month after our purchase, Switzerland introduced a new law preventing foreigners from buying property until they had lived in the country for five years!

Bill and Libo ~ 1972

I finally joined WHO in 1972 as Senior Medical Officer in the Division of Family Health. During the next two years, I again found myself involved with constant travel to many countries including Singapore, Tunisia, Thailand, Indonesia and Bali, the Philippines, Japan, Kenya, USA and Sweden, with visits to Regional Offices in Copenhagen, Manila and New Delhi. I attended meetings and conferences and advised Governments on various aspects of their family planning and human reproduction programmes.

Before I become involved with details of my WHO service I feel I must refer to a few colleagues who had a great impact on my performance during these fulfilling years. Dr Candau, the DG, and his Deputy Director, Dr Dorelle were a tremendous example to the younger generation of staff joining the Organisation. Dr Candau had been DG for nearly twenty years and had taken WHO through the difficult post-war period of development and re-creation of health services in many countries throughout the world.

Dr Mahler was appointed an ADG, obviously being groomed to be Dr Candau's successor. On his appointment he established his own team. One of his ADGs i/c Administration and Finance was an American, Warren Furth. Warren later became my senior supervisor and was wonderful to work for. My immediate supervisor, when I later joined his Division of Personnel and General Services, was Robert Munteanu. He was Romanian by nationality but had lived in Geneva for a long time. He was a manager of direct rule, being a decisive decision maker, if sometimes a degree dogmatic. He was always very well informed and prepared to listen, if on occasions difficult to persuade. I enjoyed our many sessions discussing my programmes, and I respected his loyal support.

A story about Robert deserves mention. He called me into his office one day to tell me that a colleague in another Division had remarked on my somewhat frank and direct style of communication which could at times be hurtful to him! Robert told me what I already knew, namely that the

293

colleague was Latin-American and that such people were never direct in manner and always played around the point before ever disagreeing, and that maybe I should give some thought to that when dealing with such cultures. I knew the complainant well, for in fact I had helped him several years earlier when he was applying for a post in the Organisation. He had once written three pages when commenting on a memo of three paragraphs I had shared with him! I told him that I would not be sending further memos to him because I did not have the time to read three pages of comments! Anyway, I asked Robert, "Have you told the doctor that I am British and an ex-Colonial, that I am arrogant, conceited and pompous, for I feel that if I am to understand his culture he should try to understand me and mine." Robert paused and replied, "No, Bill! I didn't tell him. There was no need to... everyone knows that about you!" I respected Robert's tolerance of me and recognised the good understanding and friendship we had developed. We laughed about this incident many times.

Another colleague whom I greatly admired was Jimmy Wright, the Director of Vector Borne Diseases. He was a true success story of WHO. He had been a field entomologist involved with the malarial control programme in Italy after the war. He joined WHO during its early stages and was a very successful field worker. With such wonderful field operational experience he inevitably later reached HQ where he soon made his mark. Finally, he became Director of the Division and after retirement became Dr Mahler's first 'Ombudsman', listening to and advising on staff concerns. He was the one who suggested that I sit on two working groups to help him. From this I was asked to be Convenor of the Steering Committee on Staff Development and Training (SDT), a post and responsibility which I held until I retired in 1983.

I had been appointed Programme Manager of the Staff Development and Training Programme in 1975. My team in SDT always considered the programme was the DG's baby and that we should do our utmost to ensure

294

its success. I shared a great confidence with Dr Halfdan Mahler but, though we had become good friends during my early working involvement with WHO, I never took advantage of that relationship. I always had access to his office, keeping him informed of events and our plans, which almost invariably he supported. Our birthdays were only days apart and so I enjoyed selecting appropriate cards for his 'day'. Libo and I always considered Halfdan and Ebbe, his wife, as our friends.

As WHO has six Regions with offices in Europe, the Americas, South East Asia, Eastern Mediterranean, Western Pacific and Africa, I undertook a considerable amount of travel. Part of my work was to meet staff to discuss, design, plan, produce and carry out training programmes in 'management', naturally involving time management. Such visits also involved discussions relating to overall programmes for the development of individual staff members, both in the professional as well as the general service staff categories.

Naturally, in the initial stages I had to use consultants to advise and assist me with running specific training programmes. Tom Attwood, David Kimber and Gordon Lippitt were my original group involved with interpersonal relationships and team-building and working. Moving into the area of modern management techniques I first attended an UNESCO programme in Paris designed and conducted by Emmett Wallace, and was so impressed that I involved him with my first major programme for senior WHO Staff. Emmett, an American, and I became very close friends, but more than that, we were an excellent duo for training in management, running programmes in Geneva, Edinburgh, Copenhagen, Manila, Tonga, Kenya and elsewhere.

Another popular and very successful consultant trainer, particularly for General Service Staff, was Miss Eleanor Macdonald. She had been a senior executive manager in an international business and after early retirement decided she needed to be involved with training women for senior positions in industry. We were lucky to hear of her training programmes and she became a regular and cherished member of our training team for programmes in Geneva, Manila, Copenhagen and others. Like Emmett she became a close family friend and indeed was present at the weddings of both our children.

I had convinced the DG of the need to include national counterpart staff in all our senior management staff training programmes. Many of these programmes were held outside the Regional Offices and I visited such diverse places as Kuala Lumpu, Penang, Singapore, Suva in Fiji and Tonga, Brasilia, Rio de Janeiro, Nairobi, Edinburgh, Kuwait and Bangkok.

These programmes in the different countries provided me with the unique opportunity of visiting fascinating areas around the world, which I would never otherwise have seen. Meeting with the people and learning of the different cultures, helped me to better understand the wonderful diversity of human behaviour, beliefs, and practices operating around us of which most of us are unaware. I formed many lasting friendships and have enjoyed the reflected glory of seeing the promotions and successes of so many of those wonderful people whom I had been privileged to meet and sometimes teach.

Contacts with so many 'nationals' led to invitations to their home countries, for example, to Moscow to The Institute of Medical Science to advise on programmes for the training in management. I also went to Prague to assist with training for the administration of TB field programmes and to the Institutes of Tropical Medicine in Amsterdam and Antwerp to assist with their post-graduate Public Health Courses. Other assignments included attending conferences on communication and maternal health in Oslo and Stockholm respectively, and visiting Shiraz and Isfahan to discuss teaching methodologies with nationals from several regions. I also assisted with the post-graduate DPH course in Teheran.

As Programme Manager of SDT in WHO I attended the UN sub-committee on Staff Training, which was part of a larger Co-ordinating Committee for Administrative Questions. The CCAQ meetings on occasions took place outside Geneva, so I was able to visit Paris and Rome. For three years I was Chairman of this sub-committee and introduced the concept that officers in the different UN agencies should assist each other in the training programmes in which they specialised - in my case 'management training' for senior and middle level managers, as well as general service staff. Accordingly I visited ILO programmes in Turin and the UN Vienna International Centre (VIC) to train staff in separate or combined agency programmes.

After my retirement from WHO in 1983, for several years I continued to receive invitations from VIC from the Atomic Energy Agency for training programmes as well as to advise the Administration on staff selections, staff development and future management development. At the end of my UN career in WHO, I could claim to have travelled from Brasilia to Brazzaville, Tonga to Turin, Australia to Alexandria, Stockholm to Singapore, Manila to Moscow, New York to Nairobi and others. During various trips I took advantage of stopping over in Sydney, Perth, Melbourne and Brisbane in Australia, and while visiting the USA I combined visits to Schools of Public Health in various Universities including Colombia in New York, Chapel Hill in North Carolina, John Hopkin's in Baltimore, Harvard in Boston and Ann Arbor, Michigan to discuss training with academic staff.

In India I visited Bombay, Calcutta, the Taj Mahal and other places of interest. In Thailand, which I visited frequently, I made trips to Kanchanaburi (bridge on the River Kwai), Ayutthaya, Chiengmai and the Hill Tribe Location, Khon Kaen and Korat while conducting several training programmes for the Asian Institute of Health and Development.

The Director was a former pupil from the London School days, Dr Krasae Chonawongse, who had previously been Minister of Health.

The programmes in Edinburgh, referred to above, continued for eight years and were part of the course for the post-graduate students studying for the Edinburgh University DPH diploma and were also attended by senior WHO staff from all regions. Sir John Brotherston was the Professor of Public Health and was responsible for persuading the European office of WHO to allow me to conduct the programmes. He was so impressed by the 'group' and 'plenary' problem-solving technique I had introduced, that he recommended the Royal College of Physicians of Edinburgh award me an Associate Membership of the College for developing a new approach to the training of post graduates. This was a great award and personal thrill for me, only surpassed a few years later when the College elected me a Fellow. Thus I was granted the qualification FRCPE, the highest medical qualification any UK physician can hold. I felt this was the final accolade to a happy and fulfilling medical career. With my decoration from the Queen for my service in Zanzibar and then this high honour from my peers in the profession, I have experienced humble pride and a sense of credit to my family. I know that Auntie Whyte and my parents would have shared my humility and pride.

My eight years in the SDT programme were certainly very fulfilling and enjoyable. Possibly the greatest thrill for me was to be told by more than a few staff members that, through my leadership and direction as Programme Manager of SDT, I had changed their direction of life and particularly their attitude to interpersonal relationships, management and communication styles as well as their own management of time. I was able to witness several members introduce improvements in their working methods and to develop close new friendships with many, who often consulted me regarding their approach to their work or their colleagues.

One colleague who was very affected by the training programmes was George Dorros who later helped me as a faculty member on an American Regional Office (AMRO) programme which we were asked to run in Brasilia in 1978. He was posted to Western Province Regional Office (WPRO) in Manila and was very active and helpful with SDT activities there. We developed a close and lasting friendship.

I considered it a great personal privilege to have been in charge of SDT over those eight exciting years, and will forever cherish the memories of so many training programmes and the participants on them, not only in WHO but also in Vienna with other UN Agencies. Many amusing stories can be told of events in many of the separate programmes, but space only allows for one. I was running 'Teamwork in Office Management' for SEARO General Service staff in New Delhi. I used a system of introduction of participants, whereby each participant was interviewed by another for two minutes and then later introduced that participant. When we had finished all the introductions I asked everyone to write on the back of their name card how they would like others to address them, for example, by Mr So and So, by a nick-name, first name etc. I turned my card round stating that I wished to be addressed as Bill. One of the Indian staff members asked to speak. "Sir, we cannot possibly call you Bill, Sir. You are my superior, Sir, and our teacher, Sir. No, Sir, I couldn't possibly call you Bill, Sir. Sorry Sir!"

"Well," I replied, "I would really like you to call me Bill and not address me as Dr Barton. But if you find that difficult may I suggest you call me Sir Bill!" And that was what I was called for the rest of the course... Sir Bill! I rather enjoyed the title but it died with the end of that course.

I was able to build up a great team for our SDT Programme and wish to mention the names of Bernadette Rivett and Judith Munzinger, two of my team who showed great personal development. The former, Bernadette, was appointed Chief of SDT in WPRO while, in time, Judith joined the

DG's team. Both moved from General Service Staff (GS) salaries to the Professional (P) scales.

Libo and I had decided to buy an apartment in Geneva so that when we retired we would be free of any mortgages and so have some security. We made so many friends that it would take a book to relate but I would be failing Libo and myself if I did not refer to one close friendship which started soon after our arrival and lasted throughout the twelve years in Geneva. The couple were John and Isabella Burton. I started work on 1st September and as Christmas approached I wondered what we might do over that holiday period. I went to ask the advice of John who, I had been told, knew about the possibilities of skiing. He told me that he and his wife had a large chalet in Champery, but he couldn't invite us to stay with them without his wife's approval!

It was arranged that the two ladies should meet for Isabella to assess whether she could tolerate Libo in the house. She obviously approved, as we then spent a wonderful week with them and Lesley and Ian who were home for holidays from the UK. It was a brilliant introduction to Swiss skiing and we spent many more holidays with John and Isabella and have treasured a close friendship ever since, only interrupted by John's death in 1998. On his retirement, John had become WHO Ombudsman and, being a member of the Steering Committee for the SDT Programme, gave me great support throughout my years in charge.

In 1972 when we moved to Geneva, the Geneva English Drama Society (GEDS) was approaching its 40th Anniversary. I was introduced to an exciting few years on stage in a wide range of theatrical experiences. I started in a *One Night Stand of One-Act Plays*. *Sketch Pad* was the short play, by David Campton.

I was privileged to learn from experienced directors and played with skilled actors. My first major role was as Sir Toby Belch in Shakespeare's

Twelfth Night, under the direction of Frank and Thelma Harling. I found that I was taller than many of the cast and so decided to reduce my height by bending my knees. I was fattened up with layers of foam rubber, all enclosed in a tight-fitting tunic and, of course, I was disguised with side-burns!

In March 1975 Barrie Philpot had been invited over from London to be the director of the latest play by Ray Cooney, *Move Over Mrs Markham*. I was privileged to be cast as Henry Lodge. Barrie Philpot was a personal friend of Ray Cooney and had been given his permission to stage the play as its amateur world premier production. It was truly an exciting and wonderful experience to be professionally directed. I will always remember the correct pronunciation of the word 'constable'! In Scotland it is pronounced 'constable' but in England, as I found out from the director, it is 'cunstable'!

In 1977 it was more Shakespeare with *A Midsummer Night's Dream*, again directed by Thelma Harling, with Frank playing Oberon. I played Peter Quince, a carpenter and leader of 'The Players'.

Jim and Jean Flux were the directors, in 1979, of my next performance as Sir Oliver Surface in Sheridan's *The School for Scandal*. This was a period costume production and introduced me to yet another stage experience, advice from the Scandalous Club - 'a weekly history of nonsense, impertinence, vice and debauchery!'

We had another professional director in Michael Deacon with *The Circle*, by Somerset Maugham. I played Clive Champion-Cheney, opposite Daphne Williams as my wife, Lady Catherine Champion-Cheney. It is a play about love, sex and the mores of society on these two very important matters!

Move over Mrs. Markham

The Circle

302

1983 was the 50th Anniversary of GEDS. The Season opened with a *Playreading of a Farce in One Act* by Terrence Rattigan. I was cast as Arthur Gosport. The highlight for me, however, was playing Alonso, King of Naples, in the truly incredible stage production of Shakespeare's *The Tempest*, directed by Jan Flux. What a production and what a great cast with whom to act in my final stage appearance with GEDS in Geneva. My eleven years in Geneva saw me in eight stage appearances with the society.

My years of experience in theatre in Geneva were extended to musical stage productions with the Geneva Amateur Operatic Society (GAOS). In 1974 I was cast as the tenor lead in the production of Gilbert and Sullivan's *Ruddigore*. As it was to be the UN Population Year, I knew I might be called upon at short notice to go overseas for a UN Conference, and so asked the director if he would allow me to have an understudy for the part. As things worked out I did have to go off, and so John Tracy had the opportunity to make his first stage appearance as the tenor lead for GAOS. He never looked back.

I was in two annual GAOS 'Music Hall' productions, in 1982 and 1983. I appeared with John Tracy in *The Wee Cock Sparra* and on my own, in my kilt, as a stand-up comic in a Scottish *Tartan Turn*, with a Harry Lauder-style act.

1976 saw the declaration by WHO of the final eradication of smallpox in the world. It was decided that there should be a special Gala Evening to be held on 22th January 1977 in WHO HQ to celebrate the event, and more especially to congratulate and say farewell to 'DA' Henderson who had been the programme leader and had masterminded the eradication. John (Jock) Copland was the brain behind the idea. He called upon several of us to compile the programme, and write sketches and songs. The programme included a Grand Souvenir Songbook, with such songs as :

OMS/WHO *(My Edelweiss)*; Smallpox *(Swannee)*; Roll Out the Vaccine *(Roll out the Barrel)*; Halfdan! Halfdan! *(Daisy Daisy)*; Variola Goodbye *(California Goodbye)*; I'd like to build the OMS *(I'd like to Teach the World to Sing)*; What shall we do with the Smallpox Virus? *(Drunken Sailor)*, and It's Goodbye to Smallpox *(Eton Boating Song)*.

Individual items were presented, including John Wickett singing his composition of 'Variola Blues'; myself in 'Lift Girls' Lament' and 'Oh Pleez DG'. I presented a short historical sketch with Bernadette Rivett in 'Smallpox and Lady Mary Wortley Montagu', as well as there being items by Jock Copland.

The climax and true highlight of the evening was the robing, crowning and triumphal procession of DA. He was awarded the Malthus Medal for increasing the world population by ten million and invested as Grand Dragon of the Order of the Bifurcated Needle. He was escorted by the Poxies, a glamorous chorus of beautiful 'girls'.

The occasion was attended by a large audience of WHO staff and recognised with a special issue of the WHO magazine *Dialogue* in February 1977, with a few photos and a selection of the songs.

While it was early in my years in Geneva, this Gala Evening was probably the most entertaining and enjoyable evening of the eleven happy years 'On the Boards' in Geneva.

When we moved to Geneva, Libo was asked to join a team of four to represent the World Association of Girl Guides and Girl Scouts (WAGGGS) at the UN. She was particularly concerned with the participation of Non-Government Organisations in the role of Youth in the United Nations Programme and attended, among many others, the UN World Conference in Bucharest in 1974.

Harry Lauder

1977 Gala Evening

In 1987, Libo was nominated by WAGGGS to be Chairman of the 26th World Conference. This was the first of these triennial events to be held in Africa -the venue was Kenya and the Conference was opened by the President, Arap Moi. It was a co-incidence that Libo was born in Kenya and had joined the movement whilst at school there. This caused a ripple of applause when mentioned in her summing-up speech.

Libo and President Arap Moi
at the WAGGGS' 26th World Conference - Kenya 1987

My farewell party from WHO was one that I wished for and enjoyed. My Supervisor, Mr Munteanu, Director of Personnel and General Services, gave a small drinks party for Libo and me in his office, for my staff and a few personal friends who included Rik Davis and Ralph Henderson, my squash opponents, and others. He had also invited the DG and ADG, Mr Furth and some of the staff of Personnel. Short speeches were made and so my career with WHO ended, with a feeling of great satisfaction and personal fulfilment, especially my eight years with SDT.

Dubai

Libo and I had decided that immediately after my retirement from WHO in 1983, we would take time off to allow us to prepare for Lesley's wedding, planned for 10th September of that year. The service was to be at St Martin-in-the-Fields, Trafalgar Square, with the reception later in the former Commonwealth Club in Northumberland Avenue. Lesley had become engaged to Owen Crisp from Toronto the previous Christmas when, with Ian and Kathy King from Kenya, we were having a family skiing holiday in Champery.

With the bride and groom in Toronto, the parents in Geneva and the wedding of 150 guests to take place in London, a great deal of planning and logistical arrangements had to be made. The Commonwealth Club could not have been more helpful, and we were also offered bedroom accommodation as the club was empty over the weekend. Lesley's godfather, Gus McKnight, my old school friend, who had become Minister of St Andrew's Church in Brussels, came over and helped in the service.

I had given considerable thought to the idea of establishing a company, '*Barton Associates*', upon retirement. This would be a team of 'experts' in various medical and para-medical disciplines to be available to go out to advise any country or organisation requiring any special expertise. I had made many contacts during my careers and travels with the LSH&TM and WHO, and I started taking initial steps to establish *Barton Associates*.

After Lesley's wedding, however, I was approached by the Director General of Health and Medical Services of Dubai, Dr Juma Belhoul, who was visiting Geneva. He wondered if I would consider visiting Dubai to assess if I could advise him on how to establish an improvement in the administration and management of the Department. He had remembered meeting me on my visit to UAE and Dubai in 1976, and having heard of my retirement he approached me. Events developed and after a visit in November 1983, at which I submitted my proposals of how I could help, I was finally invited to Dubai and stayed for three years. We arrived in May 1984 and were provided with a bungalow in the Medical compound, free water and electricity, a transport allowance and of course no Income Tax. We had two months' home leave every year with first class air passages, so were able to fly to Toronto on the allowance.

While we were in Dubai, Ian and Kathy decided to marry and we flew to Kenya for the event in November 1984. Their wedding was a very different setting to Lesley's, being on the Watamu beach in front of the family plot, no. 44. Kathy arrived on a dhow, appearing round the corner from Mida Creek. She was in a pink tinted dress, and the low sun across the sea was a backcloth for her as she sailed in and was carried ashore to join her father. An arch of palm trees decorated with bougainvillaea enclosed a small altar with a cross from a piece of drift-wood. The Catholic Priest who had baptised Kathy married them just in time before the sun set.

Both families were able to visit us in Dubai, as did other family from Kenya and the UK.

During the years I was Personal Adviser to the DG I prepared an outline plan for the improvement in the administration and management of the Department. I wrote a set of Medical Standing Orders, Rules and Regulations for the Administration and staff to follow. I introduced regular meetings of the Medical Directors of the four hospitals to plan a united policy for their management, rather than an Administration dictated at a whim by them individually according to their mood or temper! I was also involved under the leadership of Dr Jimmy Harries, Sheikh Rashid's family physician, in organising and running a course in Tropical Medicine directed by the Liverpool School of Tropical Medicine.

Dubai had an indigenous population of 75,000 but the total population of the Emirate was around 300,000. Other than the 75,000 locals the rest were 'foreigners' from Europe, India, Pakistan, Syria, Egypt, Jordon, Lebanon, the Philippines, Sri Lanka, Korea and many other countries. All 'foreigners' had to hand over their passports and were at the mercy of their national supervisors. In time it became difficult to endure the 'master and slave' attitude which operated throughout the Gulf Emirates, and after three years I decided to leave.

We loved our time in Dubai and made many lasting friendships among all communities. We enjoyed the sport, parties and above all, for me, the opportunity to take part in further theatre and musical shows. I enjoyed a wide-raging experience of plays, music-hall, pantomime and light opera, including compering a stage production and giving stand-up comic performances.

The first play was *The Lady's not for Burning* by Christopher Fry, playing Edward Tappercoom, a justice. This play in period costume was directed by Jan Beaumont.

In 1986, the second play, *The Dining Room* by AR Gurney Jr, was a unique experience under the professional direction of Neil Fucci. The scene, 'The Dining Room' was set as a theatre in the round. Three actors and three actresses play out the performance, a collection of eighteen short cameos dealing with the inter-play of characters, young and old, tragic and comic. Quick costume changes with instant switching of inflection of voice and mannerism, from a redolent child to the actions of an adult, was the real challenge. The players each acted out a variety of roles, from boys to grandfathers, from little girls to housemaids etc. Each player had eight or nine different roles covering, in all, 51 parts.

Compering a production by Alison Clarke which she called *Honour and Obey - A Light-Hearted Look at Love*, was a new stage experience. As the narrator, seated at the edge of the stage, I had to compose the script and, with appropriate humour relating to the theme of the evening, light-heartedly introduce each of eight separate scenes from a series of famous plays such as *The Taming of the Shrew*, *The Importance of Being Ernest*, *The Proposal*, *Blithe Spirit* and others. In all, seventeen players were involved in the production.

The Dubai Drama Group, under the direction of Neil Fucci, combined with the Dubai and Sharjah Singers and Orchestra in presenting a production called *Concerted Effort*. The Players staged extracts from *A Midsummer Night's Dream*; a collage from *Hamlet, As You Like It, Who's Afraid of Virginia Wolf?* and *Chess*. Their contribution ended with an improvised one-act murder mystery loosely in the style of Agatha Christie. I had my great moment to play Hamlet in his famous speech to 'The Players': "Speak the speech I pray you," while again playing in The Players in *A Midsummer Night's Dream*. Music-hall, pantomime and light opera were all within the repertoire of the Dubai and Sharjah Singers.

Being cast as Frank, the prison Governor, in *Die Fliedermaus* by Johann Strauss, was for me the acme of all my musical stage performances. Not only was it a fun part, allowing me great scope in the drunken scenes, but musically it proved to be of enormous pleasure as I was involved in the many lovely songs with multi-talented singers. Making my entrance into my Prison Governor's office in a 'drunken' state at the beginning of Act III, I had to remove my hat and cast it at the stand. I practised hard and perfected throwing my hat onto the hat stand so that at every performance I managed it without a single failure!

From this sublime I moved on to accomplish my greatest theatrical desire... playing in panto. Firstly I appeared in *Jack and the Bean Stalk* as the Ogre. The next year I was Grizella, one of the ugly sisters, in

Cinderella, playing opposite Malcolm Burke as Lucretia. After my panto appearances I felt I had accomplished everything 'On the Boards'. But there was still more music hall to come in the form of *An Edwardian Evening*, this time playing 'A Wee Cock Sparra' with Malcolm Burke, instead of with John Tracey as in Geneva.

Finally, Dubai saw me launched as a stand-up comic in the Scottish Harry Lauder style, appearing as a guest artist at various annual dinner functions, including The Sailing Club and Caledonian Ball, as well as the Dubai and Sharjah Singers Dinner. All this was the result of a 'turn' I performed at a Dubai Drama Group in-house members' party!

While I was involved with the theatre, Libo attended several courses in different subjects including, macrame, photography and teaching English as a foreign language. We certainly would have stayed longer in Dubai had it not been for the attitude of the locals as expressed earlier.

Overleaf: Appearances in *Cinderella* and *Die Fliedermaus*

We had rented out our apartment in Geneva to the Japanese Mission and so had an income from that for the three years we were in Dubai. After those years away from the scene, we came to realise that our notion for *Barton Associates* was no longer feasible and that we could not afford to live in Geneva on our pension from WHO and the Colonial Office. In due course we sold our apartment which allowed us to buy our home in Exmouth and help our family with purchasing theirs. The families were settled in Kenya and Canada and so we had decided to return to our roots, the UK, which geographically would be halfway between the two.

312

Extended Family

The next generation of our family started to arrive on 6th July 1987 with the birth of our first grandchild, Alistair Euan Crisp, the son of Lesley and Owen in Toronto. We received the news on the 7th as we were about to depart for the funeral of Aunt Bunny. The Lord gave Euan and the Lord took away Bunny.

Hurriedly we arranged to visit Toronto to see this new member of the family. As we came through the arrival gate, there he was, and we still proudly show our first photo of little Euan with his 'young' maternal grandparents. A thrilling moment indeed for the family.

As Libo and I, Ian and Kathy and both her parents had been born in East Africa or India, so it was that any children born to Ian and Kathy in Kenya, would be the third generation born outside of the UK. Accordingly, any of their offspring should, if possible, be born in the UK otherwise they would lose their rights to British Citizenship, if that is what they chose.

In December 1989 Kathy was nine months pregnant, and so she and Ian flew to the UK for her delivery which was expected early January in Exeter. This was delayed and so, reluctantly, Ian had to return to Kenya before eventually Jennifer was born. Kathy started labour at 3.00 am and wished Libo and I to be present at the delivery!

Unfortunately, Kathy fainted during the delivery and panic stations ensued with all the baby's heart sounds being monitored. I have to say at this point that I am glad that in the '50s, fathers were not allowed in the delivery room! In due course, on 13th January 1990, this wonderful baby girl was presented to us. We were proud that we had been there to watch her fight for her life, although both of us were helpless to do anything to assist her.

What a true delight Jennifer has been - our first granddaughter, so feminine and graceful. The old Scottish saying 'A man's nae a man till he's had a daughter' ran through my thoughts. Good old Ian!

Later that same year, on 15th August, young Tristan Blake Crisp was born without fuss in Toronto and again we were soon over there to be presented... he is the spitting image of his father Owen.

1993 saw the family further extended when, on 20th January, Kyle William Adler Crisp arrived, again in Toronto and it was not long before we went over to be with them all. He was quite different in looks from his two brothers Euan and Tristan.

Later that summer, Ian, Kathy and Jennifer arrived in preparation for the delivery of Michael William Barton. Ian was able to attend several preparation sessions for fathers and nearly fainted each time! Kathy was booked for her last ante-natal at 2.30 pm on the 12th July but at lunch she announced that she had started labour and so we took off. We met the lunch-time rush hour into Exeter, and whilst still fifteen minutes from the hospital Kathy was having contractions every few minutes!

We just made it, and wonderfully we were met at the entrance by the same midwife who had delivered Jennifer three years earlier. Ian, who had gone in with Kathy, appeared about twenty minutes later to tell us we had a Barton grandson, remarking "I can't think what all the fuss is about. It was a piece of cake... all over in a few minutes." Little did he know how close he was to being sloshed for such a comment, but we were all glad for Ian's sake, and of course for Kathy and Michael that it had gone so smoothly!

The 'close' family has remained at five since 1993 and looks like staying so — one girl and four boys.

Owen and Lesley

Our 'extended' family shows no such limitations...

With my work pattern and Libo's involvement with International Guiding, it is obvious that we travelled a great deal. This gave us the opportunity to see many new countries and to come face to face with a wide range of cultures and people. We felt truly blessed with such an opportunity and it was not long before we had a long list of new friends, creating an extended family spread all over the world.

As I tended to stay for longer spells in certain countries, Indonesia, the Philippines, East Africa and several other places, I found that I had the chance to meet many people, as ships passing in the night. Manohar Bamne in Bombay, David and Paul in Kampala, Bambang and Ketut in Jakarta and Bali, Robinson Grenada and Winnie Togonon in Manila and Boonyiam and Supoj in Bangkok, to name a few.

Euan, Tristan and Kyle

Ian, Kathy, Jennifer and Michael

Jennifer and Michael

We were blessed in time with being able to meet their parents, to see a few married and to meet their wives and families. We were able to help several get launched into worthwhile jobs and so to improve their status in life. One or two we were able to assist with their education at school, college or university. It has been a joy to see several of them really succeed and move abroad, to Germany and the USA for example.

Like all families, as the 'children' grow up and move away one loses the original closer ties, this being particularly so with our 'family' being so scattered around the world, but we remember the few lines 'though miles divide and distance parts, whatever time may send; they cannot alter faithful hearts nor sever friend from friend.' And so it is with our 'extended' family.

In Conclusion

I earlier made it clear that the main purpose of this biography was to satisfy my children's request to relate the 'story' of my early life and to leave for them some record of my career in medicine; a story which they could share later with their own children or possibly answer questions the grandchildren may pose.

Accordingly, I decided not to express my personal views, emotions or feelings about the world I discovered as I travelled around it; about politics, religion, relationships with my children as they grew into adulthood, my own personal friendships or involved details of what has often been called 'our extended family'.

I have had a very stimulating and blessed life, both in my chosen profession as well as being happily married with two loving children and five grandchildren. I have been honoured to meet and to mix with a wide range of people including royalty, professional giants and colleagues, as well as the more ordinary citizens of the wider world, rich and poor alike. I only wish I had had more time to write in detail about many of the wonderful people I have met at the crossroads of my fascinating professional and family journey.

I realise as I write that I have said nothing about the social life and activities of the many spheres in which Libo and I have lived. I only hope that I have been able to persuade Libo to pick up this challenge as a counterpart to this, my story. I must, however, make it clear that without Libo's great and enduring love and support, my success in my medical career and life in general could not have happened. Never once did I hear concern or criticism about the importance of my work being in competition with family life. Nor did she fail or refuse to support me or stand by my side, as I had to play certain tiresome roles or undertake less enjoyable social functions. We grew up, together realising more and more that we were lucky to enjoy being large fishes in small ponds at very early ages.

It is often said that behind every successful man stands a supportive wife. I know that for me it was always a thrill and reassurance to have, always by my side, a beautiful wife who was also a wonderful mother.

Libo

The Author

Epilogue

In retirement the question one often asks oneself is "I'm so busy how did I ever find time to work?" The answer is really quite simple; when working one never had the time to spend doing the things one had often wanted to do. Faced with retirement, I quickly realised that at work I always had a secretary to type for me and at home a wife to cook for me, or at least I could go to the refectory for a meal.

I studied the Adult Education Programme run at our local Community College and noted that there were classes for both these topics so I enrolled. For two terms I attended a programme entitled 'Gentlemen's Relish!' intended for retired males, 65+ year olds, run by Mrs Maggie Maguire. The class fully equipped one to produce meals, soups, main dishes and desserts of many varieties, which I have been able to turn out as required from time to time.

I also enrolled with a group of young female would-be secretaries on a course for touch-typing. As I had no intention of sitting for any efficiency tests, I could progress at my own pace and gain confidence. This course was followed up by one on word-processing. After these two programmes, and equipped with a PC, I felt confident to undertake another programme on Genealogy, run by Oswald Moss, who was a tremendous help to me over the following four years while compiling the family trees of our four parents, i.e., Barton, Godly, Belcher and Palmer.

Meanwhile, I had undertaken to produce a video on 'The Sultanate of Zanzibar' for the family, and also to present to the Museum in Muscat, Oman which had no records of the Zanzibar Thweni dynasty which had originated in 1867 from the Sultanate of Oman. The video, which runs for

25 minutes, was made from slides I had taken on a 35 mm reflex camera when we were in Zanzibar between 1956-63. I wrote the script for the video and provided the voice-over for it, with Alan Tibbitt of *Video EX* handling the production.

After making the video, Alan later contacted me thrice asking me to help him by writing the scripts for commissions he had for producing videos. The first was for use in fund-raising for the West of England School for Children with Little or No Sight, in which I appeared and again provided the voice-over. The second was a publicity video for the Honeylands Centre for Children with Learning Difficulties, while the third was a training video for the Royal National Institute for the Blind. All these video productions proved to be very interesting; yet another aspect of theatrical experience.

My interest in the musical aspects of theatrical work was developed when I joined the renowned local Budleigh Salterton Male Voice Choir, under their new Musical Director, Marion Room. We practised weekly and gave numerous fund raising concerts during the year. We were not allowed to use music at the concerts and so had to be word and note perfect for each concert. It was a wonderful opportunity for me to relearn sight reading, and as I was placed among the first tenors I really had to maintain serious practice in voice production and breathing.

Regarding my great interest in sport, I continued to play squash until I was 66, before moving over to regular swimming!

My major personal activities since retirement have been in charity work for disabled people. Firstly, I spent four years with the Leonard Cheshire Foundation in helping to establish their first Home in Exmouth, acting for a period as Chairman of the Management Committee. In recent years I have been more closely involved with Exmouth Fellowship for the Physically Disabled.

With such a blessed life it has been a joy in retirement to be involved in providing help for those less fortunate. With the completion of this biography relating to my medical career, I feel I have not been quite as idle as I may have thought over these last twelve years and now, with our decision to move from our lovely home in Foxholes Hill to a flat in a new development close by, I can turn to a new phase and develop still further interests.

* * * * *